This is a most helpful compilation, whi
think very seriously about the whole issu
To those who love the Scriptures, and se
will prove enormously helpful.

D0514250

When it comes to the debate about reconciling evolutionary theory to the Christian faith, some theistic evolutionist friends give the impression that, 'They think it's all over!' 'It *isn't* now!' is my response after reading this collection of very accessible essays from a variety of scientists and theologians, who beg to differ from that conclusion. Read, be challenged and be ready to think again.

Steve Brady, *Principal, Moorlands College, Christchurch*

This collection of fine essays makes an essential contribution to the ongoing discussion among Christians about how to relate biblical revelation with ongoing scientific efforts to understand the history of life on earth. Although addressed primarily to Christian believers, the book should be helpful to a wide segment of the public who want to expose their thinking to top-quality cutting-edge arguments for a view of the history of life that gives fuller weight to divine revelation. Here you can find views that are informed in a balanced way by the best current science and biblical revelation. This reviewer believes the book will helpfully focus discussions of a Christian view of neo-Darwinian evolution on the key issues.

Richard A. Carhart, *Professor Emeritus of Physics, University of Illinois at Chicago*

Naturalism has infiltrated Christian culture in the West. In assembling such a wide range of relevant high-level scholarship into one volume, and discussing the question biblically, philosophically and scientifically, this work deserves to be studied widely. The volume challenges much of the naturalistic inroads that undermine the biblical message in the year of Darwin's 200th anniversary. It should encourage the reader to question seriously the clamour to embrace neo-Darwinian theory.

Gary Habermas, *Distinguished Research Professor and Chair, Department of Philosophy and Theology, Liberty University*

The title of *Should Christians Embrace Evolution?* poses a question that thoughtful Christians must face, in light of the arguments for theistic evolution being offered by Denis Alexander in England and by Francis Collins in America. To meet the challenge of an evolutionary philosophy that explains life as the product of natural causes alone, we all need help from Christians with expertise in science and theology. Each of us must in the end come to a personal decision about which experts are sufficiently trustworthy that we should accept their guidance in forming our views about which things are real and which are only imaginary. The experts in science and theology who have contributed chapters to *Should Christians Embrace Evolution?* are of the trustworthy kind, and their words of wisdom will be very helpful to Christians who are struggling to sort out conflicting claims and arrive at the truth.

Phillip E. Johnson, *Professor of Law Emeritus, University of California, Berkeley, author of* Darwin on Trial

This book is much needed. As a nuclear physicist, I have observed reconciliation between science and theology in numerous areas, not because of modified theology, but because continuing scientific discovery has overturned nineteenth-century perspectives that sought to challenge biblical theology. The current progress in molecular biology is beyond Darwin's wildest imagination, and readers would be well advised to examine the evidence. As one who lived under Communism, I understand too well that the more a society seeks to enforce an idea, the more important it is to question it.

Dalibor Krupa, *Research Professor of Theoretical Physics at the Institute of Physics of the Slovak Academy of Sciences, Bratislava, Slovakia*

Well-informed, up-to-date and powerfully argued, this collection of theological, philosophical and scientific essays by distinguished authors shows that the theistic evolution on offer from Denis Alexander, Francis Collins and Kenneth Miller conflicts not only with the best biblical exegesis, but also with a sober assessment of the scientific data.

The theological contributors show that accommodation to Darwinism undermines orthodox teaching about creation, the fall, and redemption itself. The scientists show that the complex information common to all life could not arise from materialistic processes, and that the popular 'junk DNA' and human chromosomal fusion arguments for Darwinism dissolve under scrutiny. Evangelical Christians pondering whether they should embrace Darwinism owe it to their integrity to read this book.

Angus Menuge, *Professor of Philosophy, Concordia University Wisconsin, author of* Agents Under Fire: Materialism and the Rationality of Science

The value of the present volume is that it endeavours to deal with the underlying metaphysical assumptions of evolutionary theory and to analyze their implications for classical Christian theology. The book is therefore a fine antidote to superficiality in philosophy of science and in the thinking of many religious believers today, who naively think that evolutionism can or must be swallowed whole in order for Christianity to survive in the modern world.

John Warwick Montgomery, *Professor Emeritus of Law and Humanities, University of Bedfordshire, UK; Distinguished Professor of Philosophy and Christian Thought, Patrick Henry College, Virginia, USA; Director, International Academy of Apologetics, Evangelism and Human Rights, Strasbourg, France*

This excellent collection of essays by theologians and scientists addresses in detail the question of whether Christians have too readily embraced neo-Darwinism and adapted their theology to suit. The scientific rigour and theological clarity of this volume will encourage all those who have not bowed the knee to Darwin and challenge those who have. The arguments it presents are cogent and powerful. It is a much-needed contribution to what has become a one-sided debate.

Alastair Noble, *former Inspector of Schools and Head of Educational Services, Scotland*

The question posed has caused much recent debate. The answer given by these authors is an emphatic 'No!' First, they demonstrate with compelling logic that theistic evolution has serious theological consequences for the gospel. Secondly (and this should make us weep), the theistic evolutionary project is so unnecessary. As the second part of this first-class survey makes clear, there is actually no compelling reason to accept Darwinism anyway. Homological arguments have bitten the dust, junk DNA turns out to be anything but junk, and as for the origin of life itself, biologists haven't got a clue. In terms of recent discoveries in molecular biology, Darwinism is not only wrong but also irrelevant, a Victorian relic.

Colin Reeves, Professor of Operational Research in the School of Mathematical and Information Sciences (MIS) at Coventry University

This book is a formidable challenge to the enterprise of theistic evolution, which necessitates the accommodation of Christian theology and biblical hermeneutics to the essentially atheistic neo-Darwinian paradigm. This means that the authority of science (specifically Darwinian evolutionary theory) is substituted for the authority of Scripture and made normative for biblical interpretation and Christian belief. The result is a contemporary gnostic (to borrow a term from one of the contributions) theology that undermines the authority of Scripture and renders theologically unintelligible the core elements of the Christian gospel and in particular the death of Christ. This exposure of the theological import of theistic evolution is presented in the book with clarity and biblically informed acumen by the relevant contributors.

The book also examines the claimed evidence for Darwinian evolution (specifically the theory of common descent) in homology, the fossil record, chromosomal fusion and the human genome.

The implication of the scientifically orientated contributions is that the subordination of the historic evangelical faith to the passing demands of the neo-Darwinian paradigm by theistic evolutionists has more to do with 'intellectual pacifism' than compelling scientific reasons. The response of the contributors to this theological capitulation is (in their own words) an 'unequivocal no'. That is the right response and this book will enable Christians concerned with safeguarding the integrity of the Christian gospel confidently to make that response.

Patrick J. Roche, Tutor in Philosophy of Religion, Irish Baptist College

Should Christians
Embrace Evolution?

Should Christians Embrace Evolution?

Biblical and scientific responses

Edited by
Norman C. Nevin

INTER-VARSITY PRESS
Norton Street, Nottingham NG7 3HR, England
Email: ivp@ivpbooks.com
Website: www.ivpbooks.com

First published 2009

British Library Cataloguing in Publication Data
A catalogue record for this book is available from the British Library.

UK ISBN: 978-1-84474-406-0

Set in Monotype Garamond 11/13pt
Typeset in Great Britain by Servis Filmsetting Ltd, Stockport, Cheshire
Printed and bound in Great Britain by Ashford Colour Press Ltd, Gosport,
Hampshire

*Inter-Varsity Press publishes Christian books that are true to the Bible and that communicate
the gospel, develop discipleship and strengthen the church for its mission in the world.*

*Inter-Varsity Press is closely linked with the Universities and Colleges Christian Fellowship,
a student movement connecting Christian Unions in universities and colleges throughout Great
Britain, and a member movement of the International Fellowship of Evangelical Students.
Website: www.uccf.org.uk.*

CONTENTS

CONTRIBUTORS

David Anderson has a master's degree in mathematics from the University of Oxford and a bachelor's in theology from the University of Glamorgan (Wales Evangelical School of Theology). He was involved in church planting in the UK before moving to Eldoret, Kenya, where he currently serves as a missionary and a lecturer at a pastors' training college.

Geoff Barnard was for seven years a Senior Research Scientist in the Department of Veterinary Medicine, University of Cambridge, UK. He has been a Senior Lecturer in Biological Sciences at three other UK universities, and a visiting scientist at the Weizmann Institute in Israel.

Alistair Donald is a Church of Scotland minister with an interest in apologetics and is currently Chaplain at Heriot-Watt University. He holds a PhD in environmental science.

Steve Fuller is Professor of Sociology at the University of Warwick. Originally trained in history and philosophy of science, he testified on behalf of intelligent design theory in *Kitzmiller v. Dover Area School District* (2005). Among many books, he is the author of *Science vs. Religion?* (2007) and *Dissent over Descent* (2008).

Greg Haslam is Senior Pastor at Westminster Chapel, London. He has pastored for thirty years and travels widely as a conference speaker, preacher and lecturer. He is the author of several books including *Preach the Word!*, *A Radical Encounter with God*, *The Man Who Wrestled with God* and *Moving in the Prophetic*.

Phil Hills has been in pastoral ministry for the past twenty-three years and has led churches in Coventry, Birmingham and Swansea. He is currently pastor of the Elim Church in Dundonald, Belfast. He has a master's degree in theology from Manchester University.

R. T. Kendall is is an author, speaker, and teacher, and was pastor of Westminster Chapel, London, for twenty-five years.

Andy McIntosh has a PhD in Aeronautics from Cranfield and is Professor of Thermodynamics and Combustion Theory at the University of Leeds (contributing here in a private capacity). He has worked for the Royal Aircraft Establishment and has researched for thirty years in combustion and thermodynamics, and more recently in biomimetics (learning from nature for engineering advantage). He is author of *Genesis for Today* (2001).

Alistair McKitterick is lecturer in Biblical and Theological Studies at Moorlands College, a Christian Bible college in Christchurch. He has degrees in both physics and theology.

Norman C. Nevin OBE is Emeritus Professor of Medical Genetics at the Queen's University, Belfast and Head of the Northern Regional Genetics Service.

Michael Reeves is the Theological Advisor for UCCF. Previously he was an associate minister at All Souls Church, Langham Place, London. He is the author of *The Unquenchable Flame: Introducing the Reformation*. He holds a doctorate in systematic theology from King's College, London.

Andrew Sibley is studying towards a PhD in theology at Exeter University examining the science, theology and philosophy of the Intelligent Design arguments. He has an MSc in Environmental Decision Making and works as a specialist weather forecaster in the environmental arena. He is the author of *Restoring the Ethics of Creation*.

John C. Walton is Research Professor of Chemistry at the University of St Andrews.

FOREWORD

This is a highly significant book because it persuasively argues that Christians cannot accept modern evolutionary theory without also compromising essential teachings of the Bible.

It may at first seem easy to say 'God simply used evolution to bring about the results he desired', as some are proposing today. That view is called 'theistic evolution'. However, the contributors to this volume, both scientists and biblical scholars, show that adopting theistic evolution leads to many positions contrary to the teaching of the Bible, such as these: (1) Adam and Eve were not the first human beings, but they were just two Neolithic farmers among about ten million other human beings on earth at that time, and God just chose to reveal himself to them in a personal way. (2) Those other human beings had already been seeking to worship and serve God or gods in their own ways. (3) Adam was not specially formed by God of 'dust from the ground' (Gen. 2:7) but had two human parents. (4) Eve was not directly made by God out of a 'rib that the Lord God had taken from the man' (Gen. 2:22), but she also had two human parents. (5) Many human beings both then and now are not descended from Adam and Eve. (6) Adam and Eve's sin was not the first sin. (7) Human physical death had occurred for thousands of years before Adam and Eve's sin – it was part of the way living things had always existed. (8) God did not impose any alteration in the natural world when he cursed the ground because of Adam's sin.

As for the scientific evidence, several chapters in this book show that deeper examination of the evidence actually adds more weight to the arguments for intelligent design than for Darwinian evolution.

What is at stake? A lot: the truthfulness of the three foundational chapters for the entire Bible (Genesis 1 – 3), belief in the unity of the human race, belief in the ontological uniqueness of human beings among all God's creatures, belief in the special creation of Adam and Eve in the image of God, belief in the parallel between condemnation through representation by Adam and salvation through representation by Christ, belief in the goodness of God's original creation, belief that suffering and death today are the result of sin and not part of God's original creation, and belief that natural disasters today are the result of the fall and not part of God's original creation. Belief in evolution erodes the foundations.

Evolution is secular culture's grand explanation, the overriding 'meta-narrative' that sinners accept with joy because it allows them to explain life without reference to God, with no accountability to any Creator, no moral standards to restrain their sin, 'no fear of God before their eyes' (Rom. 3:18) – and now theistic evolutionists tell us that Christians can just surrender to this massive attack on the Christian faith and safely, inoffensively, tack on God, not as the omnipotent God who in his infinite wisdom directly created all living things, but as the invisible deity who makes absolutely no detectable difference in the nature of living beings as they exist today. It will not take long for unbelievers to dismiss the idea of such a God who makes no difference at all. To put it in terms of an equation, when atheists assure us that *matter + evolution + 0 = all living things*, and then theistic evolutionists answer, no, that *matter + evolution + God = all living things*, it will not take long for unbelievers to conclude that, therefore, *God = 0*.

I was previously aware that theistic evolution had serious difficulties, but I am now more firmly convinced than ever that it is impossible to believe consistently in both the truthfulness of the Bible and Darwinian evolution. We have to choose one or the other.

Wayne Grudem
Research Professor of Theology and Biblical Studies
Phoenix Seminary, Phoenix, Arizona, USA

PREFACE: A TWENTY-FIRST-CENTURY CHALLENGE

Phil Hills

The twenty-first century is witnessing an aggressive attack on the credibility of Christian faith. Daniel Dennett likens people of faith to drunk drivers in that they are not only a danger to themselves and others but are doubly culpable because they have allowed religion to cloud their rationality. He asserts that religion is one of the greatest threats to scientific progress. Christopher Hitchens has written to explain how religion poisons everything and is invested with ignorance and hostile to free inquiry. Richard Dawkins in his best selling book, *The God Delusion*, makes it abundantly clear that, in his opinion, science and faith are completely incompatible. The underlying argument for all of the above is that evolution has made faith utterly redundant and anyone who tries to hold on to religious conviction in the face of scientific enlightenment is significantly lacking in reason.

For many years scientists who were Christians pursued their scientific education and research without the fear of being derided for their lack of credibility. However, the new atheists are being given a good hearing. *The God Delusion* is Dawkins' best-selling book ever, remaining for fifty-one weeks in the *New York Times* bestseller list. There has been a call that any scientists questioning evolution should be stripped of their academic qualifications. Some are claiming victimization, others are afraid of voicing their real position. In September 2008 Professor Michael Reiss resigned as Director of Education for the Royal Society after some Nobel laureates embarked on a letter-writing campaign calling for his resignation. They believed that his role within the Royal Society was at odds with his calling as an Anglican priest because of his suggestion that questions about creation should be discussed in school. Even Dawkins admitted this to be like a witch hunt.

In the past Christians have held various views that they believed reconciled their theology with scientific understanding and were accorded respect. However, confronted by attack from the new atheists, any view that doesn't fully accept evolution is now being denigrated by evolutionary creationists. Those Christians within the scientific community who wholly embrace evolution appear to be embarrassed by those who don't. *Third Way*, *Christianity*, and *IDEA* have recently included calls for Christians to celebrate Darwin. The Bible Society has dedicated a whole issue of *The Bible in TransMission* to theistic evolution and distributed copies of *Rescuing Darwin* to 20,000 church leaders in England and Wales. The Theos think tank and the Faraday Institute have commissioned research entitled 'Rescuing Darwin', and though they had not yet completed their research Theos wrote to *The Times* to explain that their response to the new atheists and to those Christians unwilling to accept evolution would be 'a plague on both your houses'. The Anglican Church has recently published an official apology to Charles Darwin for the way they challenged his theory following the publication of *On the Origin of Species*, and Charles Foster has declared in *The Selfless Gene*, that 'Creationism has inoculated a whole generation against Christianity'.

This is a very important time for the Christian Church and our response to this twenty-first-century challenge is critical. It is not sufficient to come up with a response that appears intellectually credible to the scientific establishment if it is not theologically accurate. If the authority of Scripture is to be observed then any theological model must begin with an exegesis of the relevant biblical texts and not a scientific paradigm. Theological rigour must not be sacrificed on the altar of scientific consensus, and it is high time to unravel the empirically-based scientific information from the metaphysical perspectives imposed on it. It is not enough to make vague assertions about the literary genre of Genesis without engaging in the hard and detailed questions that this gives rise to.

Some are engaging those wider questions. Professors Malcolm Jeeves and R. J. Berry sought to address them in *Science, Life and Christian Belief* (Apollos, 1998), and more recently Denis Alexander has published *Creation or Evolution: Do We Have to Choose?* (Monarch, 2008), in which he seeks to reconcile a commitment to the authority of Scripture with Darwinian evolution. J. I. Packer regards this work as the 'clearest and most judicious' to be found on the subject, yet this of itself should give rise to concern as Alexander explicitly states that evolution is 'incontrovertible' and he therefore seeks a theological model that will fit with the science. However, Alexander, although not a theologian, does seek to address the significant theological questions that arise from embracing evolution. His theology might be described as novel but it could certainly not be described as mainstream. It must not be assumed though, that there is anything easy about this exercise. Evolution, as intended by the title of this book, specifically refers to the Darwinian mechanisms of mutations and natural selection and the commitment to common ancestry that are central to the ruling scientific paradigm.

As recently as summer 2007 the Faraday Institute (of which Alexander is the Director) invited Professor Michael Ruse to address the question, 'Can a Christian be a Darwinian?' Ruse concludes there are two major obstacles in providing a positive answer. First, the special nature that Christian theology ascribes to humanity is in direct contradiction to a Darwinian understanding that makes no distinction between any organisms, each one being necessarily best adapted for their particular environment. The second obstacle is reconciling the concept of a benevolent God with one who purposefully chooses to use suffering and death as the means of evolving life. These are not inconsequential questions and any Christian who embraces evolution must be able to posit intelligent answers if their position is to be considered credible. It is not acceptable to say, 'Evolution is true, we just haven't got a theology that fits with it yet', because that would demonstrate that commitment to the authority of Scripture is secondary!

In the face of the new atheists' claim that evolution has rendered faith utterly redundant there is a flood tide arising that demands that Christians must embrace evolution or acknowledge that they are opposed to science. This book believes that this is a false premise. It is written to set out a clear theological framework on the relevant issues and to confront the questions that arise from it. It is written with a compelling conviction that science and faith are not in opposition. It is written by theologians who are committed to the authority of Scripture and to the exercise of careful exegesis. It is written by scientists who are fully persuaded of the importance of rigorous scientific investigation but who are dissatisfied with the arbitrary exclusion of possible conclusions and the failure to follow the evidence wherever it leads. This is not written for a select readership that already has expert knowledge of the subjects. It is written for ordinary men and women, who have the capacity to weigh the information, seek further clarification and draw their own conclusions.

1. EVOLUTION AND THE CHURCH

Alistair Donald

The relationship between Darwin's theory and the Church has been by no means straightforward, nor, despite claims to the contrary, is the matter finally settled. Given that the scientific evidence is in significant ways at variance with Darwinism, as outlined elsewhere in this book, Christians need certainly not feel compelled to subsume their theology to the theory of evolution. The implications of doing so are considerable, as will be made clear later in this chapter, but first it will be helpful to look at the historical context.

The relationship between evolution and the Church

Since first publication of *On the Origin of Species* in 1859 the Church has been divided in its view of Darwin's evolutionary theory. It is true that Rev. Charles Kingsley gave a fulsome endorsement four days before publication, having received an advance copy. As an Anglican clergyman he is often referred to in an attempt to demonstrate that the Church of England had no difficulty accepting Darwin's thesis. However, when Rev. Dr Malcolm Brown, Director of Mission and Public Affairs for the Church of England recently wrote, 'the Church of England owes you an apology for misunderstanding you and, by getting our first reaction wrong, encouraging others to misunderstand you still', then it is clear that Kingsley's enthusiasm was not universally shared.

Even those whom Darwin counted among his friends and mentors did not wholly support his views, due to their Christian convictions. Charles Lyell struggled to accept natural selection as the primary mechanism driving evolution and could not agree that man was descended from brute beasts. When he eventually accepted natural selection it was in an equivocal way. At the same time Asa Gray, described by Darwin as his best advocate, was challenging the utter randomness he saw in the theory and could not accept the absence of divine purpose and design in the process. He corresponded at length with Darwin while also writing articles and essays to persuade others of Darwin's essential thesis. In 1876 Gray, aware of growing religious opposition to evolution, published *Darwiniana,* to try to reconcile it with Protestant Christianity.

From a Catholic perspective, St George Mivart was endeavouring to demonstrate that there was no conflict between evolution and the teaching of the Church. In 1871, he wrote *On the Genesis of Species* and addressed, in chapter 12, the perceived theological objections. In spite of his own view that these could be reconciled, he acknowledged that there were others, such as atheists Carl Vogt and Ludwig Büchner, who did not agree. Mivart eventually lost his friendship with Darwin and Huxley and was later excommunicated from the Roman Catholic Church. However, in 1950 a papal encyclical from Pope Pious XII stated that biological evolution was compatible with Christian faith, though declaring that divine intervention was necessary for the creation of the human soul.

In 1865, the Victoria Institute was founded in recognition that Darwin's theory impinged on matters well beyond science. Its stated first object is telling: 'To investigate fully and impartially the most important questions of Philosophy and Science, but more especially those that bear upon the great truths revealed in Holy Scripture, with the view of defending these truths against the oppositions of Science, falsely so called.' The Institute was not officially opposed to evolution but perusing their *Journal of Transactions* illustrates the fact that many were challenging it. These challenges were often scientific but the objects make it clear that the motive of these challenges was the defence of Scripture.

Among Presbyterians on both sides of the Atlantic there was an ambivalent approach to Darwinism. Hugh Miller, the highly influential naturalist and Scottish Free Churchman, was no friend to young-earth views of geology, arguing against the 'anti-geologists of the Church of England', but although he died three years before Darwin's *Origins* was published we know that he was opposed to existing theories of transmutation in biology and would surely have been sceptical of Darwin. In due course many Scottish churchmen did embrace the new theory with enthusiasm. By the early twentieth century B. B. Warfield, Principal of Princeton Seminary, did so as well, although the 'Darwinism' that was endorsed by him emphatically ruled out the purely chance element that is arguably intrinsic to the theory. Warfield's predecessor at Princeton, Charles Hodge, had written specifically on the issue in 1874, bluntly branding Darwinism as 'atheism'. Arnold Guyot, a Swiss-American geologist and evangelical Presbyterian, also challenged the theory, most notably in his 1884 work *Creation, or the Biblical Cosmogony in the Light of Modern Science.* In 1886, Augustus H. Strong of the American Baptists weighed into the fray. In his *Systematics* he argued that evolution could have been the mechanism that God used to create. Philip Gosse of the Plymouth Brethren was opposed to Darwin.

The Baptist Union in Great Britain was to feel the impact of the controversy in 1887. Charles Haddon Spurgeon was their best known minister and regarded as 'the Prince of Preachers'. In the Surrey Music Hall he commanded crowds of 10,000 and at the Crystal Palace he preached to 23,654 people. In 1861, his congregation had moved to the Metropolitan Tabernacle, which seated 5,000 with room for a further 1,000 standing. He published a monthly magazine, *The Sword and the Trowel*, and in 1887 this was used to highlight the *Down Grade Controversy*. This was concerned with higher criticism, the authority of Scripture and the impact of Darwinism. Initially, two articles were published anonymously in

March and April. These were actually written by Robert Shindler, Spurgeon's friend. In the first one he spoke of the *Down Grade* being responsible for spawning the theory of evolution.

The response to these articles was enormous and Spurgeon himself wrote further on this perceived malaise, citing Darwin's theory as part of the problem. The consequences were far-reaching, with many lining up on either side of the divide. Spurgeon withdrew from the Baptist Union and the Union censured Spurgeon. Baptist Associations from various parts of Canada and America sent resolutions unanimously supporting the stand that Spurgeon had taken. Just one of those, the Baptist Association of the State of Kentucky, represented 960 ministers. It is evident from this that, at that time, there were thousands of ministers who had problems with evolution.

In response to the liberal theology of the latter part of the nineteen century, *The Fundamentals* were written between 1910 and 1915. This was a series of ninety essays intended to set out essential Christian doctrine. These included an attack on evolution by George F. Wright, a geologist and Congregational minister. As a friend of Asa Gray he had been at one time something of a leader among Christian Darwinists, but in later life he revised his position completely, asserting that special creation was wholly responsible for biological variation. Many believe *The Fundamentals* gave rise to the fundamentalist movement within Christianity. This is interesting because some of those who wrote *The Fundamentals*, like B. B. Warfield, in fact subscribed to a form of theistic evolution.

George McCready Price, a Seventh-Day Adventist and avowed creationist, regularly attended the meetings of the Victoria Institute held between 1924 and 1928. He produced numerous anti-evolutionary works, including *The New Geology*. During this time Sir Ambrose Fleming was appointed President of the Institute (1927), but the influence of those sceptical of Darwinism was waning and some were looking for an opportunity more effectively to gather and organize opponents of evolution. In 1932, Sir Ambrose Fleming, Douglas Dewar and Captain Bernard Acworth, all leading members of the Victoria Institute, founded the Evolution Protest Movement. At its first public meeting in 1935, with 600 in attendance, the scientific credibility of evolution was challenged and some religious implications identified. Since that time it has changed its name to the Creation Science Movement and continues to pursue its original objectives.

In 1946 Henry Morris wrote a short book seeking to attack evolution. In 1961 he co-authored *The Genesis Flood* with John Whitcomb and cited George McCready Price as a key influence. This book went through thirty-nine reprints and sold over 200,000 copies, making a significant impact on American evangelicals. It sought to interpret geology in light of a global flood. Morris subsequently was involved in founding the *Creation Research Society* and then the *Institute for Creation Research*. He is regarded by some as responsible for the rise of the modern creation science movement. The Presbyterian Church of the United States (now the PCUSA) revisited its own position in 1969. They officially declared that there is no contradiction between the theory of evolution and the Bible and overturned their previous statements of 1886, 1888, 1889 and 1924.

In the early 1990s the Intelligent Design (ID) movement emerged, from roots in the previous decade. It is often incorrectly maintained that ID was an offshoot of biblical creationism, but in fact the movement originated among scientists who were formerly Darwinists but had come to be sceptical of the theory because recent advances in science, particularly biochemistry and information science, seemed to be incompatible with Darwinism.

This short overview demonstrates two primary points. First, the Church has been divided over its view on Darwinism since 1859 to the present time. Secondly, the division over evolutionary theory has not come from one particular wing of the Church but from a wide variety of denominational perspectives.

The implications of embracing evolution

As highlighted in the Preface, there is currently a call for the Church to embrace evolution, and it is asserted that there is no contradiction between Christian faith and Darwinism. In order to consider this claim carefully we need to identify the implications for the Church of embracing evolutionary theory. There are obviously many who believe that evolution is the mechanism that God used to create the variety of life on this planet. However, for those who are serious about the supremacy of Scripture, it is essential that any apparent theological tensions that arise from this are rigorously reviewed. It would be premature to say the least to commit to a scientific position without having a clearly worked out theology that accords with it, particularly when so much of the scientific evidence does not necessitate a Darwinian explanation.

One significant difficulty in trying to reconcile evolution and the Bible is that Darwinian evolution does not allow that there is a hierarchy of life within the natural world. Natural selection ensures that each species is best adapted to survive and thrive within its own environment but it cannot ascribe a special significance to humanity. The Bible on the other hand describes man and woman as the pinnacle of God's creative work. Humankind is seen as both special and different to the other life forms and is given dominion over them. The greatest demonstration of this special nature is seen in Christ taking on himself human flesh and laying down his life at Calvary as Redeemer.

Humankind is identified in the Scriptures as being created in the image of God. Theologians wrestle with this concept, attempting to understand exactly what this means, and there are several different views normally posited. However, there is no dissent from the view that the Bible declares humanity as unique within creation. This was not the position of Charles Darwin. His friend and mentor, Charles Lyell, debated the issue with him. Lyell could not accept that humans were descended from beasts in the same way that other organisms had evolved, though he supported much of Darwin's theory.

If Christians are to embrace evolution they must have an evolutionary theory that ascribes a special significance to humanity and recognizes the primacy of humankind within the evolutionary framework or else they must impose this special nature onto humanity apart from evolution. In his recent book, Denis Alexander, Director of the Faraday Institute for Science and Religion, St Edmund's College Cambridge, finds the special nature of humanity not in the evolutionary process but in the intervention of God. He argues that the image of God is not imparted to *Homo sapiens* through evolution but by a special revelation to a particular couple, Adam and Eve, and this revelation makes them *Homo divinus.*[1]

In his suggested model, Adam and Eve were living among up to 10,000,000 other *Homo sapiens*, so how was the image of God imparted to them or their progeny? Obviously, the vast majority of the earth's future population would not be descended from Adam and Eve. How then, are they created in the image of God? If one's reading of the biblical text allows a global flood that destroys all the living, then it could be argued that those who followed the flood were direct descendants of Adam, through Noah, and they could be said to bear the image of God in that way. However, if one's reading of the biblical text excludes a global flood, there must be some other explanation for how humanity as a whole is created in the image of God. As mentioned earlier, the Catholic Church adopted a position that necessitates divine intervention for the creation of the human soul and in this way God's direct intervention sets man apart as unique.

The issue of humanity's special position before God also requires that those embracing evolution explain why humans will not evolve into a different species. The alternative is to explain how this new species fits into the eternal purposes of God that are identified in the Bible. While there are wide-ranging eschatological interpretations, they all concern themselves with the eternity of humanity not its extinction.

When Christians embrace evolution it is usually with a conviction that this is the vehicle God has used to bring about the variety of life on our planet. It seems perfectly plausible to them that God set natural laws in place and chose this process for the development of life. However, this scenario raises numerous problems. Darwinian evolution does not allow any external direction. Natural selection working on random mutations is what gives force to the evolutionary process. Although the mutation mechanism was not known in Darwin's day, the chance element was clearly emphasized and it was this that Asa Gray found so objectionable about

---

1. Denis Alexander, *Creation or Evolution: Do We Have to Choose?* (Oxford: Monarch Books, 2008), p. 237.

Darwin's position. He urged Darwin to acknowledge design and refuted the randomness that Darwin championed.

If God is immanent in his creation then to what degree is he directing the process of evolution? Darwin withstood any notion of divine direction, not least because of the pain and death in nature he had observed. He could not attribute such activity or design to a benevolent God. Theists believe in the immanence of God. They do not subscribe to the concept of a deity who started a process of creation that he is now uninvolved in. This is a concept that Darwin would not dismiss, but he totally refused to accept the immanence of God in the process of evolution. This was his great idea – natural selection not God explained the development of all life on earth!

Alexander repeatedly asserts the immanence of God in every aspect of life and this, of course, is in line with orthodox evangelical theology but it is in direct contradiction to Darwin's theory of evolution. To embrace evolution and Christianity one must reconcile natural selection with the immanence of God. It is not sufficient to simply assert that both are true. The originator of natural selection believed them to be mutually exclusive. Stephen Jay Gould held to the view (widely supported by the scientific community) that if the whole process of evolution was to start again it is highly improbable that it would result in the same endpoint. Alexander is challenging that view because it cannot be reconciled to his theology. Any theology that embraces evolution must explain, at some level, how God is directing the process of natural selection and this explanation must make clear how natural selection can then still be considered to be natural selection.

Those who believe that God has indeed chosen evolution must address the issue of pain, suffering and death that evolution necessitates in order for life to develop. Often the debate focuses on whether it is more or less glorious that God should create instantly or design an intricate process that creates different species over billions of years. However, that seems entirely secondary to explaining how God is glorified by a process that demands agony, disease, death and extinction as necessary to the evolution of life. To conclude that God deliberately designed this process makes God directly responsible for suffering and death and runs completely counter to the view of God's goodness expressed in the

Bible. Alexander will not concede that God may deliberately hide himself or his purposes because he argues that to do so would be deceitful and God is not a liar! Yet he can conceive of a God who deliberately designed a process of disease and death for the development of life.[2]

Traditionally, Christian theology holds that the fall is responsible for the entrance of sin and death into the world. It acknowledges that pain and suffering are part and parcel of this life but anticipates that they will be completely overthrown in the coming kingdom. It views death as an enemy that will ultimately be destroyed. Evolution, on the other hand, accepts death as essential to the development of new life forms. Death is not an enemy if it is part of a created order that God considers to be very good. How is the place given to death in evolutionary theory in any way compatible with the place given to death in the Bible? These questions do not go away by an appeal to the genre of Genesis, but are central to the key themes of Christianity.

Another key issue that must be resolved is how all humanity is reckoned to be 'in Adam'. The cross is unquestionably central to Christian theology and the great hope that it affords is that 'one man' has atoned for the sins of all. The parallelism of New Testament teaching is between Adam and Christ as federal representatives of humanity. In the theology being expounded by Alexander it is very difficult to understand how one among several millions and who had been predated by others could properly be said to represent the whole. This is not secondary, it is central to our understanding of Christian faith. The New Testament argues that we can have confidence that we are included in the atoning work of Christ because it is evident that we are included in Adam.

Synthesizing contradictory worldviews

Christianity is not a set of unrelated assertions about truth. It is a narrative, beginning with a creation that is good, the story of

---

2. Alexander, *Creation or Evolution*, pp. 244–247.

its fall and an account of the redemptive activity of God that will lead to the perfect order of God for life finally being established. In this narrative, something of the character and nature of God is revealed. In the person and work of Christ the truth of this world-view is intended to be established. If, therefore, some aspects of biblical interpretation or traditional theological perspectives are to be challenged, consideration needs to be given to the impact on the whole Christian story.

Christianity reveals Christ as a saviour. It explains humanity's need to be saved from their sin and their inability to save them-selves. Evolutionary theory is trying to understand humanity's propensity for good or evil. In the early 1970s, George R. Price suggested a mathematical formula to explain altruism in humanity as part of the process of natural selection. Subsequently Richard Dawkins argued strongly that the selfish gene determines the behaviour of humanity and consequently he struggles to ascribe responsibility to people. These scientists were and are following the natural course of questioning that is suggested by the evolu-tionary worldview. How will we reconcile their explanations with our gospel? This line of argument is not from fear of what might be uncovered by science but to illustrate a point. What is the minimum we will accept as essential to hold to Christianity?

If my genetic make up is responsible for my moral conduct, in what way can God hold me accountable and why do I need a saviour? Already Denis Alexander is positing a 'fall' that is no big deal and suggests that traditional Christian theology is more of a reflection of Milton's *Paradise Lost* than of the Bible (although it may be wondered where Milton got the concept from!). Death becomes then not a result of the fall but a natural part of life's evolutionary advance. It seems a very postmodern approach that allows the individual to pick various parts of opposing worldviews and to seek to synthesize them into 'my' truth.

A naturalistic definition of science rules out any consideration of a Christian worldview from the data that science uncovers. Did the fall have any impact on the natural world? Is there a bondage to decay in the creation that was not part of God's original created order? Many would argue that the answer to both of these ques-tions is yes, but such matters can never be considered in the light of methodological naturalism. If either of the above questions is answered in the affirmative then that would have important implications for all origins research. If theism is true, then insisting on naturalistic processes for the origin and development of life is based on a false premise. That is part of the problem of seeking to synthesize opposing worldviews. The evolutionary worldview does not allow any consideration of the biblical worldview.

However, if Christians choose to embrace aspects of evolution then what is inviolable in our faith needs to be established. Is God controlling and directing the development of life? Are humans the special creation of God? Is humanity responsible for suffering, sickness and pain in the world? Will God hold humanity accountable for their wrongdoing and punish sin? Is death the enemy of humankind or is it responsible for our evolution? Is God a just and loving deity who is seeking to redeem and restore the world to his original intention or did God deliberately create a world full of sickness, pain and death with the intention of creating a world without them at some future point in time? Is Jesus Christ a Saviour or a good example of the sort of lifestyle that it is preferable for people to choose? Embracing evolution has implications for each of these questions that are crucial to Christianity.

The pastoral implications

The Church seeks not only to declare the gospel to a lost world but also to offer support, comfort and insight to people dealing with the issues of life. Pastors spend a great deal of time in hospitals, in the homes of the bereaved, at funeral services and with people in crises, seeking to apply the truth of God's loving care in difficult times. However, if Christianity is to embrace evolution we must consider what the most appropriate way forward will be in offering help and counsel to those who are hurting.

Traditionally, counsel and comfort have been expressed in the context of a fallen world that was not God's design and where death is our enemy which Jesus Christ came into the world to confront and overcome in order that it might ultimately be destroyed. If, however, the fall had no impact on the natural order, and sickness, suffering and death are the chosen order of God to develop life, our pastoral message needs to change significantly. It should therefore be clear that it is also highly questionable whether or not Church ministers are best placed to give this support. Surely scientists, who properly understand evolutionary theory, would be better equipped to explain to grieving relatives the reason for the demise of their six-year-old. As elderly parents lie dying in agony from wasting diseases, should we be explaining the evolutionary advance that may one day come from the deleterious mutations that their body is now suffering?

Evil in the world is understood very differently by evolutionary theorists than it is by those committed to the supremacy of Scripture. The Bible teaches that Christ came into the world to destroy the works of the evil one. This is demonstrated in the ministry of Jesus as he healed those who are afflicted by disease and sickness, showing his power and the nature of a kingdom that is to come. According to Jesus the thief comes 'to kill and destroy' (John 10:10) but according to Darwin it is evolution that kills and destroys. According to those urging Christians to embrace evolution this killing and destruction is the design of God for the development of life.

There is much more to embracing evolution than suggesting different ways of interpreting the creation passages of Scripture. A clear understanding of the theory is essential in order to fully appreciate its implications, and a commitment to the supremacy of Scripture will not allow the embracing of any aspect of evolution that compromises the key themes of the biblical text.

© Alistair Donald, 2009

2. THE LANGUAGE OF GENESIS

Alistair McKitterick

In this chapter we will discuss the language of Genesis. The question we want to ask is: what kinds of things can we reasonably read out of Genesis? What does it want to say to us or, more precisely, what kind of thing did the author intend for the reader to get from it? In order to answer this question, we will engage with a range of approaches and authors, but in particular we will respond to a number of statements made in Denis Alexander's chapter 'What about Genesis?' in his book *Creation or Evolution: Do We Have to Choose?*[1]

The overriding impression we get from Genesis is that it is to do with beginnings. The title given to the book in Hebrew (*běrē'šît*) is simply the first word, meaning 'In the beginning'. It was probably when the book was translated into Greek, round about the third century BC, that a title was first given to it to reflect its general theme, and that title was Genesis, meaning 'birth' or 'origin' (Gen. 2:4). We see this in all kinds of ways, including the early genealogies that make references to those who were the 'fathers' (or

---

1. Oxford: Monarch Books, 2008.

originators) of those who lived in tents, played the harp and flute, or introduced metallurgy (Gen. 4:20–22). But first and foremost, Genesis is an account of the origin of the world and humankind.

We are increasingly aware of the importance of recognizing our worldview in debates about biblical theology and science. Our worldview shapes our expectations and interprets our most basic and important experiences of life. It shapes answers to the fundamental questions of life, such as 'where did the world come from, and what kind of world is it?', 'what is the reason for suffering in the world?', 'who am I, and how ought I to live?', 'where is the world going to, and what will happen to me when I die?'

In this chapter I will argue that Genesis intends to give an authoritative account of the creation of the world, and to form in the reader a biblical worldview by providing answers to these foundational questions. This includes: that the world was created over a period of six days; that Adam and Eve were responsible for the invasion of death into the world; that one day there will come a solution to the problem of evil through the seed of the woman (Gen. 3:15). As we read it now in its canonical context, Genesis lays the foundation for our most important theological concepts, namely creation and redemption. For example, to properly understand why Jesus came into the world to die for sins, or the church received its great commission to go into all the world, we require the Genesis account of the fall and its effects, and the promised blessing of Abraham to all the nations of the world.

It should be immediately obvious that the kinds of answers that the author of Genesis gives to these kinds of questions will be entirely different to the answers from a Darwinian worldview. Death, for example, in the biblical worldview, is an intruder into an otherwise 'very good' world, and the consequence of human sin. For the Darwinian, on the other hand, death is the necessary method of selecting out those less well-suited to survive and pass on genes, and therefore part of the 'creative process' of life which resulted in the arrival of human beings.[2]

---

2. 'NATURAL SELECTION is a very grim natural reaper. Darwin made the bold claim that, at the very heart of evolution, many small deletions in

Reading Genesis in historical context

For good biblical interpretation, a text must be read in context. There are basically two aspects of context which must be addressed for any reliable study of the biblical text: the historical context and the literary context.

What is the correct historical context for a study of Genesis? The answer you give to this question will largely determine the kinds of intentions you think the author of Genesis had. For many years the historical context imagined by scholars for the composition of Genesis was a late Babylonian one. The so-called Documentary Hypothesis saw the book of Genesis as the result of many centuries of different texts that were reworked into a composite story, and that this process concluded when Judah was in exile in Babylon. That is, the pressing theological concern that the editor of Genesis had was how to relate to the Babylonian gods of the nation in which they were living, now that Yahweh had apparently been defeated (they would have reached that conclusion because the Jerusalem temple had been destroyed in 586 BC). Those who opt for such a Babylonian context have often done so on the basis of so-called conflicting or duplicate accounts in Genesis. If Genesis showed signs of being a roughly-stitched assemblage of contradictory accounts then it is unlikely to be the product of one consistent mind, and would fit better within a Babylonian exile context. For example, Denis Alexander points to what he calls the 'completely reversed' order of the creation of humans in Genesis 2 compared to Genesis 1.[3] He then spends considerable time reading Genesis in light of the Babylonian mythologies and cosmogonies.[4]

---

bulk – many small wanton deaths – feeding on the throwaway optimism of minor variation, could, in a counter-intuitive way, add up to something truly new and meaningful. In the drama of traditional selection theory, death plays the star role.' Kevin Kelly (Executive Editor of *Wired* magazine), *Out of Control: The New Biology of Machines* (London: Fourth Estate, 1995 [1994]), pp. 479–480.

3. Alexander, *Creation or Evolution*, pp. 158.

4. Ibid., pp. 160–163.

The obvious alternative historical context is the one suggested by biblical tradition, especially the Gospels, namely that it was essentially Moses who authored the Pentateuch in the middle of the second millennium BC, and would probably have done so from a tent in the wilderness, having recently led the Israelites out of Egypt. Those who opt for the Mosaic view (allowing for some later revisionary work) do so for a variety of reasons.[5] One reason is that it is more traditional. Academic support for this view, however, is that Genesis contains details that could only have come from that era. Kenneth Kitchen observes that the many details of the covenants entered into by the patriarchs could only have come from a second millennium BC context. Other observations include specific things like appropriate terminology (Joseph as 'domestic', then 'steward', Potiphar as 'dignitary'), and even the right price for the era for slaves (Gen. 37:28).[6]

Reading Genesis in a Babylonian literary context

But what about the widespread practice of reading Genesis in the light of other Babylonian texts? There are certainly many similarities between Genesis and the more ancient Mesopotamian accounts in terms of subject areas. There is the making of people in *Atrahasis* as well as a great flood; there is the plant of immortality in the *Epic of Gilgamesh* (Gilgamesh loses it to a snake, thus condemning him to be mortal); and in the Sumerian king-lists, the great ages of the kings decline after a great flood. Kitchen suggests that such traditions could have been brought with Abraham as he travelled west from Ur. Nonetheless, in typical understated fashion, Kitchen concludes that Moses, in light of his Egyptian

---

5. See the excellent work on the topic by Duane Garrett in *Rethinking Genesis: The Sources and Authorship of the First Book of the Pentateuch* (Ferne: Mentor, 2000).

6. Kenneth A. Kitchen, 'The Patriarchal Age: Myth or History?', *BAR* 21 (Mar/Apr 1995); http://cojs.org/articles/BAR%201995%20Mar-Apr/The%20Patriarchal%20Age.pdf.

education and upbringing, would be 'by far the least unfitted' to be the author/compiler of Genesis.[7] More recently, Duane Garrett has argued the same thing.[8] Despite this real possibility of Moses as author, most commentators still read Genesis 1 – 11 as responding to a late Babylonian literary context.

In 1876 George Smith first published the *Babylonian Genesis* (also known as *Enuma Elish*), the epic story of how the Babylonian god Marduk defeated the salt-water goddess Tiamat and then went on to create the world and human beings. Since that time, the common assumption has been that Genesis must be read in light of, and as a response to, this and other Babylonian texts. I shall call this Assumption A. It is quite common, therefore, to read that Genesis is derived and dependent upon them. For example, in the last century Hermann Gunkel wrote that the text of Genesis 1 compels us to 'seek the origin of the Israelite tradition in Babylon', and other biblical texts 'show the path along which the Marduk myth was transformed into Genesis 1'.[9]

There are several dependencies suggested between Genesis and Babylonian texts. Genesis 1 and 2 are said to be read in the light of *Enuma Elish* where Marduk divides the body of the salt-water goddess Tiamat and uses half of it to roof up the sky, and then goes on to form humanity out of the blood of her general Kingu in order to relieve the gods from their chores.[10] The flood narratives of Genesis 6 to 9, on the other hand, are read in light of such texts as the *Epic of Gilgamesh* and *Atrahasis*, where humans are to be

---

7. Kenneth Kitchen, 'The Old Testament in its Context: 1 From the Origins to the Eve of the Exodus', *Theological Students' Fellowship Bulletin* 59 (1971), p. 9.

8. Garrett, *Rethinking Genesis*, especially pp. 79–83.

9. Hermann Gunkel, 'The Influence of Babylonian Mythology Upon the Biblical Creation Story', in Bernhard Anderson (ed.), *Creation in the Old Testament* (Issues in Religion and Theology, vol. 6; London: SPCK, 1984), pp. 46–47.

10. Stephanie Dalley (transl. & ed.), *Myths from Mesopotamia: Creation, the Flood, Gilgamesh, and Others* (Oxford: Oxford University, 1998), p. 253–255, 260–261.

destroyed because they annoy the gods. Gordon and Rendsburg, for example, write that 'there can be no doubt that the Israelite flood story has Mesopotamian precursors (either the Gilgamesh Epic itself, or parallel, less well-known, flood traditions). This demonstrates very clearly that Israel did not live in a vacuum, but rather was part and parcel of the ancient Near Eastern cultural world'.[11] Others have suggested the Canaanite religion as the appropriate literary background for reading Genesis. In Day's 1985 book, *God's Conflict With the Dragon and the Sea: Echoes of a Canaanite Myth in the Old Testament*, he argued that Genesis should be read in the light of the mythology found in the Ugaritic texts of the conflict between the storm-god Baal against the sea-god Yam.[12]

It is important that we understand the correct relationship with such texts because it sets the reader's expectations for interpreting Genesis. If the literary context of Genesis is the *Babylonian Genesis* then the author of Genesis does not primarily want to tell us *how* God created the world, but rather wants the reader to know that the Israelite deity Yahweh did it, rather than the Babylonian god Marduk. The emphasis is significantly shifted away from what the text says and is focused instead on what is not said. It is no longer *that* God created the sun and moon that is stressed, for example; instead the author of Genesis relegates the sun and moon from gods in a polytheistic pantheon to 'mere' lights in the heavens.

This shift in emphasis is very powerful, once you accept it. It gives the impression of reading the biblical text responsibly, because you are reading it 'in its historical context'. It also means that what looks like a fairly innocuous text, such as 'now the earth was formless and empty' (Gen. 1:2), becomes a code for a cosmic battle that can be read out of the text once the right assumptions are adopted. Commentators will read Genesis as if

---

11. Cyrus H. Gordon and Gary A. Rendsburg, *The Bible and the Ancient Near East* (New York/London: Norton, 1997), pp. 50–51.

12. J. Day, *God's Conflict With the Dragon and the Sea: Echoes of a Canaanite Myth in the Old Testament* (Cambridge: Cambridge University Press, 1985).

God were quelling the rebellious elements to produce life and the world. This is particularly seen in the way that the term 'chaos' is used.

Chaos

The language of mythological battles between the gods has been modified by the use of the term 'chaos'. The term chaos has a well-established mythological use, in that it was one of three pre-existing beings that Hesiod describes in his *Theogony*, whilst the Roman writer Ovid depicts the primordial matter this way:

> One [body] was the face of Nature; if a face;
> Rather a rude and indigested mass:
> A lifeless lump, unfashion'd and unframed,
> Of jarring seeds, and justly Chaos named.[13]

Chaos is commonly depicted as more than just disorder, rather, as an opposing force that God (or the gods) must work against in order to bring out his good creation. For example, Bernard Anderson describes Tiamat, the sea-water goddess of *Enuma Elish*, as part of the 'primeval, watery chaos' and makes a comparison with Genesis 1:2.[14] The conflict theme is sometimes expressed in the term *chaoskampf*, particularly associated with the German scholar Hermann Gunkel. He asserted that the Hebrew word for the 'deep' in Genesis 1:2, *tehom*, was derived from the Babylonian goddess Tiamat, and that therefore the Genesis creation account found its origins in Babylon. Similarly, Görg has suggested an Egyptian origin for the phrase *tōhû wābōhû* (empty and unproductive) that

---

13. Ovid, *Metamorphoses*, transl. Sir Samuel Garth, John Dryden, *et al.* (1836), p. 17; http://classics.mit.edu/Ovid/metam.1.first.html.

14. Bernhard W. Anderson, *Creation Versus Chaos: the Reinterpretation of Mythical Symbolism in the Bible* (Eugene: Wipf and Stock, 1987), p. 17.

carries the sense of a 'menacing reality' and is itself another representative of primordial chaos.[15]

A similar conclusion regarding chaos is found in Brueggemann's reworking of Genesis 1 in his more recent work *Theology of the Old Testament*. Initially, he reads the creation narrative in light of Israel's exile, and says 'the chaos already extant in v. 2 represents the reality of exile – life at risk and in disorder'.[16] He states that 'we are bound to conclude that Israel understood Yahweh's activity of creation to be one of forming, shaping, governing, ordering, and sustaining a created world out of the "stuff of chaos", which was already there'.[17] Towards the end of his book, however, he is more specific about what he means by chaos, and subsumes many mythological names drawn from Babylonian and Ugaritic texts that are associated with *chaoskampf*, calling them by one name, 'Nihil'. And this personified rebellious Nihil is said to be there from the beginning.

> That is, in the sovereign act of creation, whereby Yahweh orders chaos, Yahweh provisionally defeated the power of Nihil but did not destroy or eliminate the threat of chaos . . . Thus is posed a primordial dualism in which Yahweh has the upper hand but is not fully in control, and so from time to time creation is threatened.[18]

This is a particularly powerful rereading of the text, because it subverts the normal meaning of *creation ex nihilo*. Normally that phrase would mean that God creates unopposed and unhindered. With Brueggemann, however, the phrase evokes once more the 'creation out of conflict' theme.

---

15. M. Görg, 'תֹּהוּ *tōhû*', in G. Johannes Botterweck, Helmer Ringgren, Heinz-Josef Fabry (eds.), *Theological Dictionary of the Old Testament*, vol. XV (Grand Rapids: Eerdmans, 1986), p. 571.

16. Walter Brueggemann, *Theology of the Old Testament: Testimony, Dispute, Advocacy* (Minneapolis: Fortress, 1997), p. 153.

17. Ibid., p. 158.

18. Ibid., p. 534.

Genesis as demythologized text

A second and related assumption (which I shall call Assumption B) that is commonly brought to the interpretation of Genesis 1 is that it has undergone a process of demythologization. It is quite clear now that Genesis 1 does not mention dragons or demons explicitly, and yet Assumption A says that it is derived from mythological texts. This implies that the author must have deliberately removed such explicit mythologies. The reason that the author did this, it is argued, is to make Genesis a polemic, that is, a radical response and reaction against Babylonian or Canaanite 'theology' to correct it, or to 'assert' Israelite theology instead.

A few examples will serve to illustrate this point. Day asserted that Genesis 1:2 was a demythologized text that originally would have referred to a cosmic battle between gods. Therefore the author of Genesis, by demythologizing this battle, was claiming that Yahweh, in contrast to the Canaanite gods, created unopposed.[19] Gunkel, similarly, wrote that Genesis 1 retains sufficient indicators that show that it is 'essentially a faded myth' that has 'lost much of its mythological character and almost all of its polytheistic nature'.[20] Wenham, in his Word commentary on Genesis 1, writes that 'Gen 1:1–2:3 is a polemic against the mythico-religious concepts of the ancient Orient . . . The polemic intent of Genesis is even more clear in its handling of the sea monsters and the astral bodies'.[21] Finally, Alexander writes 'Genesis 1:1–2:3 may be read as a polemical

19. Day, *God's Conflict*, cited in Richard S. Hess and David Toshio Tsumura (eds.), *I Studied Inscriptions from Before the Flood: Ancient Near Eastern Literary and Linguistic Approaches to Genesis 1–11* (Sources for Biblical and Theological Study Old Testament Series; Winona Lake: Eisenbrauns, 1994), p. 32.

20. Gunkel, 'Influence of Babylonian Mythology', in Anderson (ed.), *Creation in the Old Testament*, pp. 46, 49.

21. Gordon Wenham, *Genesis 1–15* (Word Biblical Commentary, vol. 1; Waco: Word Books, 1986), p. 37.

and sometimes satirical attack on the Babylonian and Sumerian creation stories that were widespread in the Near East during the period 500–2000 BC'.[22]

The important point for us to notice is the impact that this approach makes on the way that we read the language of Genesis. It focuses the attention on what is 'missing' from the text, and forces the reader to 'read between the lines'. The true meaning of the text would only be found when read in the light of ancient Near Eastern mythologies, rather than read for what it says of itself. Once again, the shift of emphasis is away from the textual description of *how* God created, and towards a polemical statement of victory over opposing forces.

There are two very important implications of this approach to reading Genesis: it becomes entirely *compatible with*, and *necessary to*, an evolutionary rereading of Genesis. It is firstly compatible with an evolutionary rereading because evolution requires life to form out of pre-existing lifeless matter, to bring living creatures from nature 'red in tooth and claw'. It requires staggering coded complexity to arise out of increasing entropy; it is order out of primeval chaos. If the real, hidden, demythologized message in Genesis is one of Yahweh overcoming the forces of Nihil, Assumption B, then this is very compatible with theistic evolution, which requires God to create life, and ultimately humanity, through the 'war of nature' that Darwin described.[23]

But secondly, it is absolutely necessary for an evolutionary rereading because it takes the focus away from the chronology and history of Genesis, and reduces it into a polemic against the theology of Babylon or Canaan. If Genesis is primarily a polemic against ancient mythology, then it is no longer in conflict with a theistic evolutionary interpretation. This second aspect is most clearly seen in the many and repeated assertions that Genesis is not concerned with sequence or chronology. We will respond to these two implications in order.

---

22. Alexander, *Creation or Evolution*, p. 160.
23. Charles Darwin, *On the Origin of Species* (Ware: Wordsworth Editions, 1998 [1859]), closing paragraph.

Genesis without any demythologization

Despite the common tendency to read Genesis as derived from
Babylonian myths or epics, scholarship has now solidly rejected
this position. Firstly, if Moses is accepted as the author (somewhere between the fifteenth and thirteenth century, depending
upon your dating method), then it simply makes no sense to read
Genesis as a polemic against Babylon, because Babylon only came
to prominence as an empire after the ninth century BC. It is worth
re-emphasizing that Moses was writing in an Egyptian (or at least,
wilderness) context, as mentioned earlier, and not a Babylonian
one. He was therefore hardly likely to write a polemic against a
nation that posed no political or theological threat.

Secondly, the linguistic evidence has conclusively shown that
Genesis does not reveal any demythologizing. Regarding the
phrase 'barren and empty' (Gen. 1:2), David Tsumura says that
'the phrase *tōhû wā bōhû* has nothing to do with primeval chaos; it
simply means emptiness and refers to the earth in a "bare" state,
without vegetation and animals as well as without humans'.[24] Claus
Westermann summarizes the position this way:

> There is no sign of either personification or mythological allusion in
> the biblical use of [*tōhû*]. . . The course of the debate about the mythical
> explanation of *tōhû wābōhû*] indicates clearly that the arguments for a
> mythical background are becoming weaker and weaker. The discussion
> can now be considered closed.[25]

Likewise, regarding the word 'deep' in Genesis 1:2 Tsumura
concludes: 'I have thoroughly reexamined the problem from a
linguistic point of view, and it is now clear that it is phono-
logically impossible to conclude that *těhôm* ocean was borrowed

---

24. David T. Tsumura, 'Genesis and Ancient Near Eastern Stories of
    Creation and Flood', in Hess and Tsumura (eds.), *I Studied Inscriptions*,
    p. 33.
25. C. Westermann, *Genesis 1–11: A Commentary*, transl. J. J. Scullion
    (Minneapolis: Augsburg, 1984), p. 103.

from *Tiamat*.'[26] Ouro agrees: 'The Hebrew term *tehom* is simply a variant of the common Semitic root **thm* "ocean", and there is no relation between the account of Genesis and the mythology of *Chaoskampf*.'[27]

In a more general way, Kenneth Kitchen has written that 'the attempts made in the past to establish a definite relationship between Genesis and Babylonian epics such as *Enuma Elish* have now had to be abandoned; in content, aim, theology, and philology, there is divergence and no proven link'.[28]

Finally, Alan Millard concludes:

> . . . it has yet to be shown that there was borrowing, even indirectly. Differences between the Babylonian and the Hebrew traditions can be found in factual details of the flood narrative . . . All who suspect or suggest borrowing by the Hebrews are compelled to admit large-scale revision, alteration, and reinterpretation in a fashion which cannot be substantiated for any other composition from the Ancient Near East or in any other Hebrew writing.[29]

That is, the view that says Genesis is primarily to be read from a Babylonian historical context is likely to result in a misreading of the author's intention because it will assume that the text is answering questions that the author never had in mind. Likewise, if the reader thinks that the language of Genesis is primarily reflecting Babylonian or Canaanite texts then again they are likely to misread the real message of the text. Such a misreading is exemplified in Alexander's denial of a chronological order in Genesis 1 and 2.

---

26. Tsumura, 'Genesis and Ancient Near Eastern Stories of Creation and Flood', p. 31.

27. Roberto Ouro, 'The Earth of Genesis 1:2: Abiotic Or Chaotic? Part II', *Andrews University Seminary Studies* 37.1 (1999), pp. 39–53, 45.

28. Kitchen, 'The Old Testament in its Context'.

29. Alan Millard, 'A New Babylonian "Genesis" Story', first published in *Tyndale Bulletin* 18, (1967), pp. 17–18, now published in Hess and Tsumura (eds.), *I Studied Inscriptions*, p. 127.

Genesis and sequence

Many authors have seen the accounts of the creation of humanity in Genesis 1 and 2 as evidence of a plurality of sources and the main proof that there is no logical or chronological sequence intended. Futato writes:

> There may be some chronological sequence in these chapters, but such chronology is 'accidental,' i.e., the author's primary intention is to narrate the material topically.[30]

Similarly, Alexander claims that '[t]he text has no interest in providing us with chronology but has quite different purposes',[31] and that instead '[t]he purpose of Genesis 2, like Genesis 1, is to teach theology'.[32] The argument centres on the order of creation between animals and humans. In Genesis 1, God created human beings at the end of his creation sequence, and after the animals. In Genesis 2:19 we have a phrase that is translated by the NIV as 'Now the LORD God *had formed* out of the ground all the beasts of the field and all the birds of the air', a translation which maintains the chronological sequence of Genesis 1. The NRSV, however, reads 'So out of the ground the LORD God *formed* every animal of the field and every bird of the air'. That is, in the NRSV the order of creation is reversed, namely humans and then animals, and is therefore chronologically out of order with Genesis 1.

The issue is centred upon whether or not the verb *wayyiṣer* has the pluperfect sense of 'had formed', or just the perfect sense of 'formed', which Alexander considers a 'more natural translation'.[33] But what drives his decision to call this latter a more natural translation is not the text itself but rather his assumption that the

---

30. Mark D. Futato, 'Because it Had Rained: A Study of Gen 2:5–7 With Implications for Gen 2:4–25 and Gen 1:1–2:3', *Westminster Theological Journal* 60 (1998), pp. 1–21.

31. Alexander, *Creation or Evolution*, p. 165.

32. Ibid., p. 166.

33. Ibid., p. 164.

language of Genesis cannot be chronological. He imagines an ancient rabbi giving a 'withering look' to anyone who enquired about the chronology of Genesis 1 and 2. Instead, he concludes that the message of Genesis 2 is to highlight 'the role of human-kind in caring for the earth'.[34]

But Futato and Alexander's presuppositions have led them astray. Firstly, they have overlooked the linguistic evidence that points to the pluperfect sense of the verb being required in this context. John Collins, building on the work of R. Buth and D. W. Baker, identifies criteria for when the verb form *wayyiqtol* (the same form as the key word *wayyiser*) should be translated with the pluperfect sense, and concludes that Genesis 2:19 is one such instance.[35] But the main evidence for requiring a pluperfect translation (and therefore a chronologically consistent reading) is the theological teaching of the text, which Alexander has simply missed.

In the previous verse, 2:18, God declares that he is to make a suitable helper for Adam. In order to build the excitement, the narrative delays the fulfilment of this announcement, and does so by reminding the reader that he had formed all the animals *from out of the ground*. All the animals are brought to Adam for naming, and the reader is left waiting to see which will be Adam's helper. The narrative has therefore built up a sense of tension, the mark of an expert narrator, and this tension is brought to a climax by the statement that no suitable helper was found (2:20).

The unravelling of the tension comes when God puts Adam into a deep sleep and forms Eve *from the flesh of Adam*. That is, the reason for the pluperfect reminder that God 'had formed' the animals 'from out of the ground' is to point to Eve as the climax of the creation process. It is Eve, and only Eve, who was *not* made from out of the ground, but rather from Adam's flesh. And this is why Adam sings his song over her, 'bone of my bones, and flesh of my flesh' (v.23), and why in marriage they

---

34. Ibid., p. 165.

35. C. John Collins, 'The *Wayyiqtol* as "Pluperfect": When And Why', *Tyndale Bulletin* 46 (1995), pp. 117–140, p. 127f.

are declared to be united into 'one flesh'. In this reading of the text, Eve is no mere 'afterthought' simply for Adam's benefit, but rather the climax of the creation sequence (world→fish and birds→animals→Adam→Eve). This creation theology flows naturally from the text if the pluperfect is seen as building the tension of the narrative. That is, the creation theology of Genesis 2 depends upon a consistent chronological sequence of creation between Genesis 1 and 2, namely the creation of animals followed by the creation of humans. I rather think that the 'withering look' of the aforementioned ancient rabbi would be directed at Alexander for missing the central theological message of the text because of his rejection of a consistent chronology between Genesis 1 and 2.

The language of Genesis

So how should we read the language of Genesis? It hardly needs saying that there are many more rich theological seams that could be mined in these texts, and much more that could be made of the narrative style and structure. But the language of these chapters that we have considered is not less than chronological and historical, and to omit or deny this is to lose a central aspect of the author's intention. Gerhard Hasel sums up a discussion of the historical dimension of Genesis this way.

> There is no doubt that time and its progression functions in a most profound way in the Bible. This is evident from the beginning. Genesis creation is intended to be the beginning or opening of history. History begins with time and space and consists of functions in time and space. The Genesis creation account is part of a history which contains numbers and time sequences.[36]

---

36. His article discusses the relationship of the two genealogies of Genesis 5 and 11 to the rest of the Genesis creation narrative: Gerhard Hasel, 'The Meaning of the Chronogenealogies of Genesis 5 and 11', *Origins* 7 (1980), pp. 53–70; http://www.grisda.org/origins/07053.htm.

It needs to be made clear that this is no 'modernist' or even 'scientific' rereading of the text. Despite Alexander's best attempts at eradicating chronology, the church down through the ages has always followed Jesus' own example of reading Genesis as the creation of Adam and Eve 'in the beginning', that is, not after a long unspecified period of time where death reigned over the world. The language of Genesis is not coded or demythologized. It is historical, chronological and intentional. It reveals the theologically important aspects of the history of the world so that we can understand what it means for God to have established his covenant and redeemed his people from sin.

© Alistair McKitterick, 2009

3. ADAM AND EVE

Michael Reeves

Evangelical Christians have generally resisted the demythologization of the events of the Gospels, whereby, for example, the resurrection of Jesus is interpreted as a mythical portrayal of the principle of new life. Indeed, they have argued strongly that it is the very historicity of the resurrection event that is so vital. However, when it comes to the biblical figures of Adam and Eve, there has been a far greater willingness to interpret them as mythical or symbolic. The simple aim of this chapter is to show, in sketch, that, far from being a peripheral matter for fussy literalists, it is biblically and theologically necessary for Christians to believe in Adam as first, a historical person who second, fathered the entire human race.

Adam was a real, historical person

The textual evidence

The early chapters of Genesis sometimes use the word '*ādām* to mean 'humankind' (Gen. 1:26–27, for example), and since there is clearly a literary structure to those chapters, some have seen the figure of Adam there as a literary device, rather than a historical individual. Already a question arises: must we choose between the two? Throughout the Bible we see instances of literary devices used to present historical material: think of Nicodemus coming to Jesus *at night*, or the emphasis in the Gospels on Jesus' death *at the time of the Passover*. Most commentators would happily acknowledge that here are literary devices being employed to draw our attention to the theological significance of the historical events being recounted. The 'literary' need not exclude the 'literal'.

The next question then must be: does the 'literary' exclude the 'literal' in the case of Adam? Not according to those other parts of the Bible that refer back to Adam. The genealogies of Genesis 5, 1 Chronicles 1 and Luke 3 all find their first parent in Adam, and while biblical genealogies do sometimes omit names for various reasons, they are not known to add in fictional or mythological figures. When Jesus taught on marriage in Matthew 19:4–6, and when Jude referred to Adam in Jude 14, they used no caveats or anything to suggest that they doubted Adam's historical reality or thought of him in any way differently to how they thought of other Old Testament characters. And when Paul spoke of Adam being formed first, and the woman coming from him (1 Cor. 11:8–9; 1 Tim. 2:11–14), he had to be assuming a historical account in Genesis 2. Paul's argument would collapse into nonsense if he meant that Adam and Eve were mere mythological symbols of the timeless truth that men pre-exist women.

The theological necessity

We can think of the passages cited above as circumstantial evidence that the biblical authors thought of Adam as a real person in history. Circumstantial evidence is useful and important, but we have something more conclusive. That is, the role Adam plays in Paul's theology makes Adam's historical reality integral to the basic storyline of Paul's gospel. And if that is in fact the case, then the historicity of Adam cannot be a side issue, but must be part and parcel of the foundations of Christian belief.

The first exhibit is Romans 5:12–21, where Paul contrasts

the sin of 'the one man', Adam, with the righteousness of 'the
one man', Christ. Paul is the apostle who, in Galatians 3:16, felt
it necessary to make the apparently minute distinction between
a singular 'seed' and plural 'seeds', so it is probably safe here to
assume that he was not being thoughtless, meaning 'men' when
speaking of 'the one man'. Indeed, 'the one man' is repeatedly
contrasted with the many human beings, and 'oneness' underpins
Paul's very argument, which is about the overthrow of the one
sin of the one man (Adam) by the one salvation of the one man
(Christ).

Throughout the passage, Paul speaks of Adam in just the same
way as he speaks of Christ (his language of death coming 'through'
Adam is also similar to how he speaks of blessing coming 'through'
Abraham in Gal. 3). He is able to speak of a time before this one
man's trespass, when there was no sin or death, and he is able to
speak of a time after it, a period of time that, he says, stretched
from Adam to Moses. Paul could hardly have been clearer that he
supposed Adam was as real and historical a figure as Christ and
Moses (and Abraham).

Yet it is not just Paul's language that suggests he believed in
a historical Adam; his whole argument depends on it. His logic
would fall apart if he was comparing a historical man (Christ) to a
mythical or symbolic one (Adam). If Adam and his sin were mere
symbols, then there would be no need for a historical atonement;
a mythical atonement would be necessary to undo a mythical fall.
With a mythical Adam, then, Christ might as well be – in fact,
would do better to be – a symbol of divine forgiveness and new
life. Instead, the story Paul tells is of a historical problem of sin,
guilt and death being introduced into the creation, a problem that
required a historical solution.

To remove that historical problem of the one man Adam's sin
would not only remove the rationale for the historical solution
of the cross and resurrection, it would transform Paul's gospel
beyond all recognition. For where, then, did sin and evil come
from? If they were not the result of one man's act of disobedience, then there seem to be only two options: either sin was there
beforehand and evil is an integral part of God's creation, or sin is
an individualistic thing, brought into the world almost *ex nihilo* by

each person. The former is blatantly non-Christian in its monist or dualist denial of a good Creator and his good creation;[1] the latter looks like Pelagianism,[2] with good individuals becoming sinful by copying Adam (and so, presumably, becoming righteous by copying Christ).

The second exhibit that testifies to the foundational significance of a historical Adam to Paul's theology is 1 Corinthians 15:21–22 and 45–49. Again, Paul unpacks a tight parallel between the first man, Adam, through whom came death, and the second or last man, Christ, through whom comes new life. Once again, Adam is spoken of in the same way as Christ; and once again, Adam is seen as the origin of death as Christ is the origin of life.

At this point in 1 Corinthians, Paul is at the apex of a long argument dealing with problems that the Corinthian Christians had with the body. As the ultimate answer to their pastoral problems, Paul set out to give them confidence in the reality of their own future bodily resurrection by demonstrating the historical fact of Jesus' bodily resurrection. The historical reality of Jesus' resurrection is the lynchpin of his response. That being the case, it would be the height of rhetorical folly for Paul to draw a parallel between Adam and Christ here if he thought Adam was not a historical, but a mythical figure. For if the two could be paralleled, then Christ's resurrection could be construed mythically, and then Paul's entire letter would lose its point, purpose and punch.

If I have accurately represented Paul's theology in these passages, then it is simply impossible to remove a historical Adam from Paul's gospel and leave it intact. To do so would fatally de-historicize it, forcing a different account of the origin of evil that would require an altogether different means of salvation.

---

1. In monism, evil would originate in God himself; in dualism, evil would be a rival force, eternally existing beside God and before creation. In the former, God is not truly good, in the latter he is not truly God.

2. Pelagianism (named after its instigator, Pelagius) was the fifth-century teaching that individuals are born entirely innocent, with no taint of original sin. Having been demolished by Augustine, it was officially condemned as heresy at the Council of Ephesus in 431.

Denis Alexander's 'third way'

Denis Alexander has proposed that there is a way of avoiding the sharp dichotomy between the traditional view of a historical Adam and the view that such a position is now scientifically untenable. That is, while we should definitely view Adam as a historical figure, that should not entail believing that he was the first human.[3] According to Alexander's preferred model, anatomically modern humans emerged some 200,000 years ago, with language in place by 50,000 years ago. Then, around 6,000-8,000 years ago, God chose a couple of Neolithic farmers, and to them he revealed himself for the first time, so constituting them as *Homo divinus*, the first humans to know God and be spiritually alive.

It is an ingenious synthesis, to be sure, deftly side-stepping the theological chasm opened by denials of a historical Adam; it has, however, created for itself profound new problems. The first is raised by the question of what to make of Adam's contemporaries, those anatomically modern humans who, he says, had already been populating the world for tens of thousands of years. He wisely manoeuvres away from understanding them as anything less than fully human, emphatically affirming that 'the whole of humankind without any exception is made in God's image, including certainly all the other millions of people alive in the world in Neolithic times'.[4] To have stated otherwise would have landed him in a particularly unpleasant quagmire: the aboriginal population of Australia, who, according to Alexander, had already been living there for some 40,000 years before Adam and Eve were born, would otherwise be relegated to the status of non-human animals; and presumably the parents of Adam and Eve, also being non-human animals, would then, along with the Australian aborigines, be a legitimate food source for a hungry *Homo divinus*.

---

3. Denis Alexander, *Creation or Evolution: Do We Have to Choose?* (Oxford: Monarch, 2008), chs. 9–10. Throughout this chapter I will speak of this proposal as Denis Alexander's; it is, however, a substantial elaboration of a theory put forward by John Stott, who coined the phrase '*homo divinus*' in his *Understanding the Bible* (London: Scripture Union, 1972), p. 49.

4. Alexander, *Creation or Evolution*, p. 238.

However, in avoiding all that, Alexander's proposal founders on, if anything, even more hazardous terrain. The crucial move is made when he explains what exactly set Adam and Eve apart from their contemporaries. When they were born, he suggests, there was already a vast Neolithic population to be found in God's image; what then happened to set Adam and Eve apart as *Homo divinus* was simply that 'through God's revelation to Adam and Eve . . . the understanding of what that image actually meant, in practice, was made apparent to them.'[5] It was not, then, that Adam and Eve were now freshly created in God's image; they had already been born in God's image, children of a long line of bearers of God's image. The difference was that they now understood what this meant (a personal relationship with God).

The first problem with this is biblical. In Genesis 1 and 2, it is, quite specifically, Adam and Eve who are created in God's image (the event of Gen. 1:27 being presented afresh in Gen. 2:18–25). It is not just that *some* beings were created in God's image, and that this could later be realized by a couple of their descendants. Quite the opposite: Genesis 2:7 seems to be an example of the text going out of its way to emphasize a direct, special creative act to bring the man Adam into being. That problem might be considered surmountable, but it has created a second, theological problem that seems insurmountable. It is that, if humans were already in the image of God prior to Adam and Eve, then we are left with one of two scenarios. Either, there was, before Adam and Eve, a first human endowed with the image of God; at which point we are left with two 'Adam's: the first creature actually to be in God's image, and Adam, the first human in God's image to realize what that meant. Or, if the image of God was something that slowly evolved in humanity, then we are left with a collection of first humans in God's image and multiple 'Adam's.

Quite apart from the sheer awkwardness of such a position, its consequences would quickly snowball. If, as Alexander maintains, being in the image of God is about having a personal relationship with God, then all those humans in God's image who had

---

5. Ibid.

not received the revelation of what that meant must have been sinning. Created in God's image, to relate to God, they were not relating to God. In fact, though he does not use the word, the picture Alexander paints is one of humanity immersed in idolatry, for, he says, 'religious beliefs existed before this time [of Adam and Eve], as people sought after God or gods in different parts of the world, offering their own explanations for the meaning of their lives'.[6] Thus the model has sin before the fall.

Presumably God ignored that sin (though on what basis we are not told). But if he did so, that would clash with what Paul says in Romans 1:18–32. There Paul explains that the wrath of God stands against all humanity, not because of a failure to heed a specific revelation of the meaning of being in God's image, but because of a refusal to acknowledge the revelation of God made plain in creation since it was created. In fact, given Romans 1:18ff, it seems that Alexander's religious/idolatrous pre-Adamic *Homo sapiens* must have been under the wrath of God. But even if Romans 1 can be squared with this model, it does at the very least seem strange that God should create the opportunity for sin and idolatry without yet providing any possibility for righteousness and true knowledge of God as he would later do for Adam.

And what of Adam himself? When he was chosen to receive the revelation of the meaning of being in God's image, he must have been sinful already. He was not relating to God as he was created to do. Was he then declared temporarily sinless? Or was he always sinful, the only change being that in the events of Genesis 3 he sinned for the first time *knowingly*? And if the latter, why was Adam's previous, unconscious sin excusable, when later even unconscious sin is said to bring guilt (Lev. 5:17; Ps. 19:12)?

The fact that God creates the opportunity for sin long before creating any opportunity to know him reflects what is perhaps most troubling about this synthesis, that here is a God somehow constrained to work with a less-than-ideal situation. Indeed, throughout the proposal, one gets the sense that God is having to work by someone else's rules, as if in someone else's universe.

---

6. Ibid., p. 237.

This comes out clearly in Alexander's comments on the creation of woman. According to him, Eve was a person with human parentage as real as Adam. She was not taken physically from Adam's side. Instead, the purpose of Genesis 2:21, he says, is to affirm male-female complementarity.[7] Undoubtedly that is one of the purposes of that text; however, by making Genesis 2:21 only mythical/symbolic, he becomes unable to ground that male-female complementarity in any ontological reality. If Eve had a physical origin independent of Adam, then while God might for his own inscrutable reasons want to affirm male-female complementarity, he would have no ontological basis for doing so. In other words, his affirmation here (and, one must assume, at least some of his other affirmations) floats independent of reality. God, in effect, pulls his theology out of thin air. But a God who is forced to graft meaning onto events (or non-events) that do not themselves carry any such meaning does not look like a sovereign creator.

Finally, the way Alexander's model compels him to read the Genesis text leads one to feel that he is trying to fit a round peg into a square hole. The creation of woman again serves as a helpful example: 'When Adam recognised Eve as "bone of my bones and flesh of my flesh", he was not just recognising a fellow *Homo sapiens* – there were plenty of those around – but a fellow believer.'[8] Not only does this ignore the specifically physical content of what is being said (something that is essential to later biblical references to this passage, cf. 1 Cor. 6:16–17; Eph. 5:28–31); but also it makes little sense of the previous search for a 'helper' for Adam. If Genesis 2:18–20 indicates anything, it is that there was no other member of Adam's kind present. If it was merely a search for another believer, why look among the beasts of the field and the birds of the air? Why not mention the humans being brought to Adam? And could God not simply have revealed the meaning of being in God's image to any one of the *Homo sapiens* around and so produced the required 'helper'?

---

7. Ibid., p. 197.
8. Ibid., p. 237.

A similar rationale drives his interpretation of Genesis 6:2, where the sons of God intermarry with the daughters of men. As Alexander sees it, this is a simple case of the spiritually alive family of Adam intermarrying with contemporary *Homo sapiens* who had not received the revelation of God and so were spiritually dead. The application is clear: 'Then, as now, don't marry unbelievers!' for 'it is clear that judgement follows, as described in 6:5ff with the account of the flood'.[9] Yet if Genesis 6 were about the godly marrying unbelievers from outside the line of Adam, why did the judgment of the flood not follow when 'godly' Cain took a wife from outside the line of Adam, as Alexander holds?[10]

My suggestion is that, for all its ingenuity, Alexander's 'third way' of holding to a historical Adam, but without believing him to be the first human, is unable to provide a coherent reading of the Genesis text, and creates more theological problems than it solves. Some of those problems (such as his reading of Gen. 6) are admittedly small, little more than indications that his model is probably internally incoherent and jarring with the biblical account; others (such as the implications for his understanding of God as sovereign creator) are so serious they make his argument seem incurable.

Adam fathered the entire human race

Adam's headship over humanity
Debates about Adam's relationship to the rest of humanity always tend to come back to the old debate between Augustine and Pelagius.[11] Pelagius had not called the physical connection between Adam and the rest of humanity into question, but, he argued, for the purposes of salvation, any such connection was almost entirely irrelevant. According to Pelagius, salvation and damnation are determined by the individual from start to finish: a person is

9. Ibid., p. 199.

10. Ibid., p. 241.

11. See note 2.

damned, not by virtue of any underlying connection with Adam, but by imitating his sin; correspondingly, a person is saved, not by virtue of any underlying connection with Christ, but by imitating his righteousness. In other words, salvation and damnation are not about having another's status, but imitating the one whose fate you wish to share. Augustine's response showed (among many other things) that this simply could not be squared with Romans 5:12–21, where people are said to be condemned on the basis of Adam's sin and justified on the basis of Christ's righteousness. As Augustine understood Paul, it is that God deals with all humankind through one of two men: Adam, the original man and original head of all humanity, or Christ, the first and head of God's re-created, new humanity.

Why should questions about the identity of Adam and his connection to the rest of humanity keep coming back to the Augustine-Pelagius debate? There seem to be two reasons: 1) the issues of the debate are inescapably foundational in that they really represent a debate between the Christian gospel and an entirely different approach to God and salvation; 2) the terms of the debate still manage to address even the most sophisticated modern formulations. Take, for example, the notion that Adam and Eve are symbols of what was, in fact, a whole (probably Neolithic) population, and that sin emerged in that population and from there spread to all humankind. Here the problem of Pelagianism has simply been shunted away from the bulk of humanity to a primordial few so far removed in time that the problem appears negligible.

It seems that the terms of the Augustine-Pelagius debate are so hard to evade that denials of Adam as the destiny-determining head of humanity inevitably lead towards construing personal destiny individualistically, at least to some extent. And the greater the extent of personal self-determination, the greater must be the tendency to regard Christ as more example than Saviour.

Headship has ontological roots
Once again, Denis Alexander has shrewdly avoided such pitfalls in his synthesis. Proving that he is well aware of the imperative theological need to acknowledge Adam as the head of the old

humanity, he proposes a different way of integrating that theological fact with his view that Adam was not the first human. The way he does this is simply by divorcing Adam's legal or federal status as head of humanity from any notion that Adam was the natural head or father of the human race. At some point, then, God constituted Adam as the federal head, not just of every *Homo divinus*, but of every *Homo sapiens*. As such, when Adam sinned for the first time (knowingly), God could impute that sin to every *Homo sapiens*, regardless of their lack of ontological connection to Adam. At that point, the unenlightened *Homo sapiens* of Australia (to pick one previously mentioned people group unconnected to Adam's Neolithic community) became guilty before God.

However, by divorcing Adam's federal headship from his natural, physical headship, Alexander runs into what are now familiar problems. The first is that, once again, God is making theological affirmations that have no ontological basis. Adam is being declared to be something (the head of humanity) that he is, in physical reality, not. As a result, God's imputation of sin to the unsuspecting Australian aborigines just looks arbitrary. There is here no basis for a connection between Adam and the *Homo sapiens* at the other end of the earth from him, and so God's declaration that they should share the guilt of Adam rests on nothing other than divine whim.

This, though, is not how the concept of headship functions scripturally. Rather, it is, if anyone, specifically the offspring who are affected by how God judges an individual in the Bible (hence the Old Testament preoccupation with genealogies). In choosing examples one is spoilt for choice, but take, for instance, how the blessings on Abraham, Jacob and David affect their offspring, or how the curse on Jehoiachin affects his. Conversely, Levi is considered to have acted 'in' Abraham only because he was 'still in the loins' of Abraham (Heb. 7:9–10). In other words, an individual's headship or corporate nature is never portrayed as being detachable from real connections.

If we were to move from talking about how we are born 'in Adam' to how Christians are 'in Christ', the necessity for real connection should become clearer. In the New Testament, Christians are never shown being given new birth or righteousness on the basis of a divine decree that has no grounding in what has actually happened to them. Instead, by the Spirit, a real, ontological union is established with Christ and the believer is incorporated into Christ's body. If the Spirit did not establish any such union, then the Christian's righteousness really would remain a legal fiction. And the principle works both ways: in both union with Christ by the Spirit and union with Adam by the flesh, what is essential is the relevant ontological connection. Neither can be a legal fiction if the Judge of all the earth is to do right.

There is another problem with suggesting that God could establish federal headship (for either Adam or Christ) without providing any ontological basis for it. Let us take again the example of the Christian's union with Christ as the parallel of union with Adam. Imagine God establishing the righteousness of an individual by a free divine fiat, but without the Spirit actually uniting the Christian to Christ. What would be lacking? The Spirit. The model would thus not be Trinitarian. If Paul's Adam-Christ parallel holds here, then the demands of consistency push the suggestion that a *Homo sapiens* could be united to Adam without any real connection into just such a sub-Trinitarian understanding of salvation.

While on Trinitarian grounds, it is worth noting how the logic of 1 Corinthians 11:3 seems to imply that, just as it would be odd to allow for a husband to be head of his wife without any ontological connection with her, so it would be worrying to suggest that God the Father, as head of Christ, need have no ontological connection with his Son. To import such an ontologically light view of headship into the Trinity would tip one into Arianism or tritheism.[12] Of course, in both cases nobody is seeking to do any such thing, but we are surely entitled to ask why headship is treated so differently in different instances.

Biblically and theologically, then, it seems that if Adam was not in physical reality the father of all, he could not have been head of all. Thus, quite apart from circumstantial biblical evidence

---

12. In both Arianism and tritheism, the Son is an entirely different being to the Father: in Arianism, he is not truly the uncreated God; in tritheism (belief in three Gods) he is a different God to the Father.

that seems to suggest that Adam is the one man from whom all humanity came (Acts 17:26); theologically we are compelled to say that since Adam clearly is seen as the head of all humanity, he must be the father of all humanity.

'That which he has not assumed he has not healed'

Even before Gregory Nazianzen neatly articulated it,[13] a good part of the Christology of the early post-apostolic church was shaped by the thought that whatever Christ did not assume in his incarnation could not be 'healed' or saved. In essence it was an attempt to systematize the thought of Hebrews 2:11–17, that Jesus had to be one with those he came to save, sharing their flesh and blood so that that very flesh and blood could be taken through the curse of death into the new life of the resurrection. Thus in the incarnation Christ did not take on angelic flesh – that would do us no good – but our flesh, so that he might truly be like us and truly save us. It was this theology that protected the church from those heresies that undermined Christ's real humanity and so undermined the salvation he brought.

If, however, Adam was not the progenitor of all humanity, but merely a member of one of any number of disconnected branches of *Homo sapiens*, then Nazianzen's maxim begins to look rather worrying. If Christ did not assume my flesh, but the flesh of another humanity, then he is not my kinsman-redeemer. For, if the post-apostolic church was right in its reading of Hebrews 2 and its understanding of the incarnation, then what was important was not that Christ assumed *any* humanity, but quite specifically *our* humanity.

Conclusion

When theological doctrines are detached from historical moorings, they are always easier to harmonize with other data and

---

13. Gregory of Nazianzus, Epistle 101 (*Nicene and Post-Nicene Fathers*, 2nd series, vol. 7), p. 438.

ideologies. And, of course, there are a good many doctrines that are not directly historical by nature. However, it has been my contention that the identity of Adam and his role as the physical progenitor of the human race are not such free or detachable doctrines. The historical reality of Adam is an essential means of preserving a Christian account of sin and evil, a Christian understanding of God, and the rationale for the incarnation, cross and resurrection. His physical fatherhood of all humankind preserves God's justice in condemning us in Adam (and, by inference, God's justice in redeeming us in Christ) as well as safeguarding the logic of the incarnation. Neither belief can be reinterpreted without the most severe consequences.

4. THE FALL AND DEATH

Greg Haslam

'For as in Adam all die, so in Christ all will be made alive' (1 Cor. 15:22).

It is one thing to embrace without reservation the Darwinian account of the origins of mankind and its assertion that universal suffering and death occurred long before the first *Homo sapiens* appeared on the earth, quite another to square this with the Bible. Darwinism insists upon the necessity that eons of time elapsed in order to allow a vast array of complex organisms to evolve on earth in the meta-narrative of evolution, and that the presence of billions of fossilized but now extinct organisms offers clear proof that 'trial and error' experimentation, death and destruction were all present from the start. Nevertheless, this scenario seems to be in conflict with the data of biblical theology and its account of God's perfect creation in the beginning.

Yet, in theory it should not prove difficult for believers who respect both the inspiration and authority of the Bible *and* the integrity of the findings of generations of research scientists to reconcile these complementary narratives. After all, isn't 'all truth God's truth', as Christian philosopher Arthur Holmes famously affirmed? We would expect then, that the life and earth sciences of biology, palaeontology and zoology, along with related disciplines like cosmology, astronomy, radiometric dating and genetics, would combine their testimony to offer reliable explanations for how evolution's 'particles to people' scenario coheres with the teaching of God's holy and infallible word. Nevertheless, the Bible does not sit comfortably with this 'death before Adam' scenario, at least not without a great deal of intellectual 'sleight of hand' and some radical re-interpretations of its clear statements.

Christian scientists like Denis Alexander, Francis S. Collins and Davis A. Young persistently defend various forms of 'theistic evolution' as they seek to accommodate the claims of 'old cosmos' evolutionism within a biblical framework. Their atheistic colleagues deny the very existence of an infinite, personal creator God. But in spite of their differences, they are all in agreement concerning their assumptions that death, disease, birth defects, struggle, suffering, inordinate pain, carnivorous violence, bloodshed and destructive ecological disasters of every kind, were all prevalent on earth from its earliest beginnings. This is simply the way things are, have always been, and will continue to be. This is nature being true to itself and perhaps the way God designed the world, if God exists at all. However, the NT endorses the accuracy of Genesis directly and indirectly over *200 times*, and cites Genesis 1 – 11 *107 times*. Jesus refers to Genesis twenty-five times to reinforce important doctrines (e.g. Mark 10:6–8; Matt. 23:35; 24:37–39), and Paul similarly endorses the historicity of Genesis 1 – 3 (e.g. 1 Cor. 11:8–10; 15:21–22; 1 Tim. 2:11–15). Romans 5:12–21 offers us one of the most difficult challenges to any attempt to mythologize Genesis 1 – 3.

The coherence and importance of Paul's argument here is based upon his belief in the reliability of the history of the Genesis account of creation and God's rapid forming and filling of the cosmos, culminating in the fiat creation of the human race from the first perfect pair, Adam and Eve; then the reality of a historic space–time moral fall of Adam, the head of the human race. Adam fell downwards, not upwards, an event that unlocked the safety catch of God's protection over his perfect world and allowed the entrance of evil in every form, including death, suffering and decay due to Adam's rebellion. This was followed by God's promise that total recovery hinged upon the coming of another unique man, the 'seed of the woman', whom the New Testament calls 'the last Adam', Jesus Christ (1 Cor. 15:45). He alone can undo and reverse Adam's fall by his perfectly righteous life and the universe-transforming effects of his substitutionary death and resurrection (see Gen. 3:15, the *proto-evangelium* or first announcement of the gospel).

'As in Adam all die'

The biblical doctrine of the universal reality of sin in the human race is a truth that needs little demonstration. We are all confronted with its reality in ourselves and others every day. The daily news and worrying trends in the statistics of violent crime, fraud, warped values, premature deaths, wilful injury and large-scale corruption, affect the lives of millions of people everywhere. The question arises, how did such an appalling situation ever arise in the original creation that God pronounced to be 'good'?

Romans 5:1–21 is the apostle Paul's answer, and part of the larger argument of this letter as he unfolds what Bible expositor John Stott attractively entitles, 'The Privileges of the Justified' in his classic publication *Men Made New,* based upon Bible readings delivered at the 1965 Keswick Convention,[1] and subsequently expanded in his exposition of the whole letter to the Romans.[2] Paul here unfolds the rich blessings and redemptive effects of the gospel in the lives of believers – reconciliation with God, justification from sin, freedom from the law's condemnation, and victory over death – all entirely due to the work of God in Jesus Christ. In Romans 5:12–21 Paul offers a coherent, but somewhat difficult argument designed to explain how these great achievements

---

1. John R. W. Stott, *Men Made New – An Exposition of Romans 5–8* (Leicester: IVP, 1966).
2. John R. W. Stott, *The Message of Romans* (The Bible Speaks Today; Leicester: IVP, 1994).

became possible. Adam represented all who physically descended from him. Christ represented all who are spiritually connected to him by faith. Both men were genuinely historic figures, or we have no trustworthy message. Christ restores the world to how it was in the beginning – a perfect creation, not a primitive chaos or a less evolved condition.

Paul therefore draws an extended analogy between Christ's work of redemption and Adam's ruin of the human race through sin. His argument presupposes the historical existence, unique-ness and significance of the contrasting deeds of both men, along with the effects they have upon our lives. The apostle's dominant purpose is to illustrate the doctrine of justification by faith as the primary means of recovering God's favour and our reconciliation with God that imparts assurance of salvation to all believers. Our union with Christ is the basis of this, since he alone can undo the destructive effects of our union with Adam in his rebellion against God. The words of the Puritan writer Thomas Goodwin (1600–79) vividly capture Paul's dominant idea here: ' . . . these two [i.e. Adam and Christ] between them had all the rest of the sons of men hanging at their girdle.'[3] Let's examine the case Paul marshals to support this reality.

> Therefore, just as sin entered the world through one man, and death
> through sin, and in this way death came to all men, because all sinned
> (v.12).

This is the first key assertion in Paul's parallel case for the fact that the human race experiences corruption and catastrophe, then recovery and re-creation due to the actions of these two men. The words, 'just as. . .' begin the analogy, but it is not completed until verses 18–19 where Christ's great achievements are unfolded precisely. At a fixed point in history 'sin entered the world'. It did not exist on earth before this moment, though Paul was no doubt aware of the angelic rebellion that had previously occurred in the

---

3. *Christ Set Forth*, section III, ch. 4 in *The Works of Thomas Goodwin* (London, 1862).

invisible realm prior to man's fall; however this did not render inevitable Satan's invasion of earth, for that outcome depended upon Adam's response to temptation for good or ill, in Eden. The entrance of evil into this world was foolishly permitted by *'one man'*, a clear allusion to the narrative of the fall in Genesis 3, and an endorsement of its historic reliability. Bible commentator C. K. Barrett observes, 'It need not be said that Paul, a first-century Jew, accepted Genesis 1 to 3 as a straightforward narrative of events which really happened.'[4] And Professor C. H. Dodd concurs, 'Paul bases his answer on a current doctrine of Jewish rabbis, that through the fall of Adam all men fell into sin . . . It is a good enough argument for those who accepted the rabbinic doctrine of the fall', something Dodd himself had doubts about, but readily conceded that this was truly Paul's position.[5]

For the very first time, in the nascent history of God's earth, sin unlatched the door by which moral, spiritual, and physical disaster invaded the good world God had created. Its all-pervasive effects spread to all of Adam's subsequent progeny who were as yet non-existent, apart from his newly-created wife Eve. There's no doubt that this was Paul's conviction in stating these facts, since he repeats this theme throughout this section of Romans to help ensure that his readers grasp this concept: for example, '. . .from the time *of Adam*. . .' (v.14), '. . .the many died by the trespass of *the one man*' (v.15), 'the result of the *one man's sin*' (v.16), 'by the trespass of *the one man,* death reigned' (v.17), 'the result was condemnation for *all men*' (v.18), 'through the disobedience of *the one man* the many were made sinners' (v.19).

There was no exception to this deadly contamination then: '. . .because all sinned'. This cannot simply mean that we have all merely emulated Adam's sin (which of course we have), nor that every human being has plunged into his or her own historic 'fall' just like Adam did (which, in a lesser sense, we have also done),

---

4. C. K. Barrett, *A Commentary on the Epistle to the Romans* (London: A&C Black, 1957).

5. C. H. Dodd, *The Epistle of Paul to the Romans* (London: Hodder and Stoughton, 1944).

but rather that we were all somehow implicated in and affected by Adam's first sin. What Adam did, he did *for* and *to* us all. He was our God-appointed representative in his decision and actions. He was the 'federal head' of the human race, and his actions affected us all regardless of our consent that this be the case, or lack of it.

'All *sinned*' is an aorist verb denoting a once-for-all past event. Adam's one sin was thus counted against all. It is '. . . *in Adam* all die' (1 Cor. 15:22). The only explanation for this is that 'in Adam' we all 'sinned', and were implicated in his damning act of eating the forbidden fruit, because he represented us. We are all most certainly guilty of voluntary transgressions that we've committed subsequently, but this doesn't explain why 'death came to *all*', in other words, all humankind – male and female, every age and ethnicity, everyone. Paul is aware of the difficulties in accepting this for reasoning minds, and so he digresses to explain this fact very carefully in verses 13 to 17:

> for before the law was given, sin was in the world. But sin is not taken into account when there is no law. Nevertheless, death reigned from the time of Adam to the time of Moses, even over those who did not sin by breaking a command, as did Adam, who was a pattern of the one to come (vv. 13–14).

Paul asserts that death passed to those who had never personally violated a known law of God, since no such written laws existed in the early earth. Yet people died from Adam onwards, including the whole world during Noah's universal flood (Gen. 7). Between Adam and Moses there was no written law of God and so, though personal sin existed ('*sin was in the world*'), it could not be technically charged or legitimately reckoned up against people. They had not sinned as Adam did in voluntarily transgressing a known law. Yet they were still treated as sinners from birth onwards, and eventually died a sinner's death. Not entirely for their own personal sin but *Adam's*, which had been imputed to them. Adam's sin was reckoned as theirs from conception. We are all born into sin (Job 25:4; Ps. 51:5). And this is why in verse 14, Paul seems to have had in mind another category of puzzling deaths, namely that of very young infants, even children still in the womb, along with such unusual cases as the mentally handicapped who have diminished personal responsibility and are often incapable of understanding or exercising faith, some of whom also die young. The big question is 'Why?'

Once again, Paul is clear that these apparently 'innocent' deaths, due to no personal transgressions committed against God's written law, are a consequence of their physical and spiritual connection to historic Adam. The only adequate explanation of their death – moral, spiritual and physical – is their solidarity with Adam in his one act of sin. Someone might suggest that this is simply due to the inheritance of a 'fallen sinful nature' from Adam, which is indeed a reality. But though this is a biblical fact about us all since we experience the down-drag of sin in our warped human nature, why should we *inherit* this? God could protect us from this couldn't he? But instead, he allows the transmission of pollution to us, since universal condemnation flows from Adam's sin, not just our sinful nature alone, in Paul's theology. He says repeatedly, even our corruption is due to Adam's '*one* sin'. This explains why we inherit a sinful nature. It is part of God's condemnation and judicial sentence upon the whole of mankind due to Adam's deed. Later, Paul announces the good news that we can also be justified through Christ's righteousness, not because we are inherently 'holy', even though we experience regeneration by God's Holy Spirit. Justification is entirely due to the 'alien' righteousness and obedience of 'last Adam', Jesus Christ, that's imputed or 'reckoned' ours though faith in him, not our own goodness.

In much the same way then, we are condemned in Adam due to *his* transgression and not *our own* subsequent spiritual pollution. The latter is actually a grim *consequence* of that condemnation, along with our subsequent moral weakness, mortality, and liability to disease and death that entered God's perfect world as a result of the space-time fall of Adam, Adam's 'one sin'. Encouragingly, Adam's sin is a picture of the reverse pattern of 'the one to come', Jesus Christ, who undoes this solidarity in Adam by introducing the new reality of our radical union with himself and his righteousness, by faith in him. Adam is a 'type' of Christ, a kind of 'model' of him in reverse. We might find this concept strange, but it happens to be the key to our deliverance. We are all either 'in Adam' or 'in

Christ', and only the latter location can undo the deadly effects of our former connection, and not simply undo them, for Christ transcends them!

Paul is now ready to explore some clear contrasts between Adam and Christ, whilst reinforcing the striking parallels between their opposite, but not equal, achievements. Adam's 'one' sin is the cause of God's curse coming upon humankind, entering God's good world and thus damning and polluting Adam's descendants. Not one of us could annul this curse ourselves by our own efforts or personal righteousness, for we do not have the resources to accomplish this even if we wanted to. We were securely, irrevocably and irreversibly ruined and condemned, and our own righteous deeds could never have undone this because (1) they are never truly righteous, (2) they cannot sever our federal connection with Adam which was God's covenant arrangement, and (3) because none of us even wanted such deliverance due to the depraving effects of sin within us. Only the grace of God in Christ could reverse our lost condition, in his capacity as our God-appointed and new, covenant head. It is to be expected that his gains would far surpass Adam's losses, just as his divine personhood and perfect manhood transcend Adam's fallen humanity. This is the point Paul drives home in the remaining verses of this chapter.

'So in Christ shall all be made alive'

Paul's theology of 'federal headship' asserts the fact that vast possibilities follow directly from the divine appointment of just two representative men: namely, Adam and Christ. Ultimately billions of lives will be affected, due solely to their actions rather than our votes, consent or personal deeds. This should not surprise or offend us, for to a lesser extent this is how most earthly states and governments operate. The lives of whole cities and nations are affected by the decisions of appointed kings, presidents, and elected ministers, regardless of the form of government that prevails – republic, parliamentary democracy, monarchy or totalitarian dictatorship. The people have little say and must live with the consequences of their ruler's decisions for good or ill, whether we chose this or not.

Paul's logic here is clear then. He describes the origin of our misery and lamentable condition in four stages, followed by the remedy:

1. '*Sin entered the world*' (v.12). Therefore it wasn't there before. It invaded the earth at a fixed point in history, in the comparatively recent past.
2. '*Through one man*'. A clear reference to the historicity of the narrative of Adam's fall told in Genesis 3. Fascinatingly, Eve ate the forbidden fruit first, but Adam had the major leadership role before God and Eve did not. Humankind is lost in Adam, not Eve, though she rebelled first. In *Adam* all die – federal headship again.
3. '*And death through sin*'. The first occurrence of Adam's liability and subjection to the experience of spiritual, moral, and physical death. Something that was not the case before this.
4. '*And death passed to all men because all men sinned*'. The consequences of this one sin then extended to all of Adam's descendants on account of his representative role on their behalf. Thankfully, this is not the end of the story!
5. '*But the gift is not like the trespass*' (v.15). God has planned for the possibility of the reversal and recovery of all that was lost in Adam by sending Jesus Christ.

However, it would be a mistake to conclude that both Adam and Christ are commensurate and equal in the impact of their distinctive roles upon humankind. Paul's theology of the respective roles of Adam and Christ therefore continues in a vital parenthesis to the flow of his argument, which will resume and reach its climax in verses 18–21. He first pauses to exalt Christ's total contrast with, and supremacy over Adam, in terms of his superior gains that far outstrip Adam's losses. Their respective roles are still in mind, but this time in terms of vastly different outcomes. In Paul's thinking, the reality of the representative roles of Adam and Christ display the principle of divine imputation, that is, the reckoning, or crediting to our account of the actions of each appointed 'head'. Yet here as elsewhere in the scriptures, the *antitype* always transcends the *type,* the *shadow* is always eclipsed by the full *reality* shining in Christ. The 'trespass' and the 'gift' are not equal and opposite in their effects, for the latter outperforms the former in every way. 'But the gift is *not* like the trespass,' Paul asserts (v.15a). The apostle presents this fact in a series of stunning contrasts we'll sum up under three headings.

The respective influences achieved by both Adam and Christ

> But the gift is not like the trespass. For if the many died by the trespass of the one man, how much more did God's grace and the gift that came by the grace of the one man, Jesus Christ, overflow to the many! (v. 15)

We are reckoned as guilty and condemned on account of the sin of Adam. As a result, universal death afflicts all born of Adam, without a single exception. But we can be regarded as innocent and pardoned due to the 'grace of one man', Jesus Christ. This brings hope of life restored, both spiritual and physical, in the new birth and then the final resurrection of our bodies, both secured by Christ. Some affirm that the 'death' that Adam experienced as a result of God's curse upon his sin, and then passed on to his progeny was only 'moral' and 'spiritual' death – corruption and separation from God along with eventual liability to eternal destruction away from his presence. They insist that the human race has always been mortal and that physical death was in the world before Adam sinned, a created reality from the beginning.

However, how could this condition be termed 'good' by God during the creation week throughout Genesis 1, when death is so ugly and destructive of all good? Genesis 3 makes clear that physical death is part of God's curse, along with all other lesser miseries God cursed sinners with. Life is hard, relationships are strained, childbirth is painful and death is certain, because of Adam's sin (Gen. 3:14–19). Through Adam's sin alone death entered the world and 'many died' (Rom. 5:12, 15), then 'reigned' over us all (v. 17). Adam lived long – over 900 years – but like all of his progeny since, he eventually died. The Bible calls death 'the last enemy to be destroyed' (1 Cor. 15:26). We had no permanent *enemies* in

Eden, least of all death! Death is an alien and recent intruder into God's world, and not a 'natural' part of human or animal life. It is only as old as mankind is, and will soon be finally gone at Christ's parousia (1 Cor. 15:50–57).

The respective attributes of God displayed in Adam and Christ

> Again, the gift of God is not like the result of the one man's sin: The judgment followed one sin and brought condemnation, but the gift followed many trespasses and brought justification (v. 16).

When Adam believed Satan and went into 'the God business', defiantly deciding moral truth autonomously himself in a bid for independence from God, his soul died, his body began to perish, he was banished from God's paradise and flaming swords totally forbade re-entry. That one sin evicted us all. Steel shutters closed, and this might have been the end for us, but for God! God was bound to display his justice, but still free to show his grace. So Christ finally overcame a multitude of sins that had overwhelmed us all. Now, brand new possibilities have opened up to us. We see God's justice and condemnation of sin dominant in the events of Genesis 3 as the result of Adam's rebellion, but also God's mercy and pardon displayed in Christ's historic triumph over human corruption as a direct result of his life-long obedience, culminating in his sacrificial death on the cross at Calvary. We were treated as guilty and condemned because of the sin of one man, but reckoned innocent and free by Christ's 'one act of righteousness' (v. 18), the sum of his whole fully-lived life and his totally saving death.

This concept offends some. Our solidarity in Adam's disobedience means that all people were constituted or put into the category of 'sinners', and treated accordingly. How could a good God damn the whole world because one man bit an apple? But this objection can only be countered by the fact that God planned that by faith-union with Christ we can be treated as righteous in Christ and as fully obedient to the Father and justified as he was. And this is for everyone! God will eventually take billions of people to heaven (i.e. the restored 'new heaven and earth' described in Rev. 21 and 22), rescuing them completely from their damnable condition because of what one man did by his life and death on the cross! Paul later concludes that God, who 'did not spare his own Son, but gave him up for us all', an abandonment to the utmost extremes of darkness, God-forsakenness, judgment and death for us, will surely also 'along with him, graciously give us all things' (Rom. 8:32). We win, at last!

The respective ultimate effects upon us due to Adam and Christ

> For if, by the trespass of the one man, death reigned through that one man, how much more will those who receive God's abundant provision of grace and of the gift of righteousness reign in life through the one man, Jesus Christ (v.17).

Whilst in no way disparaging the wonder that was Adam before his rebellion, the superiority of the person of Jesus Christ is evident here. Behind and operative under and within his full humanity was the glorious full deity of Christ. If in Adam that great tyrant death 'reigned' over all without exception, and always takes us by macabre surprise, 'how much more will those who receive God's abundant provision of grace and of the gift of life reign in life. . .?' The once badly *ruled* finally get to *reign* over death and hell with Christ! This is our certain destiny.

'All shall be well, all shall be well, and all manner of things shall be well'[6]

The apostle now concludes his case for the importance of the historic figures of Adam and Jesus Christ, resuming the statement he began in verse 12. Here is the essence of our present and future hope in Christ's triumph over Adam's sin:

---

6. Julian of Norwich, *Revelations of Divine Love* (c.1393), ch. 27; http://www.ccel.org/ccel/julian/revelations.toc.html.

> Consequently, just as the result of one trespass was condemnation for all
> men, so also the result of one act of righteousness was justification that
> brings life for all men. For just as through the disobedience of the one
> man the many were made sinners, so also through the obedience of the
> one man the many will be made righteous. The law was added so that
> the trespass might increase. But where sin increased, grace increased all
> the more, so that, just as sin reigned in death, so also grace might reign
> through righteousness to bring eternal life through Jesus Christ our Lord
> (vv. 18–21).

Paul points out that men are 'made' righteous (v. 19) in
a way that's opposite but similar to the way we were 'made'
sinners in Adam. This was not humanly reversible, for the law
can neither save nor sanctify us but only fuels our desire to
sin (v. 20). But here, the new notes Paul strikes both explicitly
and hopefully for the future of the world are 'increased' and
'increased even more'. Grace intends to undo Adam's fall completely, in an evidently superior way. This is not 'universalism',
the heretical false hope that maintains that 'all shall eventually
be saved and none shall be finally lost'; the Bible does not
support this and anyway, we have to 'receive' the gift of life
by faith to experience it (v. 17). Nevertheless, the final number
of the saved may well vastly exceed the number of the lost by
an incalculably long way. Abraham was promised that his heirs
would be more numerous than 'the stars in the sky and the sand
on the seashore' (Gen. 22:17), a promise reclaimed by Jacob
(Gen. 32:12), Moses (Exod. 32:13; Deut. 1:10–11) and several
other Old Testament prophets (e.g. Hosea 1:10; Jer. 33:22), then
echoed by the apostles in the New Testament (Heb. 11:12; Rev.
5:9; 7:9).

Take for example the fate of dying infants. Jesus assured us that,
'Your Father in heaven is not willing that any of these little ones
should be lost' (Matt. 18:14), referring to God's great mercy to all,
but particularly to young children and perhaps especially to those
who die in infancy and are incapable of responding to the gospel.
David gave voice to the hope that they would be saved when his
ill-conceived son by Bathsheba died, saying, 'I will go to him but
he shall not come to me' (2 Sam. 12:23).

The seventeenth-century Scottish covenanter Samuel Rutherford once observed, 'If Satan were the jailor and had the keys of death and hell, they would be stored with more prisoners.' He was sure however, that Christ would yet see to it that Satan would not win the greater victory over Christ in terms of lives plundered. Similarly, the gifted nineteenth-century American theologian and commentator Charles Hodge, noted in Romans 5:21:

> That the benefits of redemption shall far outweigh the evils of the fall, is clearly asserted. This we can in a measure comprehend, because 1. The number of the saved shall doubtless exceed greatly the number of the lost. Since the half of mankind die in infancy, and according to the Protestant doctrine, are heirs of salvation; and since in the future state of the Church the knowledge of the Lord is to cover the earth, we have reason to believe that the lost shall bear to the saved no greater proportion than the inmates of a prison do to the mass of the community. 2. Because the eternal Son of God, by his incarnation and mediation, exalts his people to a far higher state of being than our race, if unfallen, could ever have attained. 3. Because the benefits of redemption are not to be confined to the human race. Christ is to be admired in his saints. It is through the Church that the manifold wisdom of God is to be revealed, throughout all ages, to principalities and powers. The redemption of man is to be the great source of knowledge and blessedness to the intelligent universe.[7]

There is truly a lavishness in God's grace!

'Let God be true, and every man be a liar'

The bearing of all this upon the widespread accommodation of the Bible's worldview to the alien perspectives of theistic evolution, progressive Creationism and other concessions to dubious scientific claims that deny the historicity of Adam and the events of the

---

7. Charles Hodge, *Commentary on the Epistle to the Romans* (Eerdmans, Grand Rapids, repr. 1947), p. 178.

fall, consistently undermines and jeopardizes trust in the reliability of biblical theology to a degree that few people realize.

It is time to draw some conclusions:

- If Adam was a fictional and mythical character, as many maintain, this means that Genesis has seriously mislead generations of readers. Yet neither Jesus nor his apostles could be mistaken in affirming the historical accuracy of Genesis. Jesus was personally present at creation. Paul was inspired by the Holy Spirit. Both knew that if Adam was mythical then people might conclude that Christ was fictional too. But Christianity is based upon fact not fiction. We can trust these accounts.

- Denial of Adam's historic influence leads to doubts that Adam's sin can or should be reversed in the way that Paul asserts here, since there would be little or no need for this. If death, disease, decay and destruction were present from the beginning and declared to be 'good' by God, then why undo them? But the Bible asserts that death is the 'last enemy' that will be finally destroyed at the return of Christ. He will evict what should never have been there at all and is most certainly not 'good'!

- Doubts concerning Adam's primogeniture, his 'firstborn' status as the first human, undermine Paul's presuppositions, reasoning and conclusions, since they are deemed mistaken and outmoded ideas belonging to a more scientifically primitive age. If so, then we are completely at the mercy of the claims of modern science and sceptical biblical scholarship to tell what we can and cannot believe in the rest of Paul's writings. Yet science has often proved to be mistaken, the Bible never has.

- These doubts may compromise the gospel itself, for if there is no historical basis to Adam's disobedience then we have to question the historic reality of Christ's saving work. Similarly, such concepts as 'Adamic federal headship' (both 'first' and 'last'), Christ's substitutionary atonement, the imputation of Adam's sin and Christ's righteousness, as well as our justification and adoption as a result of the latter, are simply not 'gospel truth' if the Bible is deceptive.

- Finally, our future hope in the final consummation of all things and the sudden re-creation and renovation of the whole cosmos along with the resurrection of all the redeemed, is seriously undermined. If God's creative work was as slow, imperfect, slipshod and dangerous to life and limb as evolution asserts it was, then the creation story of Genesis 1 – 3 is wrong and this throws into question the final consummation accounts in Revelation too. If God didn't say what he meant in Genesis, why should we trust him anywhere else? If God couldn't get creation right first time in the beginning, and was forced to use a 'hit and miss', 'road-kill' method involving eons of death and destruction, then how long might we have to wait for God to re-fashion the world at the end? It could be a long wait for our final resurrection and new residence! Yet both are said to be instant outcomes of Christ's return in the Bible. Why not at the beginning also?

For all of these powerful reasons and more, we are summoned to recover our confidence that 'the God who cannot lie' has spoken to us coherently and accurately in his word about both our origin and our destiny. The whole world really is 'hanging from the belts of just two men', and it matters desperately to us all that in our own personal case we should know which of these two men we are vitally connected with.

© Greg Haslam, 2009

5. CREATION, REDEMPTION AND ESCHATOLOGY

David Anderson

Gnostic heresies are some of the very oldest, going right back to New Testament times. The apostles themselves wrote to refute Gnostic-type teachings – teachings which sought to separate the physical from the spiritual in God's created order (e.g. 1 John 4:2; Col. 2:18–23). These errors have also been amongst the most enduring. Gnosticism is ultimately not a fixed set of beliefs or an organization, but a recurring set of ideas that can surface (and in church history have surfaced) in many different forms. In this chapter I will argue that attempts to join Darwinian evolution with the Bible, by their very nature make Gnostic errors, especially when they deal with the relationship of the new creation to the old.

I also hope to show that the clash between Darwinism and Bible-based Christianity is not, as theistic evolutionists assert, because of enthusiasts (whether Christian or atheist) pushing either science or theology too far into the other's territory.[1] It is

---

1. Leaving aside for now the important point that *everything* is theology's territory (Gen. 1:1)!

rather because both Darwinism and the Bible lay claim to the same
territory, that of earth history. The theory of evolution makes
claims about the physical events in the past of the human race;
so does Scripture. Each tells a story about the critical space-time
events in the history of humanity; those stories deeply conflict.

Gnosticism

Gnosticism can be described by a number of traits. One writer
says, 'Gnosticism is a tendency: the tendency to replace the historical facts of Christianity with philosophical ideas. Gnosticism is the
tendency to de-historicize and de-physicalize the Christian religion. Gnosticism transforms history into ideology and facts into
philosophy.'[2] Under this transformation, physical facts and physical existence ultimately have their value denied. Such things are
too earthly, too common and base, for the spiritual person. Hence
for the classic Gnostic, salvation ultimately consisted in his or her
spirit – supposedly the 'real you' – being freed from the prison
of the body. The things you can touch and see have less value,
leading either to rampant immorality (because the physical doesn't
matter), or asceticism (harsh treatment of the evil body).

In biblical Christianity, spiritual truths are taught to us by God
using historical facts. Bread from heaven teaches us that we cannot
feed on bread alone; the earthly tabernacle, the copy of the heavenly one, taught the Israelites about the presence of God and how
to enter it; and more to the point, Eve's creation from Adam's
rib reveals the nature of the relationship between man and wife
(Deut. 8:3 and John 6:31–41; Heb. 8:5; Gen. 2:21–25 and 1 Cor.
11:11–12). Gnosticism, though, seeks to have the fruits of the tree
after removing its roots. The most devastating manifestation of
Gnosticism in recent centuries has been in theological liberalism.

---

2. James B. Jordan, *Creation In Six Days: A Defense of the Traditional Reading of
   Genesis One* (Moscow: Canon Press, 1999). Jordan later makes such wide
   applications of his definition as to make almost everyone outside of his
   own group a Gnostic.

Liberalism reduces the Bible's histories to myths whilst seeking to keep its lessons for outward moral behaviour. Liberalism has at least, whilst destroying Western civilization from within, helpfully demonstrated just how short a time the fruits can survive when this happens.

Being content simply to throw sticks at others' theological folly, though, won't do (Matt. 7:3–5). We contemporary evangelicals need to recognize that the same errors are being spread in broad daylight in our own camp. The inevitably disastrous results mean that cannot be a side-issue.

The Bible as an earthly book

The first step to avoiding Gnosticism is by returning to a foundational fact. The Bible's story is a single, continuous and integrated one. The first verse of Scripture tells us about what God did in the beginning; the last verse looks to what he will do at the end. It begins with an old earthly paradise where man dwells with God, and progresses to a new heavenly one where he does so in an even greater way. The whole story in between is one that is worked out in time and space. Since the Enlightenment, Westerners have learnt increasingly to make the Gnostic division between facts and ideas. It then came as a great surprise to most of us to find that the Bible is overwhelmingly made up of narratives (stories) instead of being like a Greek philosophical textbook listing lots of doctrines and their finer points. Often we don't know what to do with these stories, and they get relegated to the children's Sunday school class. The very earthiness of these stories, though, makes them an embarrassment there too. Thus children are rarely taught about Judah's intercourse with his daughter-in-law Tamar (Gen. 38), the rape of Dinah and the ensuing slaughter of the Shechemites (Gen. 34), or Jael driving a stake through the head of Sisera (Judg. 4 – 5)! Yet the Bible insists on these events, because they are a fundamental part of salvation history. The Saviour himself came from the line of Judah through Tamar, the rash actions of Levi and Simeon (and first-born Reuben's later fall) revealed God's choice of fourth-born Judah (Gen. 49:3–10), and Jael's godly actions were an anticipation of the fulfilment of the ancient promise that the serpent's head would be crushed (Gen. 3:15).

Physical is good

We need to feel the full impact of the Bible's very first verse: 'In the beginning *God created the heavens and the earth.*' All of physical reality was made by God, and was blessed by him as 'very good' (Gen. 1:31). That is why Paul could be so scathing about teachers who said that we should not marry, or were forbidden to eat this or that food. He rather forcefully called these ideas the doctrines of demons, the teachings of those who had 'abandoned the faith' – because 'everything God created is good, and nothing is to be rejected if it is received with thanksgiving' (1 Tim. 4:1–5). God made the physical world, and loves it and everything that can legitimately be done in it, such as sport, sex and sewing – it, and no other imaginary world, displays his glory and is the theatre in which the riches of his splendour are displayed. It is only by physical actions in God's physical world that salvation has come to us.

This display of his glory is chiefly in the good news of his Son (Gal. 6:14), who took on real human nature, died a real human death, and rose bodily from the grave. He experienced real tiredness, physical suffering, the agonizing pains of the cross, and ate real fish after he'd really emerged from Joseph of Arimathaea's tomb (John 4:6; 19:1–3; Luke 24:42–43). Hence Paul contended so strongly for the physical resurrection in 1 Corinthians 15 – a faith in Christ which was not grounded in confession of these earthly realities was, in the end, no faith at all (1 Cor. 15:17–19). Either the Christian faith is built upon beliefs about history, or it is not a faith that the Scriptures would recognize.

What about evolution?

The issue to which we must now turn is just how far the compromise of the gospel goes when we attempt to combine evolution with the Bible's own history. This is the question which the teachings of theistic evolutionists in general, and Denis Alexander's recent writings in particular, are begging. Alexander clearly knows that these issues are on the table, because he devotes multiple chapters to dealing with them. Our task is to judge whether or not his effort is a success.

Dr. Alexander's recent book[3] shows that he has a very organized and logical mind, and is willing to follow the results of his core beliefs wherever they take him. His foundational beliefs are that God has given us 'two books'.[4] We should look to science for truths about the physical world, and to Scripture for spiritual ones. Truth in science, he believes, is established by the rigorous process of peer review and gaining mainstream consensus. The ideas of cosmic and Darwinian evolution claim such a consensus, and therefore we can know it is true. Reading each book against the backdrop of the insights from the other, we can gain an integrated account of God's world and his workings in it.

Earth and human history

Concerning the physical past the evolutionary account claims that the world and the life forms in it have, over a period of millions of years, made a gradual rise from chaos to order. For life, this happened through the process of natural selection – competition for limited resources weeded out less fit specimens and allowed others who had gained better adaptations[5] to thrive. Eventually, through this struggle, increasingly sophisticated creatures came into being, culminating in man. This climax was reached in the last few seconds of evolutionary time. Looking at the Bible and trying to understand where its figures fit in, Adam and Eve seem most likely to have been Neolithic farmers in the east, probably 6-8,000 years ago. Darwinian orthodoxy means that this was many scores of thousands of years after the first humans, culture, art and writing

---

3. Denis Alexander, *Creation and Evolution: Do We Have to Choose?* (Oxford: Monarch Books, 2008).

4. The metaphor goes back to Francis Bacon, *The Advancement of Learning* (1605).

5. Through random genetic mutations and possibly other genetic activity.

had developed, and there were other branches of the human family (such as the Aborigines) who are not descended from Adam (neither was Eve made from his rib). It also goes without saying that such things as pain, suffering and death long preceded the arrival of Adam and Eve – in fact, they were an essential part of the process (the struggle for limited resources) that gave rise to them. Biology, says Alexander, is a package deal – you cannot have sentient beings in a world anything like ours without also having these minuses.[6]

Paradise lost

It follows logically, and Alexander unswervingly affirms, that therefore the fall was in no sense an event affecting the physical world. Adam and Eve had human ancestors who toiled and sweated amongst thorns, suffered pain in childbirth and died. If you think otherwise, we are told, then you have most likely been getting your ideas from Milton's classic *Paradise Lost* instead of the Bible.[7]

If Adam and all his supposed relatives were always subject to death, then in what sense can the wages of his sin have been death (Rom. 6:23)? Alexander answers this with another piece of dualism, setting up 'physical death' and 'spiritual death' in sharp contrast. The first is natural and intended from the beginning – it is the second, whose meaning is separation from God, which Adam incurred. (In what Alexander writes, Adam's specialness as a human basically consisted in being the first who was offered a divine relationship – this means that in the fall he lost what nobody had ever had; a non-event!)[8]

Deliberate history

We have already noted that it is the very first verse of Scripture that draws attention to God's total involvement – as its author – in the

---

6. Alexander, *Creation or Evolution*, p. 279.

7. Ibid., pp. 256, 271.

8. Ibid., p. 192.

world of space and time. Indeed, the first chapter as a whole then goes on to deal with very physical matters: light, dark, earth, sea, sun, moon, stars, land, animals, birds, man. And it is not long at all until, in Genesis 4 and 5, we meet the first of the Bible's genealogies. Whereas Gnostic-influenced modern theologians and preachers have often found them easy to ignore (Alexander finds no space in his 300 plus pages to say anything about them), the Bible writers in both testaments were very interested in genealogies.

Genesis extends the line further in chapters 10 and 11, taking us up to Abraham. We are then led through the accounts of Abraham, Isaac and Jacob and the very gritty details of faith and deception that gave rise to the twelve patriarchs. The writer of 1 Chronicles repeats the genealogy of Genesis, and takes us to King David. Abraham and David are the two picked out by Matthew, who recounts the whole line again, showing its final climax in Jesus Christ. Luke gives us the complete record to the Saviour's birth coming right from Adam (Matt. 1:1–16; Luke 3:23–38). Along the way of that line we see incest, prostitution (Judah and Tamar), bigamy, sisters married to the same man (Jacob, Rachel and Leah), and much else besides. It is the kind of material forbidden before the television watershed, but also the kind of material the Holy Spirit thinks we need to spend a lot of time reading. That's because the history is not an optional extra to the Bible's story – rather, it is essential to it. We cannot, as Alexander does, simply relegate Genesis to the status of a theological novel without denying its intended purpose. We are given an accurate history of the world and its salvation, as a bulwark against every false, competing theory. We are not intended to bring Genesis and competing histories into some kind of artificial harmony (a harmony that guts Genesis of its actual historical value) – we are supposed to use Genesis to fight and defeat those alternatives.

Cosmic redemption

What about when we go beyond humans and human relationships? What about the non-living universe? Does Scripture, then, teach that the fall was an event that had a cosmic impact throughout the physical universe itself? Is physical death the result of Adam's sin? Does giving birth hurt because Eve broke God's covenant (Gen. 3:16–19)? Alexander's first defence against these possibilities is that it is wrong even to bring them to Genesis in the first place, because Genesis is not that kind of book. We have just answered this claim. The Bible's comprehensive interest in history from Adam to Christ makes it really clear that the Bible is deliberately given as that kind of book. There is no possible spiritualizing, Gnostic and ethereal reinterpretation of 'And after he became the father of Enoch, Jared lived 800 years and had other sons and daughters. Altogether, Jared lived 962 years, and then he died', such that we can now jettison the actual historical fact of Jared being quite so old.[9] The earthly fact is an essential part of it. Jared was an ancestor of the promised seed of the woman who would be the Saviour. He was part of the chosen line, with all its splendour and sordidness. The (bare) details of his life and times are recorded because those details are the very point.

What, though, of the physical world? We will now survey some key texts. Firstly, the details of Genesis itself must be asserted. If Jared and his 800 years after becoming a father are an essential historical fact, then we must see it is necessarily arbitrary to write off any of the other historical assertions of the early chapters. There is no principle of biblical interpretation that allows us to admit that Eve gave birth to a son named Seth, whilst denying that in giving birth she suffered great pain as she would not have done if Adam had not sinned. There are no contextual markers of any kind which allow the genealogical details of Genesis 4 and

---

9. Gordon Wenham, not a young earth creationist, in his massively researched commentary on Genesis is very honest in conceding that despite his wishes to the contrary, all the existing suggestions for re-interpreting these massive ages in a symbolic fashion are not persuasive. 'To date, then, no writer has offered an adequate explanation of these figures. If they are symbolic, it is not clear what they symbolize.' Gordon Wenham, *Genesis 1–15* (Word Biblical Commentary; Waco: Word Books, 1987), pp. 130–134.

5 to be literal, whilst the details of the same people when they are named in Genesis 2 and 3 are not. If Genesis is telling us that Jared spent 962 years walking on the real earth, it is arbitrary to insist that we are not meant to believe that the same earth started to produce thorns and other nuisances at the time Adam rebelled.

Christ-like Bible interpretation

This was undeniably how Jesus and his apostles interpreted the early chapters of Genesis. Paul believed and stated without equivocation that Eve was made after Adam, from him and for him, and that a serpent deceived her (1 Tim. 2:13–14; 1 Cor. 11:8–9; 2 Cor. 11:3). Peter believed that the world perished in a flood (Gen. 6 – 9) in the same historical way that he believed that Abraham's nephew Lot escaped the destruction of Sodom in Genesis 14 (2 Pet. 2:5–8), a teaching he first heard from Jesus himself (Luke 17:26–29). The supposed 'gap' (which Alexander presents no arguments to justify but merely asserts as a fact) between the non-historical theological stories of Genesis 1 – 3 and the true histories of Abraham, David and Jesus simply does not exist. The Bible interweaves them all into a seamless whole, and they must remain together or we must reject or ruin the whole garment.

The teaching of the Apostle Paul

In Romans chapter 8, Paul gives us a thrilling exposition of the work of the Holy Spirit, and how through him all that we could not do before, all that we lost, all that we could never have, has been made a sure and certain reality. The 'old trinity' of the law, sin and death kept us in a bondage which he has burst through. By him, the godly life that the law required is realized in us. He dwells in our mortal bodies and will bring us the fullness of resurrection life even as he did to Jesus. Verses 18–24 are especially important for us here, because in them Paul explains that even the very creation itself will experience glorification in the renewal, being 'liberated from its bondage to decay and brought into the glorious freedom of the children of God' (v. 21). The Greek word translated 'decay' (*phthora*) refers to something ruined – an inferior state compared to what was previously the case; a negative privation. Something was lost!

Confirming this observation, in verse 20 Paul says that the creation was 'subjected to futility'. When did this happen? The conclusion is clear. Paul's point is that creation's destiny is inextricably linked with man's. In the future, when man experiences the final fullness of his redemption, creation will also join in this redemption. Obviously, in the past, creation was brought into bondage when man was, an event that the Bible uniformly attributes to the time when Adam sinned (Rom. 5:12–21; 1 Cor. 15:22). Man, as the star actor on the stage (made in the image of God), is the very reason for the play. When he rebels, the whole play is ruined with him. Creation must rise and fall in accordance with the rise and fall of the first and last Adams – anything else is a Gnostic separation of what God has joined.

Evangelical Christianity has always insisted as an essential of orthodoxy the belief that in the future the creation will undergo comprehensive physical change; Alexander himself teaches this. Some writers have preferred to describe this change in terms of a glorious and total renewal of the existing world. Some have seen it more as a destruction by fire followed by re-creation. We do not need to decide between those options now. The point is that the fact of a change in the physical order is agreed.

This being so, on what grounds can it be denied that God also brought change at the fall? Here, Alexander's assertion is incoherent. If words have any meaning, Paul placed the present physical world into the nexus of sin, decay and death that man's sin has brought in, and teaches us that when man experiences the final renewal the physical world will too. Alexander himself seems perplexed by these verses, telling us that this 'passage has kept commentators and PhD theology students happily busy for centuries' so 'we cannot be too dogmatic about the interpretation'! This is a poor substitute for an argument – Alexander does not go on to provide us with an alternative possible interpretation, but simply makes valid observations on other points from the text and arbitrarily concludes that therefore there is no need to deduce that Paul believed in a physical fall.[10]

His assertion here also appears to be quite untrue. I surveyed one by one the first three shelves of books on Romans in my nearest evangelical library.[11] Amongst them, I found no authors at all who taught what Alexander does – that Paul's words can be interpreted in line with the belief that the physical creation did not undergo change because of Adam's sin. Two authors (the ancient and modern heretics Pelagius and John A. T. Robinson!),[12] were silent on this question but I judged that what they did say in their commentaries could be understood as showing sympathy with Alexander's position. On the other hand, I collected quotations from twenty-two other authors unambiguously stating the traditional position. In some cases these authors were theological liberals – they explained that Paul meant to teach this position, even whilst making it clear they personally disbelieved it! Alexander appears to be projecting his own struggle against the clear teaching of this passage onto others. It is interesting to contrast Alexander's reluctance to assign meaning to Scripture with his dogmatic certainty about the suggestions of contemporary science: stone tools appeared 2.6 million years ago; we know who lived near Lake Turkana precisely 1.44 million years ago (not 1.45 or 1.43) because peer-reviewed science has a consensus; but in the case of even such apparently open-and-closed texts as Romans 8:19–22, it would apparently be wrong to be too dogmatic!

---

10. I.e., he makes the fallacy of introducing an unnecessary 'either/or' choice. Alexander, *Creation or Evolution,* pp. 278–280.

11. The Nairobi Evangelical Graduate School of Theology, which houses approximately 180 books in the section on Romans (not all of which are commentaries or refer to Romans 8:19–22), on eight shelves.

12. In agreement with Pelagius, on p. 265 Alexander teaches that we each die (spiritually) because of our own actual sin, not because of Adam's. Inconsistently, he also asserts that Adam is our federal head but does not explain what this consists in – the only way to harmonize what he writes seems to be by holding that Adam's headship is ultimately only figurative.

Biblical consistency

In unfolding his teaching about a cosmic restoration, Paul was not making a new revelation. Rather, he was unpacking what had been proclaimed by the prophets under the Old Covenant when they spoke of the days to come – he was continuing Scripture's one story. An example is found in Isaiah 11:6: 'The wolf will live with the lamb, the leopard will lie down with the goat; and the calf and the young lion and the yearling together; and a little child will lead them.' In handling such texts we have to tread carefully. Because of the intertwined relationship of the physical and spiritual sides of reality, it is perfectly possible for the prophets to use the former to illustrate the latter in a variety of ways, without the statement being intended to be understood literally. For example, on the day of Pentecost Peter under the inspiration of the Holy Spirit declared that Joel's prophecy of the moon being turned to blood had been fulfilled (Acts 2:16–21).

Concerning Isaiah's wolf and lamb, there are many other interpretative possibilities discussed amongst evangelicals. For example, some think these verses describe a future earthly millennium before the final judgment. Whichever of the options is preferred, one thing remains clear. Isaiah's prophecy brings the renovation of the whole of creation within the remit of the work of the Messiah. In particular, the harsh and contrary aspects of creation will be changed. Where creation appears to be in conflict with itself – where nature is red in tooth and claw – the Messiah will bring peace and harmony. This is what Christ will do when he deals with sin – when he judges with righteousness, smites the earth in judgment and slays the wicked with the breath of his lips (Is. 11:4). The 're' in 'renovation' is important. It is a definite work of restoration – when the knowledge of the Lord is spread throughout the nations, just as Adam and Eve in the garden once walked with God. Isaiah uses the common prophetic imagery of paradise restored – creation in harmony.

Thus in the Old Testament, as well as the New, Christ's work is described as being cosmic in scope (not just limited to an unseen realm) and that work includes a redemption of something spoilt, not merely an arbitrary introduction of something new. What Paul did was to fill in the colours of the prophet's picture of Eden restored, rather than replacing it with another picture. As well as the Romans passage, he does so in Colossians 1:14–18, telling us that Christ, by the blood shed on the cross, restored things visible as well as invisible, in earth and heaven. It is a cosmic redemption.

Signs and wonders

We move on now to consider the signs that Jesus performed during his ministry. There are firstly a number of signs in which he demonstrated his power over the physical creation. He walked on water, he instructed the waves to be still, he fed thousands from a few loaves and fishes (Matt. 14:15–33; Mark 4:37–41). These physical facts taught spiritual truths, to be sure; they revealed him as the Son of God, the Lord of Creation and thus the only one able to redeem it. In the healing signs, he manifested his role in redemption even more clearly. He came to the strong man's house to plunder it (Matt. 12:24–29). Satan's grip on humanity, drawing them into sin and thence into pain, misery and death, could not stand before the power of God's Son (Mark 1:24). The signs were ultimately the signs of redemption, and it is not only legitimate but intended for Christian preachers to use the many different signs to explain the multi-layered glory of Christ's saving work.

Darwinian thinking shatters the coherence of this orthodox understanding of Jesus' miracles. If paralysis, blindness, internal bleeding and the like are not symptoms of humanity's fall (e.g. Matt. 8:5–13; Mark 5:25–29; 10:46–52) then how is their removal a symptom of restoration from that fall? If they are not anchored in a past tragedy, how do they point forward to the removal of the cause and effects of that tragedy?

Alexander understands this reasoning and follows it. He admits that the miracles of Jesus cannot, by his logic, have this connection to the past. Instead, they are purely future-pointing signs, declaring the blessedness of the entirely new kingdom which is to come.[13] Similarly, concerning death itself, Alexander asserts

---

13. Alexander, *Creation or Evolution*, p. 273.

that 'physical death' never was presented in the Old Testament as an evil; only 'spiritual death' is. Instead, he says, it is presented as a normal and natural expectation, at least when it occurs after a good number of years. Alexander appears to have moved from the biblical distinction between physical and spiritual death to an unbiblical dichotomy. When Adam sinned, he did not simply lose his fellowship with God – he was also told that he would at a later stage return to the dust (Gen. 3:19). The two were distinct, but inseparably joined.

Why do we die?

If it is not because of sin, then why does Alexander say that human death is needed at all? His answer is that it is because the order to come is so different and we cannot inherit it in our present state; he quotes 1 Corinthians 15:50.[14] There is certainly a shadow of truth here, but the very next verse goes on to explain that *not* all will pass through death to be changed. Hence this cannot be the *primary* reason for death (Elijah and Enoch are also counter-examples) – its subsidiary nature is also indicated by its late position in this resurrection chapter.

This inevitably leads to the question of the physical resurrection which is at the heart of the Christian hope. Alexander says that such resurrection never was a part of the Old Testament believer's creed. In fact, it was basically unknown throughout most of that time, he argues, and only towards the end began to be hinted at: 'Although there are hints of the possibility of resurrection in the later books of the Old Testament, there is no developed resurrection teaching within the old covenant.'[15]

Alexander says that when the apostles started to clearly proclaim the idea of physical resurrection, it was as a new revelation

---

14. Letter to the editor, *Evangelical Times*, January 2009. See my review of this letter at http://david.dw-perspective.org.uk/writings/creation-or-evolution-dr-denis-alexander.
15. Alexander, *Creation or Evolution*, p. 245.

connected with the new kingdom to come. It was not one that inevitably flowed from the idea of a redeemer who would undo Adam's evil work and restore life in all its fullness, even surpassing it and glorifying us as if Adam had passed the original test. This is implicitly a massive concession. It implies that the apostles did not so much unfold the true meaning of the Old Testament (Acts 26:22), as replace it. If major features of the Messianic salvation were not revealed in the Old Testament and only revealed by the apostles, then it would hardly be fair for those apostles to have condemned the Jews for rejecting Jesus as a false Messiah (Acts 13:27). The apostles, though, clearly did not believe what Alexander says. Instead, they proclaimed that they were preaching the fulfilment of the Old Testament's resurrection teaching (Acts 26:23) – not as a new revelation.[16]

The big picture

As we take a step back to survey these ideas, we realize that we are now seeing not just the dim shadow, but a full-blown development in broad daylight in the evangelical camp of classical Gnostic teaching. In Alexander's thinking, the future inheritance of Christians is not a creation redeemed, restored and glorified. It is creation replaced. So he says, this present order was inevitably from the beginning a place of suffering and death, long before Adam sinned. Christ brings us out of this old and unpleasant order into an inherently different one. It seems that he is at heart not the last Adam of Christianity (1 Cor. 15:45), but the legendary Gnostic redeemer who liberates our spirits from the prison of our package-deal carbon-based pain-racked bodies into something else entirely.

The present world is evil and has always been evil: we must wait for the new age to arrive to be free from it. The Old Testament is the book of the Gnostic 'demiurge' who made a bad world – the

---

16. Though without doubt, there was a great deal of filling in of the details that was, as in many other areas, part of the apostles' work.

New introduces us to the one who can liberate us. It is ironic that in his postscript Alexander chastises creationists for supposedly not spending enough time on the issues to do with the care and maintenance of the present creation. It is only the orthodox theology of creation and redemption which makes such care meaningful or worthwhile. If Christ's coming kingdom is Alexander's disconnected replacement for the doomed old one, why would we bother caring for it?

What would Jesus say?

The idea that resurrection was not a part of the Jewish creed is not new. The Sadducees, the forerunners of modern liberal theologians, had the same idea. On one occasion they sought to prove to Jesus that it could not happen, through a story about a woman who had a succession of seven husbands. If there was a resurrection, whose husband would she be? Jesus' rebuke to them was stinging – they did not know the Scriptures, or the power of God. In fact, he said, the resurrection was not merely hinted at darkly towards the end of the Old Testament. Rather, it was clearly taught right at the start of the Bible, in Exodus chapter 3 when God spoke to Moses at the burning bush (Mark 12:18–27; Exod. 3:6). Alexander makes no reference to these words of the Son of God which so embarrassingly contradict his own claims. His observation that death is treated throughout the Old Testament as normal and inevitable gives no help. The Old Testament (as part of the Bible) is a unified story, and must all be read that way. It begins by telling us how death came into the world – because of sin. Adam acts as the head of humanity, on its behalf, and so when he has sons those sons are in his image – the fallen image (Gen. 5:3). Sin, once let loose, is everywhere and devastates everything it touches – so that one of those sons even murders another (Gen. 4:1–8). Sin spreads everywhere, and hence so does death (Rom. 5:12–14). Death is thoroughly routine, because of the all-pervasive nature of sin – Adam's fall ruined the whole race, not just himself. The reason why death is 'normal' could not be clearer.

Christ the non-Gnostic Redeemer

We must now consider more closely the way in which Christ achieved the work of redemption, i.e. his death and resurrection. Why did Jesus have to die physically, and why is the physical resurrection so important? In my opinion Alexander's presentation makes the physical death of Jesus logically inexplicable. If Adam's sin had no effect on the physical world (as adherence to orthodox evolutionary theory requires), and if Jesus did not come to redeem a fallen physical creation, and if the wages of sin is not physical death, then there was no necessity for Jesus to experience one.

If Adam was offered and then lost a purely spiritual benefit (of friendship with God), Jesus did not need to be crucified to undo Adam's work. Alexander never discusses the incarnation, but his theory begs the question here also. Why must Christ come in a real humanity in any case? As far as bearing the punishment for sin goes, if sin had no consequences for the physical integrity of the creation or the life of man in particular, the atonement is incoherent.

If that were the case, there would be no logical reason why Christ could not have come only as an appearance (like the Old Testament Christophanies) or as a spirit and suffered (if sufferings are needed at all) only spiritual abandonment. The old Gnostics saw what consistency required of them here. That is why they adopted a Docetic Christology, teaching that Christ did not come in the flesh but only appeared to do so. Their theology, like Alexander's, had no real need for any other idea.

Did Jesus teach Nicodemus that death was not physical?

In an incisive review of Alexander's book, Professor Andrew McIntosh has asked this very question, saying 'Why did Jesus die physically if the wages of sin is not physical death?'[17] Alexander's

---

17. *Evangelical Times*, October 2008.

reply was that, 'The answer is in Hebrews 9:11–28, and the fact that Jesus died to save us from eternal separation with God, the "second death" (Matthew 1:28; Revelation 2:11). Paul in Romans (6:21–23 and other chapters) is speaking of spiritual death. As Jesus explained to Nicodemus in response to his question (John 3:4), rebirth is spiritual, not physical (v. 5).'[18]

This answer, then, seeks to rely upon a very polarized physical/spiritual distinction. But studying the texts that Alexander has quoted does not bring this out as a necessary distinction. It can only be seen in them if the reader first reads them with that idea in mind. In my opinion, Alexander's answer simply ducks the question. He gives reasons why Jesus had to undergo some kind of punishment, but not why that punishment had to be partly physical. Alexander mentions but does not expound John 3 in his book, so it is hard to know in what sense he believes Nicodemus to have been misunderstanding the nature of death or instead how he sees the observation on rebirth to imply a conclusion about the nature of death or the necessity of Jesus' physical death. It seems like a classic case of a text being distorted because of the reader's prior beliefs. There is nothing in Jesus' words to deny that there is a second physical coming forth (the resurrection); the words 'rebirth is spiritual, not physical' are neither included nor implied in John 3:5.

Conclusions

In this chapter we have highlighted the writings of Denis Alexander. The arguments made, though, apply to all consistent theistic evolutionary schemes. If evolutionary theory gives an accurate history of the past and the development of the earth and life, then the fall must necessarily be an event with no significant impact on the physical order or humanity or his exposure to death in particular. The curse cannot have involved physical penalties.

---

18. *Evangelical Times*, January 2009 – Alexander also states this in *Creation or Evolution*, p. 265.

By consequence, the scope of redemption cannot include anything in these realms. Christ cannot have redeemed what Adam never lost. Following the logic further, there is no logical necessity for the physical sufferings or death of Christ. His sign miracles can only have pointed towards something entirely new that was coming, not something that was regained for us by his atoning death. The physical resurrection cannot be a recovery and glorifying of a life that Adam lost our access to, but becomes instead a neutral doorway into a different mode of existence. Each of these ideas contradicts biblical thinking.

We have furthermore seen that theistic evolution, when it turns its attention to matters of redemption and the new creation, is a comprehensively Gnostic scheme. It is based on an anti-biblical dualism which is rejected by Scripture from the first verse onwards. Alexander's *Creation or Evolution* sharply and consistently separates the 'book of nature' from the 'book of Scripture', theology from history, fact from idea, spiritual from physical. This in turn leads to the separation of Christ from Adam, redemption from creation, the new order from the old, resurrection from death, and ultimately renders the gospel's claims about the coming and work of Christ incoherent.

Alexander writes in a manner as to indicate that he thinks that making the connections he rejects is for simple and unlearned people.[19] If, he argues, we can extract the theological fruit from Genesis, then only a fundamentalist woodenly wedded to words could insist that God requires us to hold to the historical roots also. This procedure and this argument have always been the hallmarks of Gnostic scholarship. The enlightened elite rise above the crude, earthly, flesh-and-blood world of the masses. The spiritually minded leave behind the low earthly passions of the carnal world of bodies and men having sex with their daughters-in-law, and rise to nobler heights. God, though, has decisively set his face in Scripture against the reasoning which tries to be more spiritual than he is.

---

19. E.g. see his ridiculing of the idea that Eve was made from Adam's rib in *Creation or Evolution*, p. 197.

Theistic evolutionary writers use many of the same words as orthodoxy, but uncovering the meanings behind them reveals radical differences. The good fruits of the historic truths may not all have rotted and fallen off at the very instant that the roots started to be removed. Christian history, though, and especially the history of theological liberalism, show us what lies down that road. The Gnostic empire is not dead, and one of its seats of strength is amongst evangelicals who seek to weld Darwinism on to the biblical story. For this reason, we need to be quite clear about what the Bible teaches – the future is at stake in more ways than one.

6. THE NATURE AND CHARACTER OF GOD

Andrew Sibley

There are a number of questions that arise out of the science-faith dialogue that relate to origins, especially when some theistic leaders within science advocate what many believe to be a rather extreme view that denies the miraculous in creation, demands acceptance of theistic evolution, and insists that science must be done within strong methodological naturalism. This dualistic approach gives priority and independence to science, and in effect elevates science into the religion of *scientism*. It calls into question the power and nature of God and allows secular forces to shape the way Scripture is interpreted. This approach weakens Christian faith, and encourages a deistic view of God. Neither is this approach consistent with Christianity's mission in the world.

Is God a deceiver?

Theistic evolutionists sometimes comment that if creationism were true, then surely God would be a deceiver because all of the scientific evidence supports evolution and not special creation.

Denis Alexander repeats this claim in his recent book in order to dismiss the arguments of biblical literalists and uses as an example the work of Philip Gosse in *Omphalos* who argued that God created everything with an apparent age, including the evidence of fossils, for the purpose of providing a test of faith for Christians.[1] I doubt though whether Alexander could find a modern proponent of Gosse's ideas amongst creationists if he tried. Even in his day Gosse's ideas were out on a limb, as nineteenth-century scriptural geologists for instance interpreted fossils as being of organic origin as relics of the Noahic flood, an interpretation shared by present-day creationists. The seventeenth-century Danish scientist Nicolai Steno, a member of the Medici Accademia del Cimento in Florence who later converted to Rome and became a Catholic Bishop, took a similar view in his rejection of the popular neo-Platonic plastic theory of fossil formation. The inorganic theory, favoured by the Jesuit Athanasius Kircher, asserted that fossils formed naturally in the earth due to the actions of the *anima-mundi* or 'world-soul'. Steno's approach, written in *Prodromus to a Dissertation on Solids Naturally Enclosed in Solids*, gave equal weight to Scripture and nature in his scientific studies and by allowing Scripture to inform his work successfully forced acceptance of the organic origin of fossils, but not without a prolonged struggle that continued after his death. The same dispute erupted in the early Royal Society where Robert Hooke accepted the biblical flood and favoured the organic origin of fossils against the inorganic arguments of Martin Lister and many others in that institution.[2]

However, while that is an interesting account, it is necessary to consider the case in question. It may be pointed out that God did not deliberately set out to create things that look old, but that in creating he made things complete and whole; thus Adam and Eve, the animals and plants were created as mature entities having the appearance of age, not because of a desire to deceive on God's

---

1. Denis Alexander, *Creation or Evolution: Do We Have to Choose?* (Oxford: Monarch Books, 2008), pp. 139–142, 213, 240.

2. See A. Cutler, *The Sea Shell on the Mountaintop* (London: William Heinemann, 2003).

part, but out of his sovereign choice to make beings with physical maturity, an entirely sensible decision bearing in mind the need for parental care towards the immature.

Alexander further argues that there are molecular fossil relics in the genetic code that can only be interpreted in terms of an evolutionary history involving a common ancestor, and that this is an 'overwhelmingly convincing body of data'.[3] However, there is increasing evidence that many of these 'junk' or 'fossil' pieces of DNA do in fact have important functions within the cell, thus they are not 'left-over' from our past and common descent is not a necessary explanation. This is discussed more fully in chapter 10. Furthermore an inductive examination of the history of science shows that the most reliable scientific theories can be overthrown and shown to be untrue within a short period. Newton's theory of gravity has been replaced by Einstein's thoughts, and the 'billiard ball' approach to sub-atomic particles has been replaced by a quantum mechanical approach involving a wave-particle duality. Thomas Kuhn also saw the development of science in terms of competing paradigms.

Michael Polanyi has further noted that there is an unavoidable personal commitment within science that resembles the work of an artist, or even a religious search for truth, and that this needs to be acknowledged. The idea then that there exist absolutely objective facts within science is false because of personal participation and the nature of science that is an evolving social practice.[4] Different social groups also bring their own foundational commitments to the table as Alvin Plantinga for instance has argued. All knowledge claims are then based on untestable foundational assumptions, and the interpretation of all data sets is based upon beliefs that lie outside of science. Christians therefore are perfectly at liberty to bring knowledge from faith into their scientific work and question the foundational beliefs of naturalistic science; Plantinga calls this approach Augustinian or theistic science. He

---

3. Alexander, *Creation or Evolution*, p. 213.

4. M. Polanyi, *Science, Faith and Society* (London: Oxford University Press, 1946), pp. 19–27, 42–70.

further asserts that if God acts indirectly in creation, then it logically follows that he must also at some point in the past have acted
directly, and asks what warrant people have to presuppose that
God is not able to act in such a way.[5] While recognizing the benefits of methodological naturalism in science as a good 'general
counsel', Plantinga argues that it cannot insist upon a 'principled
proscription' of direct divine intervention.[6] What is shown though
is that no body of data is so well established as truth in science that
it could be claimed that God is a deceiver.

Furthermore, according to Polanyi, science is a balance between
excessive criticism and unbridled intuition that requires human
judgments. Such judgments themselves are dependent upon the
conscience, which should seek after truth.[7] This type of approach
incidentally falls under the umbrella of critical realism. However,
it often seems as though proponents of the theory of evolution
have a defensive antithesis towards criticism, especially from out-
siders, and as a result their research is perhaps driven by excessive
intuition with insufficient concern to ground their work in reality.
This approach would appear to be shaped in part by an overbear-
ing institutional peer pressure that can be very aggressive towards
dissenters. Fear of exclusion from the peer community can then
focus the minds of theistic scientists towards ungrounded intuition (or excessive criticism), which may dull the conscience and
cloud judgment.

In the arena of understanding origins, peer pressure often
affects the way the evidence is interpreted, and I would suggest
that Alexander's judgment, like many theistic evolutionists, is to
accept evidence for evolution with insufficient criticism, but then
because of an overall commitment to truth an excessive criticism
is applied to interpretations of those Scriptures that speak about
origins. The interpretation that is then placed upon the creation

---

5. A. Plantinga, 'Methodological Naturalism?' in R. T. Pennock (ed.),
*Intelligent Design Creationism and its Critics: Philosophical, Theological and
Scientific Perspectives* (Cambridge MA: The MIT Press, 2001), pp. 346–355.

6. Ibid., pp. 355–357.

7. Polanyi, *Science, Faith and Society*, pp. 19–27, 42–70.

account is determined by the need to fit Scripture within the prevailing scientific thinking of secular institutions. Within this framework Scripture can never be interpreted according to a proper theological understanding, but is at the mercy and whim of the latest scientific claims. Giving secular science priority in the science-religion dialogue is surely an inadequate situation for understanding theological truths, especially when scientific truths are known to change through time. As Samuel Taylor Coleridge has urged, the first chapters of Genesis should be read 'without prejudice'.[8] Genesis does indeed need to be read without the intruding peer pressure of secular scientific institutions. Instead a proper balance between science and faith needs to be found, with a sharpened conscience and appropriate judgment.

To claim so strongly that God would be a deceiver on the basis of particular sets of scientific findings being true is at best disingenuous and does not take into account the provisional and fallible nature of science, nor does it take into account personal and social commitments and untestable foundational beliefs that form the basis of all science. There is something amiss when it is suggested that God might be deliberately misleading people, when it is already known that science is a fallible practice and ideas will probably change in the future as new data arise. Common design remains a perfectly valid explanation, not because God chooses to deceive, but because of a common blueprint on the part of the designer for biological life that remains a logical possibility.

Evolution and deistic or pagan conceptions of God

A further question that arises is whether theistic evolution, or at least some versions of it, are really in harmony with the creation account and a proper understanding of the Creator, or are they closer to pagan or deistic conceptions of the divine? Alexander

---

8. S. T. Coleridge, *Specimens of the Table Talk*, vol. 1 (New York: Harper & Brothers, 1835), p. 39; Quoted by A. N. Wilson, 'Why I believe Again', *New Statesman*, 2nd April 2009.

makes some very useful comments about the inadequacy of 'nature' as a concept because it means that nature might exist independently of God; he asserts that he prefers to speak of 'creation' and 'Creator'. The naturalistic view, he notes, is really influenced by ancient Greek pagan beliefs, but was reintroduced into Western thought in the seventeenth and eighteenth century by Enlightenment deists. Nature, as a concept, reduces everything to an autonomous machine, perhaps initially given a spark by a distant, disinterested and impersonal deity who has little concern for its working and continued existence. However, according to theism the creation is entirely dependent upon God for its formation and ongoing existence, and a proper theistic approach must recognize that God is both transcendent and immanent with creation. Alexander's comments appear thoroughly orthodox in this regard.[9]

While there is little doubt about the desire of theistic evolutionists to maintain their commitment to theism, it is pertinent to ask what follows logically from the scientific acceptance of some forms of theistic evolution, especially those that claim that it must be understood within methodological naturalism where all evidence of God's handiwork is excluded from science by definition. This version of theistic evolution maintains that all of God's activity in the creation is in terms of indirect action, where it is believed that God has so fine-tuned the laws of nature that human beings and life as we know it were bound to arise. In this view, God's actual involvement is hidden from view and science must be carried out as if God has not acted directly in nature, except to fine-tune the laws and regularities of nature at the beginning. Howard Van Till argues that God has given the creation functional integrity, which he argues forms an important understanding that enables scientists to carry out their work.[10] However, the first question to ask is whether this view of theistic evolution is even feasible in light of the probabilistic nature of quantum mechanics, and to a

---

9. Alexander, *Creation or Evolution*, pp. 28–33.

10. H. Van Till, *When Faith and Reason Cooperate*, in Pennock, *Intelligent Design*, p. 158.

lesser extent chaos theory. For instance, Richard Swinburne has questioned whether this approach would actually work within a universe characterized by uncertainty, and John Polkinghorne has also cautiously recognized that quantum mechanics leaves creation open to the possibility of God's interactive direct involvement in the created order.[11]

But more importantly, methodological naturalism in effect establishes a dualism between the spiritual and material that is not part of Judeo-Christian theology, which recognizes instead that God seeks to bring all things in heaven and on earth together under Christ (Col. 1:20). However, the division of matter and spirit does have echoes in Gnosticism, and the idea that science and faith are separate realms of thought has in fact been influenced by the neo-Platonism of the twelfth-century Islamic scholar Averroes. The work of Averroes was later brought more fully into Christian thinking through institutions such as the University of Padua, and one of its most notable students, Galileo, who was educated, and subsequently taught, at that institution. Galileo's well-known statement on the difference between truth in science and truth in Christian faith was set out in a letter to the Grand Duchess Christina of Lorraine in 1615, in which he attempted to hold to the integrity of Scripture and accept advances in science. Accordingly, God's Holy Spirit is interested in teaching us 'how to go to heaven, not how heaven goes'. Galileo argued for three further basic points: first, the book of nature and the book of Scripture cannot be contradictory as both proceed from God, second, science can provide truths that are independent of Scripture, and third, Scripture cannot be used to deny truths that are established through the scientific method. This approach though, effectively sets up a dualism between truth in science and truth in Scripture where it is believed that science gives truth in the material realm and Scripture gives moral and spiritual truths, although I don't think Galileo was fully aware of the implications

---

11. R. G. Swinburne, *The Existence of God* (Oxford: Oxford University Press, ²2004), pp. 346–349; J. Polkinghorne, *Faith, Science and Understanding* (London: SPCK, 2000), pp. 77, 110, 175.

for Christian theology. Galileo did in fact criticize Kepler for apparently ascribing occult properties to the planets and moon – Kepler had tried to fit their orbits into the Platonic shapes.

But by asserting that material truth can be arrived at independently of God's special revelation in reality idolizes or deifies science and the scientist. Roy Clouser has argued that if attributes that properly belong to God, such as self-existence and absolute trustworthiness, are ascribed to created things then those claims are in effect pagan.[12] So if the process of science is given a level of trustworthiness that is independent of God, then in effect it is developing along neo-pagan lines. There is a tendency in many minds to confuse science, which is a valid process of investigation, with scientism, that in effect becomes a religious belief that elevates scientific knowledge above knowledge in theology and philosophy. This was most fully realized in the philosophy of Auguste Comte who attempted to set up a religion of science where he considered that all truth would one day come through science. This influenced Charles Darwin and later Thomas Huxley, who argued for a non-conformist version of Comte's ideas.

But accepting strong methodological naturalism forces Christians involved in science to allegorize Scripture until it has little relevance to the material world, and even does damage to its theological content as well. The scientific process is instead dependent upon fallible human faculties and evidences that are subject to the fall of creation. As will be discussed later, throughout Scripture significant theology is interwoven with material events. A proper and more humble approach to Christian involvement in science must be to weigh scientific claims carefully against Scripture and not carelessly dismiss the biblical historical accounts when it suits because of pressure from secular institutions. Steno's approach outlined in *Prodromus*, which allowed Scripture to speak about material events alongside studies in nature, successfully predicted the organic origin of fossils and advanced science. It is of course possible that fallible human beings sometimes interpret

---

12. R. Clouser, *The Myth of Religious Neutrality* (Notre Dame: University of Notre Dame Press, 1991), p. 194.

Scripture wrongly, but a much more considered and judicious approach is required to balance claims in science with biblical interpretations. Science cannot be done independently of theology and Scripture because both are revealed in the material. There are also questions about understanding God's purposes in the world that are being worked out through the mission of the church, and whether methodological naturalism is in harmony with that mission because God is bringing all things, whether spiritual or material, together under Christ.[13]

The other aspect of theistic evolution that has echoes of Enlightenment deism or pagan beliefs is the idea that God makes things make themselves. In other words it gives a creative power to nature that should properly belong to God. Alister McGrath quotes Charles Kingsley who, while praising William Paley's contribution in *Natural Theology*, argued that God makes all things make themselves, and credited Charles Darwin for providing the explanation for this mechanism.[14] However, while Paley argued that there are designed contrivances in creation, as far as I can see he did not argue that the whole of nature resembled a machine. Paley was writing in response to Erasmus Darwin's *Zoonomia* and David Hume's *Dialogues Concerning Natural Religion* and he asserted that even the regularities of nature require an explanation in terms of a divine mind.[15] It was in fact Erasmus Darwin in *Zoonomia* who argued strongly that the Great Architect of the cosmos as the 'power of generation' 'makes the maker of the machine' and referenced Hume's *Dialogues*.[16] In part VII of the *Dialogues*, Hume's character Philo appeals his argument to Hesiod's *Theogeny* and Plato's *Timaeus*, as well as the writings of

13. N. T. Wright, *Surprised by Hope* (London: SPCK, 2007), pp. 130, 269–276.

14. C. Kingsley, 'The Natural Theology of the Future', *Westminster Sermons* (London: MacMillan, 1874), p. xxvii, quoted in A. McGrath *The Open Secret* (Oxford: Blackwell Publications, 2008), pp. 268–269.

15. W. Paley, 'Natural Theology', in W. Cooper (ed.), *Paley's Watchmaker* (Chichester: New Wine Press, 1997), p. 31.

16. E. Darwin, *Zoonomia; Or the Laws of Organic Life*, vol. 1 (New York/Boston: Thomas and Andrews, ²1803), pp. 400–401.

the Hindu Brahmins.[17] For Plato the creator was the demiurge, an impersonal force or lesser deity that fashioned the cosmos out of pre-existing matter thus leaving it imperfect. David Sedley has recently argued that the demiurge should be interpreted metaphorically as having the appearance of an impersonal force at work in nature,[18] an idea not that dissimilar to the now discredited plastic theory of fossil formation.

I would suggest then that the idea that God makes creation make itself has strong echoes of pagan metaphysics and should be rejected by those committed to robust theism. Thomas F. Torrance too has been critical of the type of deistic reductionism that leaves the whole of nature as a vast machine because that would then mechanize knowledge.[19] Instead God created (Heb., *bārā'*) energy and matter out of nothing, but then formed man out of the dust of the ground, taking raw materials of clay and fashioning the human form (Heb., *yāṣar*) in the same way a potter shapes a pot. In other words, God has imposed higher levels of order within creation than more basic regularities.[20] In the same way an artist paints a picture onto a carefully chosen canvas, although both the picture and the canvas are designed, but at different levels. Or a poet writes her thoughts in a book, but the words are not reducible to the paper and ink. Within this framework, science should expect to find regularities in the created order, but also to find higher levels of order involving shape and machine-like contrivances. Of course regularities in laws of physics and chemistry can produce shape as well, such as the snowflake for instance, but in biology there is a much higher degree of complexity that is not

17. D. Hume, 'Dialogues Concerning Natural Religion', in N. Kemp Smith (ed.), *Dialogues Concerning Natural Religion* (Indianapolis: Bobbs-Merrill Educational Publishing, ²1947), p. 180.

18. D. Sedley, *Creationism and its Critics in Antiquity* (Berkeley: University of California Press, 2007), pp. 98–107.

19. T. F. Torrance, *Christian Theology and Scientific Culture*, vol. 1 (Belfast: Christian Journals Limited, 1980), pp. 15–23.

20. See M. Polanyi, 'Life's Irreducible Structure', *Science* 160 (1968), pp. 1308–1312; Torrance, *Christian Theology*.

reducible to physics and chemistry. While a good design argument should include such machine-like order, the whole of creation cannot be turned into a machine as Enlightenment deists, pagan metaphysics and forms of theistic evolution imply.

How does God reveal himself?

The Apostle Paul, in Romans 1, explains that there are a number of ways in which God reveals himself to humanity. These include: the revelation of the prophets in the Old Testament (that includes the writing of Moses) (v. 2); the revelation of Jesus Christ and his resurrection (v. 4); the revelation of righteousness that comes through the preaching of the gospel (vv. 16–17); the revelation of the created order (vv. 19–20); and also the revelation of God's wrath against those who suppress the truth in their wickedness (v. 18). Three of these revelations also come by or with power (Gk *dynamis*);[21] the power of the resurrection, the power of the preaching of the gospel, and the unchanging permanence (Gk *aidios*) of God's power revealed through creation (v. 20). The Greek word *dynamis* is interchangeably used for miracles in Scripture, for instance in Acts 2:22 where Peter asserts that Jesus was accredited to us by God through 'miracles (Gk *dynamis*), signs (Gk *sēmeia*) and wonders (Gk *teras*)'. The word *dynamis* incidentally also forms the basis for the English word 'dynamite'. While Alexander acknowledges the possibility of miracles in terms of the ministry of Jesus and the Exodus and the language of signs, wonders and power, he seeks to deny the miraculous in the creation, suggesting that the regularities of nature are unchangeable because they are given by God.[22] But Paul, as well as expounding upon God's unchangeable

---

21. Greek definitions are sourced from: W. E. Vine, M. F. Unger and W. White (eds.), *Vine's Complete Expository Dictionary of Old and New Testament Words* (Nashville: Thomas Nelson Publ. 1985). Also used: A. Marshall (transl.), *The Interlinear NASB-NIV Parallel New Testament in Greek and English* (Grand Rapids: Zondervan, 1993).

22. Alexander, *Creation or Evolution*, pp. 36–38.

power, further elaborates on those aspects of God's 'divine nature' that may be known from creation; that is from 'what has been made'. He writes:

> For since the creation of the world, God's invisible qualities – his eternal power and divine nature – have been clearly seen, being understood from what has been made, so that men are without excuse (Rom. 1:20).

The word Paul used for 'divine nature' is *theiotēs* (from *theios*), and refers to the attributes of the one true God. This is different from *theotēs,* which would be used to refer to the personality of God. Vine notes that Paul uses the word *theiotēs* to assert that it is the attributes of God that can be known by the revelation of creation, and not the personality of God. Instead the personality of God is fully revealed in Christ.[23] *Theios* is also used at one point in Paul's preaching at the Areopagus on Mars Hill (Acts 17:29) to denote the one true God who made all things, as opposed to the idols that the Greeks considered to be gods.

The Greek word Paul used for 'what has been made' is *poiēmasin* (from *poiēma*), which forms the root of the English word 'poem' and refers to workmanship. *Poiēmasin* implies then that the created order is more than a physical act, but also a work of art or design where the craftsman brings his will, his thoughts, his love and skill into the work. A written poem is for instance an interwoven creational blend of word, thought and love or passion. The idea that creation is a work akin to human poetry is an important concept that follows from the Jewish cultural tradition where poetry, as for instance in the Psalms, is an essential expression of faith, and where the creation itself is considered a response to God's commanding word. The heavens, for instance, 'declare the glory of God . . . day after day they pour forth speech; night after night they display knowledge' (Ps. 19:1–2). According to Paul then, the poetry of the created order reveals something of the unchangeable power of God and his divine attributes, but special revelation is necessary to tell us more about the personality and purposes of God.

---

23. Vine, *Expository Dictionary,* pp. 178–179.

In John's Gospel we find Jesus identified as the Word of God who creates all things: 'In the beginning was the Word, and the Word was with God, and the Word was God . . . through him all things were made' (John 1:1, 3). Similarly in Colossians Paul asserts that 'He is the image of the invisible God, the firstborn over all creation. For by him all things were created . . . and in him all things hold together' (Col. 1:15–17). Jesus was present in creation, and is revealed in Genesis 1 – 3 as speaking creation into existence, thus from a scientific perspective I would suggest that we should expect creation to present evidence of that spoken word. This is precisely what we find in the order of natural regularities and laws, and in the information content in the genetic code, creation giving up evidence of its spoken formation and existence. Torrance has argued further that there should be no division between the natural and the supernatural because both are necessarily responding to God's commanding word.[24] God then orders all creation through his word, and this approach avoids the pitfalls of God-of-the-gaps type of arguments.

The other aspect to bring out is that the miracles of Jesus recorded in the Gospels are not only described as wonders, and acts of power, but are signs (Gk *sēmeia*), thus having theological significance. At the wedding party in Cana Jesus turned water into wine as a sign that he was the true vine, a creative miracle occurring in a short space of time. Jesus also claimed to be the light of the world and healed a man born blind. He claimed to be the resurrection and the life and raised Lazarus from the grave, and he claimed to be the bread of life after feeding five thousand people from a few loaves and fish. These are described in the Gospels as being real, creative miracles that impacted the material realm, but also demonstrated aspects of Christ's divinity and signified his purpose in the world.

By asserting that the miracles of Jesus were miraculous demonstrations of power and signs, the New Testament writers then provide us with an interpretive framework where miracles are seen as real, material events, but having theological significance and

24. Torrance, *Christian Theology*, p. 122.

meaning. As Paul stated, the creation reveals something of God's *unchangeable* power and divine nature, and so there is every reason to believe that the interpretive framework of the New Testament miracles applies equally to Genesis. Within this framework the creation account should be read as a literal as well as a literary theological account containing deeper levels of truths, and this is entirely consistent with the way in which theology is revealed throughout the Bible. The account of Abraham taking his son to Mount Moriah (Gen. 22), and sacrificing a ram in his place as provided by God, also displays the same framework for understanding Scripture, where significant theology is revealed through material events. The incarnation, crucifixion and resurrection of Jesus are prime examples where the material and the spiritual are brought together in this manner. The way in which the spoken blessings of Abraham, Isaac and Jacob-Israel are worked out in their descendants' lives defies a naturalistic explanation and also reveals theological significance. Throughout Scripture, God is revealed as working out his purposes in the world by directly intervening in his creation and shaping it according to his sovereign choice.

So, although Alexander seeks to deny the miraculous aspect of the creation account, there are very good reasons from Scripture for believing that it should be understood in such a way. It is God who is unchangeable in his power and divine nature, and in his sovereignty is free to change any or all of the regularities and laws of nature at will through his commanding word. In his love and mercy God generally does not intervene very often, which provides a stable environment in which to live, although at other times he does choose to intervene directly, again according to his love and mercy.

Conclusion

Christians cannot place artificial limits on God's sovereign activity in the created order and then seek to do science with absolute integrity. Instead, uncertainties about the fallible nature of science and its dependence upon God must be acknowledged in order to maintain that integrity and avoid deifying science. God has not sought to deceive people by making things look as if they have evolved when they have not, but has clearly revealed his activity through Scripture and the creation. Forms of theistic evolution that deny any direct involvement of God in creation also have the appearance of deistic or pagan conceptions of the deity and weaken Christian faith, giving it a deistic spirit. The type of division of science and theology espoused by Galileo is a dualistic approach that has more in common with neo-Platonism or Gnosticism than with robust theism. Instead, Scripture and science must be held in a proper relationship that respects the integrity of God's word, an approach favoured by Steno that has proved fruitful to science in the past. When there appears to be a contradiction, theistic scientists cannot simply allegorize Scripture at will, as new data are likely to force a reinterpretation of the science in the future. Such an approach leaves the interpretation of Scripture and our understanding of God's activity in the world in an unstable and unsatisfactory position. Instead it is God who is unchanging in his power and love.

7. FAITH AND CREATION

R. T. Kendall

> Through faith we understand that the worlds were framed by the word
> of God, so that things which are seen were not made of things that do
> appear (Heb. 11:3).

The subject of creation puts in bold relief the seriousness of this
matter of faith.[1] Sooner or later the question of creation versus
evolution emerges for the Christian in today's world and the
matter of faith with special reference to creation is often the crux
of the whole issue. Many want to believe in God and enjoy the
venture of faith which the warriors of Hebrews 11 experienced,
but often prefer not to have to believe the Genesis account of creation. Indeed, many stand in awe of Enoch, Abraham and Moses
but fancy the possibility of side-stepping the question of creation
by God's own act. The writer of the Epistle to the Hebrews will

---

1. This chapter is an extract from R. T. Kendall, *Believing God: Studies on Faith
   in Hebrews 11* (Milton Keynes: Authentic Media, 2004), and used with permission.

not let us do that. Early in this eleventh chapter he makes us face the question of creation by God *ex nihilo* (out of nothing). He will not let us move to the stalwarts of faith until we are clear on this matter of creation by God alone. There can hardly be a more relevant issue at the present time; it is undoubtedly one of the burning issues of our generation. I suspect that the most common tool used by Satan today in his attack on historic Christianity is the theory of evolution. The masses now generally accept the theory of evolution uncritically and many leading theologians and pastors have also capitulated to the spirit of the age and have made the Bible subsidiary to the latest scientific theory. It is my view that none of us dare expect to experience faith as these great men did unless we also believe as they did concerning God's creation.

I too have a theory which I want to put to the reader. It is this: *every generation of Christianity has its own stigma by which the believer's faith is severely tested.* For example, in the first generation of the church it was to say that Jesus of Nazareth is the fulfilment of the Old Testament. This was particularly the stigma which the Jews accepted when facing the establishment that upheld Temple worship. Around the turn of the first century the cutting issue came to be whether to praise Christ or Caesar. About the turn of the fourth century the issue largely focused on the question whether Jesus Christ was co-eternal and consubstantial with God Almighty. In Luther's day it was whether one was justified by faith or works. These are but a few examples of what I mean, for I could go on and on. The most hotly contested issue of any day is that which is true but which also makes the minority view look foolish and makes the believer look a fool. Athanasius stood alone in his day when he stood for the full deity of Jesus Christ. The world is against you, they would say to Athanasius. Flashing his black eyes, he retorted: 'If the world is against Athanasius, then Athanasius is against the world.'

Things are no different today. We may think that our issue is unprecedented in weightiness in its threat to the Bible. We may fear that at long last the Bible will be disproved and Christianity made extinct. But there is nothing new under the sun. Every generation has its stigma by which the believer's faith is tested, and the issue is always that which appears to be the last blow to the Truth.

Arguments emerge that had not been thought of before; evidence is put forward which seems completely new; issues coalesce that point to the impossibility of believing what the Apostles believed. So today; we are in a post-Newtonian era. St Peter, Athanasius, Luther and Calvin had no trouble believing in creation *ex nihilo;* they also believed the world was flat (so it is argued). This is a new day, it is often said, and we must work out a faith to believe in that is consistent with modern science. The stigma of our generation, then, it seems to me, is to reject the theory of evolution and stand unflinchingly for creation by God: 'that things which are seen were not made of things which do appear.'

Behind the question of creation *versus* evolution is the very nature of faith itself, namely, whether we will believe God as a consequence of what he has said, putting his own integrity on the line; or whether we follow so-called empirical proofs at the level of nature. The nature of faith consists in this: Do we believe the word of God for its own sake or pay homage to the empirical method before we can trust the Lord?

To put it another way: the issue is whether the *internal* witness of the Spirit is prior to (or has priority over) the *external* witness. This issue is mirrored in the nature of saving faith itself. Are we Christians because we look at Christ directly or must we wait for some other indication (e.g. repentance or good works) that we are saved? The gospel message is this, that we know we are accepted because of Jesus Christ. But if we must look to our works for our assurance to be firm, then we are not enjoying a salvation by grace alone. So also with the matter of believing Scripture; do we believe the Bible is 'God-breathed' by an inner persuasion (the secret testimony of the Holy Spirit), or do we conclude that the Bible is true only in proportion to an external witness (e.g. archaeology or scientific verification)? The issue here is the analogy of nature *versus* the analogy of faith.

The stigma of our generation is to believe God's account of creation *without* the empirical evidence. In any case, nobody has proved that real empirical evidence is available in the first place. It is seldom pointed out to young people in school that the theory of evolution is just that – a theory. Much less is it acknowledged that the great impetus for believing in evolution is a godless conspiracy against Christianity. Behind the search for evidence to prove evolution is largely an emotional reaction against some people's view of God. George Bernard Shaw summed it up: 'If you can realise how insufferably the world was oppressed by the notion that everything that happened was an arbitrary personal act of an arbitrary personal God of dangerous, jealous and cruel personal character, you will understand how the world jumped at Darwin.' And yet Darwinism is yet to be proved, and it is partly for this reason that there are several theories of evolution. In any case, the purported empirical evidence for *any* of the theories is inconclusive.

I suspect that how we in our generation react to the stigma of our day is a hint how we would have reacted to the stigma of a former day. Indeed, how we respond to the test of our generation indicates where we would have stood in a previous age. Some of us are tempted to wish that we had lived in this or that era. Others might feel lucky that they were not living in a time of great persecution, as they fear they could not have stood it. There is a way to tell whether you could have stood it, and that is whether you are faithful to what is given to you now. It is as simple as that. We are no weaker or stronger than the martyrs, no more and no less intelligent, and have by nature no more or less courage; neither are we naturally any more spiritual than any who lived in a previous age. Spirituality is not a natural endowment in the first place. Jesus said: 'He that is faithful in that which is least is faithful also in much' (Luke 16:10). If we are faithful to the revelation God gives us in our day, it is sufficient proof that we would have been on the right side of the issues that matter in a previous generation. The men of Hebrews 11 are those who accepted the stigma of their own day.

One cannot help but notice that over one-half of the contents of Hebrews 11 is devoted to the book of Genesis. We can therefore see by this alone how relevant this chapter of the Epistle to the Hebrews is at the present time. The attack upon Christianity in our day centres largely in the culmination of two anti-God movements: (1) the embellishments of Hegelian philosophy and (2) the modifications of the thought of Charles Darwin. By the embellishments of Hegel's philosophy I refer mainly to the emergence of the Higher Criticism of the Bible and Marxism. These forces, combined with a denial of creation *ex nihilo,* have done more to undermine faith in the Bible than anything else has done in recent times. The modern church largely succumbed to this trend in the twentieth century, and as a consequence it is exceedingly difficult to find a churchman or theologian today who does not believe in some form of the theory of evolution. The conspiracy against the Bible has focused mainly in an undermining of the book of Genesis.

The writer of the Epistle to the Hebrews serves notice that he believes that 'the worlds (ages) were framed by the word of God, so that things which are seen were not made of things which do appear.' This statement is worded very carefully and contains everything that is needed in order to show that one cannot hold to evolution and creation *ex nihilo* at the same time. It is to be noted that the writer does not say that by faith we 'prove' that the worlds were created by the word of God. This points to the mistake many are making. Some feel a need to spend a lot of time proving certain things in order to establish faith. I sometimes wonder if this need arises out of some embarrassment for the Bible. I have a report in my files that describes the findings of a scientific laboratory which has proved the possibility of a virgin birth in higher mammals. This actually suggests to some that Jesus' miraculous birth is credible after all! It is not our task to destigmatize the faith by finding an analogy at the level of nature but rather to bear the stigma as we bear the cross of Jesus. We must be willing to be unvindicated and laughed at; and not rush to make our belief in the Bible credible to others.

Neither does the writer say that by 'science' we understand. The mistake made by many is to assume that science must be correct, and what science says is right. By the way, what is 'science'? It is often forgotten that science, as used in medicine or theology, is a nebulous term that lacks an absolute consensus. Many people listen to one scientist and think they have heard 'science' speak! Scientists are people who have more and more knowledge about less and less, and nearly every one of them specializes to such an extent that they are often ignorant of what is going on outside their own field. These scientists are quite human, by the way, and, like all natural people with biases against God, find no great difficulty in accepting some theory of evolution. The world is largely unaware of a rising number of competent, brilliant scientists (some Christian, some non-Christian) who do not believe in evolution at all.

The writer says: by 'faith' we understand. By *believing God* we understand. 'The fear of the Lord is the beginning of wisdom: and the knowledge of the holy is understanding' (Prov. 9:10). By believing God, there is a breakthrough to knowledge. By believing God, then, we understand that time and space were created by the word of God. It may be that in fifty or one hundred years, more and more scientists will believe this even by empirical knowledge. This should not surprise us. For, after all, empirical knowledge has failed to make their theory today more than theory. One wonders *how far behind* science generally is as a result of scientists' uncritical acceptance of evolutionary thinking. And yet if the majority of scientists were to deny evolution, this should not be the reason for accepting the biblical account any more quickly. For it is by 'faith' we believe in creation in the first place.

Hebrews 11:3 says it is by faith that 'we' understand. 'We' understand; others may not. 'We' do. Who are 'we'? The company of believers. The world may not understand. Many scientists may not understand. But 'we' do – we who are the family of God. Because creation really is a family secret. It is something we understand by faith. It was never meant to be understood by those outside the family. It is not a case of believing in creation and then being adopted into the family; rather, we are adopted into the family and then we discover the truth. One of the problems some Christians create for themselves is that they get defensive about a family secret, and then it becomes a family scandal. The Christian should never apologize for what has been revealed by the Holy Spirit, regardless of whether those outside the family ever come to affirm the same thing.

Apart from my conviction that God's word is faithful and true, if you were to ask why I believe that God created time and space out of nothing, I answer: the power of God in my own life. When I consider what God has done for me, I find the book of Genesis the easiest book in the world to understand. If God can save me, he can save anybody. If God can save you, he can save anybody. If God can save any of us, he can do anything.

By faith, then, we understand. What precisely is it that we understand? That the things which 'appear' – time and space and all matter – were not made of things that are visible – or that already existed. This is the essence of creation 'out of nothing'. Through faith we understand that time, space, and all matter were brought into being by the word – command – of God, so that things which are *there* were *put there* from *nothing* by the voice of God. 'And God said, Let there be light: and there was light' (Gen. 1:3). This of course runs right across pantheism, the view that all is God – flowers, birds, humans, and all nature. Nature is God. For pantheism assumes the eternity of matter, that there has always been time and space and matter. The writer of our epistle was no pantheist. Neither was he upholding panentheism – that all is *in* God, a supposed mediating position between pantheism and theism. This was Paul Tillich's position and many have followed him, for here they found what appeared to be a halfway house between atheism and Christianity. In the words of Harvey Cox, Tillich is 'the indispensable comforter of those who grew up in a faith they can no longer believe'. Those who are attracted to panentheism (but also many who have never heard of the term) subscribe to the idea of theistic evolution. Some even believe they can hold to creation *ex nihilo* and evolution at the same time. Their view is that evolution was merely God's way of bringing things to what they are today.

Those who subscribe to theistic evolution take their cue not from Scripture but from nature and 'science'. Those who believe in theistic evolution believe that the aforementioned external witness is prior to the internal witness. They assume that, since so many scientists believe in evolution, there must be something to it, so they begin with the assumption that evolution is probably true – but so is the Bible, that is, up to a point. And yet our writer tells us that what is seen at the level of nature was *not* made out of what

is visible, or which now exists. Any view of evolution takes it for
granted that what now appears, or is there, has *evolved* to its present
state, and evolved from what already existed. To superimpose the
name of God upon a system of thought that never intended to
cohere with Scripture is not only to dignify atheism but is to betray
that one does not begin with the simple statement of the inspired
word of God. What things are 'seen' *(phainomenōn* – literally, 'what
is being seen') 'were not made' *(gegonenai* – literally, 'brought into
being') by 'things which do appear' *(blepomenon* – literally, 'what
is visible'). If the writer of the Epistle to the Hebrews had seen
civilization 1,900 years in advance and wished to make a statement
that would categorically refute any view of evolution, he could not
have worded it better.

To take one's cue from nature is to assume the reliability of nature.
But nature is 'cursed' (Gen. 3:17) and consequently ceases to be a
reliable instrument or mirror by which to view the age of the world
or the way in which nature came along. It is not surprising, then,
that 'science' is always changing. A scientific dictionary nowadays
is out of date in ten years, and yet theologians keep running after
modem science. What 'science' purports to be true today, theology
will probably say tomorrow. What a pity that this is so! Theology
ought to set the pace and command scientists to respect the Most
High God. However, many scientists have sufficient integrity to
admit their own inconsistencies. One prominent scientist on the
eastern seaboard in America made the point that the evolutionists have continually failed to face up squarely to the fact that the
theory of evolution flies directly in the face of some of the best
established laws in the scientific world. Some of the foundations
which had been assumed are crumbling. We should not be surprised at this, neither should we necessarily be encouraged. For it
is by 'faith' that we understand!

  When we affirm creation 'out of nothing', we are actually
affirming what is perhaps the profoundest thing that can be said
about God – that he always was. This means moreover that he
was not always creating. The panentheistic view is that God is
Creator because it is his essential nature to create, that he has
always been creating. It follows, if that is true, that there is no

such thing as a 'beginning' of time or of space and matter. But one of the profoundest things we can say about God is that there *was* a 'beginning'; that 'before' then there was *nothing but God!* God became Creator because he chose to create.

To believe this at the present time however is not only to be outnumbered but it often means to be scoffed at and made to look like a fool or an obscurantist. But if it were not this issue, there would be another that would be just as open to mockery. For every generation has its stigma by which the believer is tested. We must not sidestep the bearing of the cross or try to destigmatize the faith. If we do not accept the stigma – that which is 'least', we need not expect to follow in the steps of these giants – who were faithful in 'much'.

8. TOWARDS A SCIENCE WORTHY OF CREATURES IN IMAGO DEI

Steve Fuller

The biblical basis of modern science – then and now

A good indicator that we live in a secular age is that merely to suggest a biblical basis to modern science is to make oneself appear antiscientific. Immediately one is reminded of Archbishop James Ussher's derivation of the exact date of creation – the night before the 23rd October, 4004 BC – by calculations derived from a literal reading of biblical chronology, a practice still admired by Young Earth Creationists. However, in fairness to Ussher, his technique reflected a 'modern' conception of fact and number that had only come into vogue in the seventeenth century and shortly after Ussher's death would be actively promoted by the Royal Society as the appropriate way to approach texts by credible authors. Indeed, Ussher understood the Bible in the spirit in which we normally understand the statements of trusted scientific experts today.[1] The

1. See Peter Harrison, *The Bible, Protestantism and the Rise of Natural Science* (Cambridge UK: Cambridge University Press, 1998), esp. p. 226.

problem is that in the four centuries that separate Ussher from us, the reliability of the Bible as the expression of the divine word has been called into question in many quarters, not least academic theology.

But truth be told, the reliability of the Bible has been always called into question in various respects and to varying degrees, spawning numerous versions, redactions and interpretations, which periodically resulted in heresies, schisms and still more drastic forms of dissent in the Christian ranks. Unlike Muslims, who have traditionally treated Muhammad as less the author than the medium through which Qur'an was written, Christians (and Jews) generally accept that human fallibility renders any account of the divine message potentially suspect.[2] Nevertheless, all Christians, no matter how heterodox, have shared the view that the content of the Bible is worth contesting because it is the privileged form of communication between God and humans. Indeed, Alister McGrath has dubbed the empowering character of one's personal encounter with the Bible as 'Christianity's Dangerous Idea', which truly came into its own during the Protestant Reformation, aided by the spread of literacy and the commercialization of book publishing.[3] On the one hand, the Reformation sparked wars of religion that engulfed Europe for more than a century and inspired virtually all of the secular revolutionary movements of the modern era; on the other, it provided the modern basis for 'agreeing to disagree' in political life, while reserving to science the right to test what is agreed to be testable.

Has the Protestant fixation on the Bible been worth the cost? Under the circumstances, it is tempting to adopt a Roman Catholic position, which downplays the unique significance of the Bible as a source of divine understanding. Instead, following Thomas Aquinas, one might argue for the irreducibly analogical character of biblical language, a reflection of humanity's own inevitably

---

2. Evangelicals, of course, affirm the divine inspiration and infallibility of Scripture, as originally given.

3. Alister McGrath, *Christianity's Dangerous Idea* (London: SPCK, 2007).

partial access to the divine message, whether it be expressed in the Bible or, for that matter, in nature itself. Rather, the Catholic stress is placed on harmonizing different sources of evidence, typically by circumscribing each to its own intellectual jurisdiction, without taking any of them as privileged or our understanding of them as final. It is just this fluid interpretive situation that theistic evolutionists wish to foster today, regardless of where they officially stand on other matters that divide Catholics and Protestants.

Of course, the 'Catholic' policy promotes considerable intellectual humility and interpretive generosity but at a high cost: namely, the loss of a unified sense of the truth that we might approximate through our own efforts as blessed by divine grace. It was just this unifying perspective that the Reformation championed as it called on Christians to read the Bible for themselves and to respond personally to its message. The example of Galileo is instructive. He proved to be a problem for the Church, while providing encouragement to Protestant scientists like Johannes Kepler, because he read the Bible as unequivocally empowering humans to make sense of nature, even if it meant identifying errors in the biblical and patristic authors, whose humanity no one had denied but the implications of which the Church wished to avoid for political reasons.

Many of Galileo's arguments were expressed as counterfactual claims that might be epitomized as follows: 'Had the biblical authors access to a telescope and today's astronomical knowledge, they would have altered what they originally wrote.' The modern scientific attitude was born of this sensibility, whereby given sufficient time all sincere inquirers would reach the truth to which they are entitled to know by virtue of their divine lineage. Our sheer mortality, the lingering consequence of original sin, simply means that whatever conclusions people have reached in their individual lifetimes must be treated as tentative and not final. Just as we contest whether our contemporaries have interpreted the Bible correctly, all of us can contest whether its original authors fully grasped the divine message, given the limited means at their disposal. If we believe that this matter may be corrected over time, then we have an obligation to enable people to live longer so as to expose them to more opportunities to eliminate the noise from our reception of God's message. At this point, upholding a scientific attitude merges with an agenda for progressive politics – albeit one that keeps in delicate balance respect for individual autonomy, collective security and corrigible judgment.

The political side of this argument did not become fully relevant until 150 years after Galileo's original challenge to the Church. However, what made Galileo a secret hero to Protestants in his own day (as demonstrated by the visits he received when under house arrest from, among others, John Milton and Thomas Hobbes) was his refusal to accept the finality of papal authority on matters of belief. Were Galileo with us today, he would regard bastions of the scientific establishment like the US National Academy of Sciences and the Royal Society of London as comparable to the Vatican in his own day. All of these institutions have sought to minimize the reasonableness of dissent by arguing that the dissenter confuses knowledge claims that belong to different domains, which nowadays are called 'science' and 'religion', which answer questions of 'how' and 'why', respectively. This argument was turned to great effect against intelligent design (ID) in *Kitzmiller v. Dover Area School District* (2005) by the Catholic theologian Jack Haught, an expert witness for the plaintiffs and devotee of theistic evolution.[4]

But what Galileo would find especially strange about *Protestant* theistic evolutionists like Denis Alexander and Francis Collins is that while they do not accept papal authority – which at least has a biblical basis in Peter's apostolic primacy – they confer Vatican-like authority on scientific institutions that have no biblical basis whatsoever. However, Galileo would have recognized a precedent for this attitude in the 'divine right of kings', a doctrine that in his day was most potently represented by England's King James I, whose Lord Chancellor, Francis Bacon, first proposed the institution that after his death would become the Royal Society. The divine right of kings explicitly yoked together secular and sacred authority by having the state church anoint each successive monarch as

---

4. Report of John F. Haught, PhD, 'Expert Pre-Trial Witness Report', *Kitzmiller v. Dover Area School District*, 1 April 2005.

the protector and executor of God's will on earth. The English Civil War was fought to overturn this doctrine, on the Christian grounds that every human being – not simply the current royal dynasty – has been created in the image and likeness of God and is thereby empowered to decide the constitution of civil society. Its chief legacy, of course, has been parliamentary government.

However, the sensibility informing the divine right of kings persisted and has arguably migrated from politics to science. To be sure, an institution like the Royal Society is governed as an oligarchy, but still it is no more accountable to those formally credentialed in science – let alone the public at large – than an absolute monarch. This would not be such a problem, if 'science' referred merely to a narrow set of technical skills, in which case it would be entitled to operate in the self-protective manner of guilds. But in fact, 'science' is reserved for the most authoritative form of knowledge in society, in which all citizens are supposed to be educated and on the basis of which a government can reasonably act without having to provide any further justification. Thus 'science' tends to connote final, if not absolute, authority. From that standpoint, if we imagine the rank-and-file scientific community and the public at large as, respectively, the landed gentry and the commoners just prior to the Magna Charta, then we have a good sense of the current state of intellectual captivity that theistic evolutionists wish to maintain in the name of keeping the peace between science and religion.

A strategy for ID to regain the initiative from theistic evolution

The main strategy used by theistic evolutionists to undermine intelligent design's credibility is to present contemporary biological science as a unified front – aka the modern evolutionary synthesis – and ID supporters as a fringe movement of well-intentioned but scientifically illiterate evangelical Christians who, were they to prevail, would reverse the direction of scientific progress, returning humanity to the Dark Ages. Closer to the truth is the exact opposite: while no one denies that much largely philosophical effort has been spent in weaving together the various strands of biology into what is properly called the 'Neo-Darwinian synthesis', those disciplinary strands conduct their normal business without need of Darwin's blessing. This is especially true of molecular biology, the cutting edge of biological research for the last half-century. It has become the securest basis for claiming intelligent design in nature, as it increasingly seems that life is the product of a *literal* genetic code.[5]

A good way to appreciate the manufactured nature of the modern evolutionary synthesis is to consider the looseness that normally surrounds the usage of 'evolution' in biology's technical literature, which can be used to talk about either convergent or divergent processes that are produced in laboratory experiments, modelled in computer simulations, observed in nature or inferred from the fossil record. Indeed, in genetics, 'evolution' technically means *any* change in a population's normal distribution of traits, a situation that ideally presumes controlled experimental conditions (i.e. not in the field), in which the geneticist designs what Michael Behe would call the 'edge of evolution', within which mutations are generated that potentially alter the balance of traits in a given population.[6] It is only when biologists feel collectively under threat that they take refuge under a specifically Darwinian rubric and rally around a purposeless sense of natural selection for their definition of evolution. Of course, biologists are not the only ones given to

---

5. On the studied independence of molecular biology from evolutionary theory, see Michel Morange, *A History of Molecular Biology* (Cambridge, MA: Harvard University Press, 1998), p. 249. The most developed pro-ID case for taking the idea of 'genetic code' literally, based on molecular biology is Stephen C. Meyer, *The Signature in the Cell: DNA and Evidence for Intelligent Design* (New York: HarperOne, 2009). Richard Dawkins is in broad agreement: See his 'Foreword' to J. Burley (ed.), *The Genetic Revolution and Human Rights* (Oxford: Oxford University Press, 1999), p. vi.

6. See Steve Fuller, *Dissent over Descent: Intelligent Design's Challenge to Darwinism* (Cambridge UK: Icon, 2008), pp. 116–117. See also the work of the US philosopher of biology, Alexander Rosenberg, who is inclined to see biology less as a unified science than a set of experimental techniques for bringing about particular effects, e.g. inducing mutations in species.

such rhetorical flexibility. After all, philosophers normally speak of 'logic' in a relatively loose way for a more-or-less inductive argument. But when forced to defend their disciplinary prerogative from interlopers, they pull back to a strict definition that equates logic with deductive reasoning, a topic over which they enjoy exclusive jurisdiction.

However, biology's easy alternation between loose and strict conceptions of evolution should not be seen as solely a rhetorical matter. It equally reflects the lack of a generally agreed sense of how the discipline's various branches relate to each other in pursuit of some common overarching intellectual vision. This needs to be kept firmly in mind when encountering the excessive claims that philosophers and biologists often make about the status of evolutionary theory. There is no canonical statement of the theory's content that goes beyond such vagaries as 'common descent with modification', which tells us nothing about how one makes and evaluates claims to knowledge in the field.[7] There are no agreed mathematized laws of evolution, let alone ones of universal scope. Instead, and quite understandably, biologists adapt more general expressions of evolutionary theory to the conventions of their own disciplines, resulting in knowledge claims that bear little more than a verbal resemblance to those made across disciplinary boundaries, leaving considerable discretion on how one constructs the so-called evolutionary synthesis.

The situation recalls the option that the original thirteen American colonies turned away from once they had successfully seceded from Britain. Palaeontology, ecology, genetics and molecular biology constitute more a *confederation* than a federal (let alone unitary) system of scientific governance. They are united only when under collective attack (e.g. by creationists or ID proponents) but remain separate in peacetime. Thus, the response that a palaeontologist would normally give to how findings in his field relate to those in molecular biology vis-à-vis evolution is likely to be rather different from the molecular biologist's view of

---

7. I cite this specific formulation because of its practised mantra-like invocation by the plaintiffs' experts during *Kitzmiller*.

how his findings relate to those in palaeontology. The difference is epitomized in the following question: When it comes to evolution, do the specific DNA differences detected amongst species provide independent corroboration or a direct test of the fossil record? The palaeontologist is likely to say the former, the molecular biologist the latter. For the former, 'evolution' refers to a theory about the history of life on Earth; for the latter, the theory is about the differentiation of life-forms, regardless of the actual history.

One would think that there is a world of difference between whether the iconic Darwinian metaphor of the 'tree of life' is supposed to be treated more like a family genealogy or a periodic table of elements, as palaeontology and molecular biology suggest, respectively. Yet, this rather deep divergence of interpretation is largely confined to the technical literature, so as to be ensconced from the machinations of creationists or ID theorists.[8] Under the circumstances, a good counter-strategy for ID is to appeal to the biological disciplines separately so that their practitioners do not think that they are collectively implicated in a common fate. Specifically, the order in which the various species came into being, about which there is relatively little controversy, should be distinguished from two others in which creationists and ID theorists have taken legitimate issue with Darwinists: *When* did the various species come into being? *By what means* did they come into being?

An 'edge' strategy for intelligent design theory

Following in the footsteps of that other lawyer who revolutionized the science-religion relationship, Francis Bacon, Phillip Johnson has suggested that ID should be seen as the 'thin edge of the wedge' that would dissociate the pursuit of science from a commitment to a naturalistic metaphysics.[9] His explicit goal was to

---

8. See Joel Cracraft and Michael Donoghue (eds.), *Assembling the Tree of Life* (Oxford: Oxford University Press, 2004).

9. Phillip Johnson, *Defeating Darwinism by Opening Up Minds* (Downers Grove: IVP, 1997).

re-acquaint science with a certain interpretation of its Christian origins, one which many have seen as politically aligned with the 'religious right' in the United States.[10] A tacit acceptance of Johnson's 'wedge strategy' has enabled a wide range of creationists to align themselves with ID, albeit much to the detriment of the outcome in *Kitzmiller*. Nevertheless, it is undeniable that Johnson's strategy has managed to consolidate for our times a distinctive Christian – and perhaps even broadly Abrahamic – take on science that stands apart from the scientific establishment. This success, however legally or politically limited, remains a thorn in the side of theistic evolutionists, given their strenuous efforts to assimilate Christian thought to mainstream science.

I would now wish to propose an 'Edge Strategy', my euphonious name for expansion of ID's constituency to the borderlands of Christianity that would serve to defuse the common caricature of ID as a sectarian right-wing movement, which turned out to be its Achilles' heel in *Kitzmiller*. The Edge Strategy aims to incorporate what I call 'Liminal Christians' – those whose orientation to the world clearly descends from Christianity but whom we would ordinarily regard as leading secular lives and operating from a liberal-left political perspective. The people I have in mind, who are often too quickly dismissed as atheists (much to the delight of today's 'new atheists'), include deists, Unitarians and a host of rationalist, idealist and humanist philosophers. All of these people share the belief that nature possesses a design that the human mind is especially equipped to master, which effectively raises us above all else in nature. This crucial assumption makes Liminal Christians natural allies of ID and opponents of Darwinism.

Liminal Christians may refrain from speculating as to why we find ourselves in this superior position (just as many ID supporters today avoid talk of the 'intelligence' that informs 'intelligent design'), but it is clear that they would never have thought humans superior had they shared Darwin's species-egalitarian view, voiced as early as his *Beagle* memoirs, when he remarked that

---

10. Barbara Forrest and Paul Gross, *Creationism's Trojan Horse: The Wedge of Intelligent Design* (Oxford: Oxford University Press, 2004).

more metaphysics may be learned from a baboon than from John Locke. Liminal Christians do not normally stress this common ground with mainstream Christians because the Liminals have historically defined themselves as non-conformists or, to recall a bit of nineteenth-century Newspeak, 'free-thinkers'. Thus, as we see even among people who today call themselves 'humanists', they are attracted to Darwinism less for its substantive intellectual position, which reduces the human to a mutant ape and reality to a meaningless mess of atoms, than for Darwinism's opposition to organized religion, which humanists hold has failed to treat humanity with sufficient respect by demanding submission to superstition, dogma and ritual.

Here we need to understand the historical horizons of Liminal Christians vis-à-vis mainstream Christianity. They debunk organized religion in order to separate the wheat from the chaff of spirituality, very much as the Protestant reformers treated the doctrines and rituals that had accrued to the Christian faith under the rule of Roman Catholicism. For Liminal Christians the Enlightenment was a further purification of Christianity that Protestantism had begun by devolving the Christian message from a central papal authority to a self-organizing faith community to, finally, the self-legislating individual, as one finds in Kant.[11] A vivid and controversial attempt at such purification is the so-called Jefferson Bible, written late in the life of the principal author of the US Declaration of Independence and inspired by the Unitarian scientist-theologian Joseph Priestley. The striking brevity of this secular scripture is due largely to Jefferson's removal of all supernatural references concerning Jesus.[12] While I do not expect mainstream Christians to approve of Jefferson's redaction, they should appreciate that it was the product of someone who

---

11. A good sense of this historical trajectory may be gleaned from Jerome Schneewind, 'The Divine Corporation and the History of Ethics', in R. Rorty, J. Schneewind and Q. Skinner (eds.), *Philosophy in History* (Cambridge UK: Cambridge University Press, 1984), pp. 173–192.

12. I purchased my own copy of the Jefferson Bible at the US National Archives in Washington, where it is sold as a devotional text.

saw himself as personally addressed by the Bible and certainly was comfortable with the idea of God as nature's intelligent designer, in whose image and likeness humanity is created.[13]

Although Darwinists seem perfectly willing to accept Liminal Christians as their own, they do not know quite what to make of them. After all, how does a Darwinist explain the continuing fascination that someone like Jefferson had with the Bible, even if only to demystify it? Was it simply an ingrained cultural habit that reveals Jefferson to have been a creature of his times? Some Darwinists might doubt the sincerity of Jefferson's project, dismissing it as a piece of satire to annoy the pious. Others might advance a more sophisticated argument, cribbed from Galileo: Had Jefferson the benefit of knowing Darwin's theory of evolution, he would have put aside his foolish preoccupation with the Bible altogether. However, none of these arguments work. Although Jefferson himself died in 1826, more than thirty years before the publication of *Origin of Species*, there are Liminal Christians who had strong, largely positive encounters with evolutionary theory yet ended up not so far from Jefferson's position. I include here Abraham Lincoln and the co-discoverer of the theory of natural selection, Alfred Russel Wallace, both of whom had a complex understanding of nature as governed by intelligent design, even Divine Providence.[14]

As suggested above, the main obstacle to the acceptance of Darwinism by Liminal Christians is its radically de-privileged position of human beings, who are cast as a transient offshoot of the great apes, themselves only marginally different in genetic makeup from other animals. Corresponding to this removal of metaphysical privilege is a tendency for Darwinists to treat the

---

13. This point is pursued in Fuller, *Dissent over Descent*, ch. 7.
14. I stress this point in a play I wrote in 2008 as the Sociology and Social Policy division president of the British Association for the Advancement of Science: 'Lincoln and Darwin: Live for One Night Only!' It was first performed in the Stanley Theatre, Liverpool on 9th September 2008 and subsequently in Oxford and Sydney during Lincoln and Darwin's joint 200th anniversary in 2009.

most distinctive features of the human condition as by-products or pathologies, in either case implying that we are lucky to have them in the first place but they may prove to be our undoing in the end. This general train of thought, which accounts for the generally pessimistic outlook found in the corpus of Stephen Jay Gould, is already present in Darwin's *Descent of Man*, where our developed forebrains are blamed for the human tendency to fixed ideas, which are the basis for wars and other forms of barbarism. Most Darwinian accounts of religion fall into this category.

In the case of distinctive human propensities that Darwinists look upon with more favour, such as art, the explanations turn on refinements in our adaptation to the environment. But this too is a mixed blessing, as it generally means that aesthetic response becomes a high-grade version of animal gratification, the 'push-pin is as good as poetry' view of art espoused by the great utilitarian philosopher, Jeremy Bentham. What drops out in the process is art's specifically *creative* dimension, that is, art from the standpoint of someone who produces rather than consumes it, what the nineteenth-century Romantic movement often characterized as a 'godlike' feature of our being. This shortcoming of Darwinism is obvious to anyone who has ever thought of themselves as an 'artist' in some sense. Not surprisingly, amongst the most influential defenders of freedom of expression as requiring distinctive legislation in the modern era – an essential but often overlooked aspect of our aesthetic lives – were two figures just on either side of the edge of Christianity: on the one side, the English Protestant John Milton (freedom of the press); on the other, the German idealist Johann Gottlieb von Fichte (author's copyright).

Living on the edge of Christianity: scientific progress as recovery from the fall

Lacking from Darwinian accounts is the idea that humans are capable of genuinely higher faculties of thought that enable us individually and/or collectively to transcend our animal natures and, in that sense, 'make progress' to some literally higher state of being. I choose my words carefully here to capture the full range of Liminal Christianity's concerns. Liminal Christians may think we can reach a higher spiritual plane, achieve heaven on earth by political means or upload our minds into more durable matter. All of these projects presume that there is more to being human than the sum total of our biological inheritance. This point is reflected in the centrality of science to the Liminal Christian worldview. Much more than with respect to religion and art, Darwinists are especially flat-footed when they try to explain science as a distinctly human achievement.

Science is not merely an extended form of empiricism that happens to allow us to adapt to the world more effectively. On the contrary, as history has repeatedly shown, science has expanded humanity's intellectual horizons far beyond our sensory encounters with nature, while at the same time placing us at greater material risk. The role of mathematics, especially once yoked to physics, is exemplary of this point. In strict Darwinian terms, it is hard to see why the people whom we regard as our best minds would be devoted to making sense of aspects of reality – the very old, the very large, the very small, the very far – that are unlikely ever to become part of ordinary human experience, especially when inquiries into these areas have the potential to destabilize our place in nature, most obviously in the case of nuclear energy. The answer common to Liminal Christians and more mainstream Christian ID supporters is that our minds are equipped with a form of knowledge that is not reducible to the cumulative sensory experience registered by our animal bodies.

Philosophers implicitly recognize this point in the idea of '*a priori* knowledge', which has always referred to more than simply our genetically programmed capacities as normally triggered by the environment. Indeed, the paradigm case of *a priori* knowledge is mathematics, whose truths we can discover without having encountered empirical versions of them in nature. For example, when reasoning with very large or very small numbers, what matters is that the calculations conform to the rules of arithmetic, *not* that we have seen external representations of the numbers. Here the Enlightenment focus on the 'light of reason' should be understood as the secular descendant of the 'divine illumination' that makes us uniquely capable of taking 'the mind's journey to

God', to recall the title of a book by the mid-thirteenth-century director-general of the Franciscan order, Bonaventure (aka John of Fidanza). This is the source of the memorable phrase 'mind of God' that remains a staple in popular physics presentations.

Bonaventure's original 'journey' was about outlining the correct order for studying the academic disciplines to bring about a level of spirituality that ultimately converges on the divine standpoint. While the whole Franciscan way of approaching our relationship to God has struck more conventional Christians as mystical, 'mysticism' here should be seen as what rationalism looks like when it is expressed in purely qualitative terms – that is, once one claims increasing closeness to God without a capacity to measure the distance to its full realization. Thus, Bonaventure's proposed intellectual journey consists in a conceptually defined ordering of stages, but he fails to specify the length of time that one should spend at each stage or even when one can tell that he or she is ready to enter the next stage.

Indeed, Bonaventure distrusted any reliance on 'external signs' of leading a divine life because it was all too easy to adapt to the letter without embodying the spirit. The original Christian context for this discussion was what it means to live in 'the imitation of Christ', to recall the title of the fifteenth-century best-selling self-help book by Thomas à Kempis. Whatever else Jesus might have wanted us to do, he did *not* simply want us to 'ape' his behaviour (note the Darwinian metaphor) but to call up his spirit in the conduct of our distinct lives, which may in practice contradict the established beliefs and practices of others who regard themselves as Christians. It was just this respect for the decision-making powers of the individual – including that they might make the wrong decision – that fuelled the Protestant Reformation's return to the Bible and the Enlightenment's championing of free expression. It is also in just this spirit that ID wishes to recover for science from its captivity in such authoritarian institutions as national academies of science that do not permit a free vote on epistemic matters.

Bonaventure lectured at the University of Paris alongside his Dominican rival, Thomas Aquinas, whose more static and stratified vision of knowledge eventually became the basis of the Roman

Catholic 'separate but equal' approach to the science-religion relationship that is championed today by theistic evolutionists. In
contrast, precisely because it lacked the status of Church dogma,
Bonaventure's vision of the progress of individual learning to full
divine illumination could migrate to more secular and collective
conceptions of human intellectual progress, eventuating a half-
millennium later in such Liminal Christians as Condorcet, Comte
and Hegel.[15] Importantly for our purposes, their accounts are not
'evolutionary' in a strict Darwinian sense, they are driven by quite
specifically human actions and guided more by their destination
(i.e. the source of light that attracts humanity) than their origin
(i.e. the darkness out of which humanity then tries to grope[16]).
Not surprisingly, philosophers of science innocent of theology but
intoxicated with Darwin have often puzzled over the teleologi-
cal dimension of these secular conceptions of progress: How can
one conceive of an end that is not in some sense the product of
ordinary inductive processes – that is, the accumulation of effects
that are always already in evidence? Put in a more metaphysically
pointed fashion: How can the contingent set of events that char-
acterize the history of science ever come to be resolved into an
overarching vision, as the theorists of progress require?

The most obvious answer to the theologically literate is that
an overriding belief in scientific progress makes any sense at all
only because we imagine that the history of science has been
engaged in a long collective quest to recover from Adam's original
closeness with God that was lost with the fall, and which we, as
Adam's descendants, dimly remember and which in turn drives
us to seek an understanding of reality that transcends our sheer
animal existence. In that case, each confirmed hypothesis reflects

---

15. John Passmore, *The Perfectibility of Man* (London: Duckworth, 1970).
16. The word 'groping' is used deliberately. It is the normal translation of
    the French *tâtonnement*, which is Pierre Teilhard de Chardin's description
    of the sense of 'creative evolution' that he endorsed. The term comes
    from the Enlightenment theorists of progress, Turgot and Condorcet.
    See Emma Rothschild, *Economic Sentiments* (Cambridge MA: Harvard
    University Press, 2004), pp. 160–161.

an instance of divine grace, that is, a moment in which God indicates his approval without at the same time exactly revealing the larger significance of that approval, since in the end it is up to 'us' – individually or collectively – to decide how to take forward our empirical knowledge as we try to make our way back to God. We are free both to seek the truth and find error along the way.[17]

A concluding cautionary tale: theodicy as the original theory of intelligent design

We have seen that there are good theological and scientific grounds for ID to resist the accommodation with Darwinism proposed by some contemporary versions of 'theistic evolution'. These grounds amount to an argument for a normatively unified sense of ourselves as inquirers and that into which we inquire. However, the quest for this normative unity poses its own deep problems, ones which the ID community has only begun to embrace. These problems constitute the field known as *theodicy*.[18] The word itself is an Anglicized version of the Greek for 'divine justice'. Nowadays it refers to a boutique topic in philosophical theology that is concerned with how a perfect God could have made such a miserable world. Put still more provocatively: how can a good God allow evil to exist? Nevertheless, theodicy was the original science of intelligent design, a comprehensive master discipline that hails from a time – the late seventeenth century – before theology, philosophy and science were neatly compartmentalized into discrete academic fields. The fundamental question posed back then was how could the divine Creator, who is described in the Bible as omniscient, omnipotent and omnibenevolent, produce a

---

17. For a brief discussion of the lineage of divine illumination in this context, see Peter Harrison, *The Fall of Man and the Foundation of Science* (Cambridge UK: Cambridge University Press, 2007), pp. 39–41.

18. I have in mind William Dembski, *The End of Christianity: Finding a Good God in an Evil World* (Nashville: Broadman and Holman, 2009). See also Fuller, *Dissent over Descent*, ch. 5.

world that is imperfect in so many respects? In what sense, then, could all this imperfection add up to ours being, as Leibniz, author of the first book called 'theodicy', notoriously put, 'the best of all possible worlds'?

From the standpoint of today's ID debates, theodicy remains interesting because it concedes at the outset that nature contains palpable imperfections, ranging from unexplained natural catastrophes and monstrous births to senseless deaths and more everyday examples of suboptimal design in organisms. Nevertheless all of these were presumed to be somehow part of an overall optimal package that manifests God's intelligent design. One clear assumption of theodicy, which always made it controversial in theological circles, is that our having been created *in imago dei* enables us, at least in principle, to second-guess God's motives. In other words, we might not only discover *how* God designed the world as he has, the stuff of the physical sciences, but also *why*. The relevant sense of 'why' here is the one implied by Leibniz's notorious slogan: God created the world as he has because any other possible world would have been worse in some respect necessary to the realization of the divine plan.

The most natural way for us today to approach the task of theodicy is to imagine God as the ultimate engineer striving to achieve multiple goals with limited resources. In that case, theodicy is about inferring how other possible divine blueprints would have been worse than the one apparently in place. Put this way, theodicy seems to be inherently conservative, justifying the *status quo*, no matter how bad things are. Voltaire capitalized on this point in his satirical portrait of Dr Pangloss in *Candide*. However, Voltaire was slightly unfair because the purpose of humanity has been always a wild card in theodicy, depending on whether our having been created *in imago dei* is taken to imply our *merely comprehending* or *outright completing* God's plan. Of course, the latter prospect has inspired more radical, millenarian forms of Protestantism and modern secular revolutionary movements.

This entire way of thinking about God's relationship to creation, in both its conservative and radical forms, also proved theologically controversial, as it suggested that God might be somehow limited by matter. Those willing to engage in debates about theodicy tend to place considerable weight on the bare fact that the biblical God takes time to create. In other words, God neither refrains from creating at all nor creates simply by thinking things into existence. God must come to grips with matter to create, however long or short a time it takes. While God by definition always manages to get his way, how he does so depends partly on the medium in which he works. In this respect, God operates with a globalized sense of 'the end justifies the means', whereby certain short-term or localized miseries are deployed to achieve long-term or more widespread benefits. Leibniz himself was enamoured of this mode of thinking, which made him an easy target for Voltaire's jibes. Indeed, Leibniz had obtained his first invitation to the Parisian court – then the centre of European intellectual life – by proposing a new crusade against Islam as the optimal way to reinvigorate the feuding factions of Christendom with a renewed sense of common purpose.[19]

Nowadays we are most familiar with Leibniz's perverse style of reasoning from economists. This is no accident, since those who practised theodicy in its declining period from the late eighteenth to the early nineteenth centuries treated the emerging science of political economy as the field's chief secular offspring. Thomas Malthus, the Anglican minister who inspired Darwin's theory of natural selection, regarded his stark economic analysis of the immiserating consequences of population growth as applied theodicy. Certainly this was how he was read by one of his fans, William Paley, who incorporated Malthus' views into his *Natural Theology*, a book normally celebrated in ID circles for its remarks about evidence for design in living organisms but ignored for its acceptance of poverty and shortness of life on a mass scale as equally evidence of the divine plan.[20]

Much more could be said about the relationship between

---

19. This tale starts the best popular introduction to theodicy, Steven Nadler, *The Best of All Possible Worlds* (New York: Farrar Strauss and Giroux, 2008).

20. Paley offers a positive appraisal of Malthus' work in *Natural Theology* (1802), ch. 26, entitled 'The Goodness of the Deity'.

theodicy and economics, but the point worth stressing here is that Paley probably appeared to Darwin just as callous as many economists today who still seem to justify widespread misery in the name of some overarching order that it ultimately serves. But whereas Darwin's contemporary, Karl Marx, responded by inventing a secular theodicy that aimed to rectify this sanguine vision of misery, Darwin simply lost faith in any possibility for redemption – spiritual or secular. While it is common nowadays for Darwinists to deride Paley for seeing intelligent design in nature where he should not have, Darwin's own verdict was that the sort of intelligence that would produce the design in nature that Paley extolled was not worthy of worship. Contrary to today's vulgar Darwinists, who complain about God's seemingly incompetent design, Darwin himself granted God an inimitable sense of craftsmanship, including its trial-and-error character, but found it bereft of the moral perfection that Paley and other theodicists had ascribed to it. After all, divine trial-and-error, under a more mundane guise, consists in the mass wastage of individual lives.

Clearly Darwin began his lifelong inquiries into natural history in order to find a rational path to God. Darwin's epigraph to *Origin of Species*, drawn from William Whewell, reminds the reader of that point.[21] Theodicy promised just such a path that would not only explain but also justify creation as the product of intelligent design. However, the deity that theodicy revealed, already in Leibniz and certainly in Paley, was much more distant and calculating than the one promised by an ordinary reading of the Bible. (Not surprisingly, theistic evolutionists use a version of this argument against ID to appeal to conventional Christians.[22]) In particular, the deity

---

21. 'But with regard to the material world, we can at least go so far as this – we can perceive that events are brought about not by insulated interpositions of Divine power, exerted in each particular case, but by the establishment of general laws.' Taken from Whewell's *Astronomy and General Physics Considered With Reference to Natural Theology* (Third Bridgewater Treatise, 1835).

22. Denis Alexander, *Creation or Evolution: Do We Have to Choose?* (Oxford: Monarch Books, 2008), p. 316.

of theodicy did little to relieve the misery immediately suffered by those in whose image and likeness God supposedly created them. Deists and Unitarians accepted those consequences and gradually removed themselves from organized forms of Christian worship, while retaining the biblical idea that humanity is raised above other animal species by virtue of its 'divine spark'. As for Darwin, he lost faith altogether in any kind of biblically inspired deity, resulting in a view of humanity that prompted his staunchest public supporter, Thomas Henry Huxley, to assert the ethical project of humanity as forced to operate in open defiance of natural selection.[23]

Huxley understood the matter exactly right. If humans are the crown of creation, as the Abrahamic faiths would have us understand ourselves, then the metaphysically levelling character of Darwin's theory of evolution needs to be actively resisted. The outstanding question is whether this resistance should be seen as merely a Sisyphean struggle – that is, an ultimately self-defeating existentialist gesture – or an attempt to overturn the Darwinian fixation that we are just another species awaiting extinction. Put another way, is our continuing concern for human rights and the sanctity of all stages of human life merely a form of expressive politics or an embodied attempt to refute the theory of natural selection, at least as applied to humans? Under the circumstances, it becomes easy to see why theistic evolutionists would want to drive a wedge between the terms on which one believes in God and believes in science; it would rule out of bounds the intensely difficult question that first theodicy and now intelligent design squarely face: Can the image of God be found, not alongside, but in the very conduct of science?

© Steve Fuller, 2009

_____

23. See especially Huxley's 1893 Romanes Lecture, 'Evolution and Ethics', http://alepho.clarku.edu/huxley/CE9/E-E.html.

9. INTERPRETATION OF SCIENTIFIC EVIDENCE
9A. HOMOLOGY

Norman C. Nevin

Difficulties over the theory of evolution have centred on evidences such as homology. A leading evolutionist, Ernst Mayr, defined homology as: '[a] feature in two or more taxa is homologous when it is derived from the same (or corresponding) feature in the common ancestor'. [1] Scientists before Darwin considered that such homologous structures were due to a common plan. Darwin, however, claimed that homology was best explained by descent with modification from a common ancestor: 'If we suppose that an early progenitor – the archetype as it may be called – of all mammals, birds and reptiles, had its limbs constructed on an existing pattern . . . the similar framework of bones in the hand of a man, the wing of a bat, fin of a porpoise, and the leg of the horse . . . at once explain themselves on the theory of descent with slow and slight modification.' [2]

---

1. E. Mayr, *The Growth of Biological Thought: Diversity, Evolution, and Interitance* (Cambridge, MA: Belknap Press, 1985).

2. Charles Darwin, *The Origin of Species* (Oxford: Oxford University Press, 1996), p. 352.

Indeed, he considered homology a central tenet of his theory, and as powerful evidence of inheritance from a common ancestor. He wrote:

> We have seen that the members of the same class independently of their habits resemble each other in general plan of their organisation. This resemblance is often expressed by the term 'unity of type'; or by saying that several parts and organs in different species of class are homologous . . . is it not powerfully suggestive of true relationship, of inheritance from a common ancestor.[3]

Some evolutionary biologists cite homology as providing one of the most compelling lines of evidence for evolution. Indeed recently, Shubin *et al.* define traditional homology as 'a historical continuity in which morphological features in related species are similar in pattern or form because they evolved from a corresponding structure in a common ancestor'.[4]

The similarities of bone structure conform to a basic pattern. However, Darwin went further and considered the homologies were best explained by descent with modification from a common ancestor. Advocates of common descent conclude that homologous anatomical structures originated in a common ancestor and were modified by random mutations and natural selection. Frequently, they point to the persistence of the five-digit pentadactyl pattern of fore- and hind-limbs of quadrupeds as evidence of homology.

It is argued that the problem of homology stems from Darwin. It is an argument advanced on the basis of no other evidence than an apparent physical and structural similarity in organisms. But if homology is defined as 'similarity due to a common descent', then to say that homology provides evidence for common descent is a circular argument.[5] In other words homology necessitates that

---

3. Ibid., p. 351.

4. N. Shubin, C. Tabin, and S. Carroll, 'Deep Homology and the Origins of Evolutionary Novelty', *Nature* 457 (2009), pp. 818–822.

5. Stephen C. Meyer, Scott Minnich, Jonathan Moneymaker and Paul   '

the first requirement is to know the ancestry and then decide that the corresponding structures are homologous. Nevertheless the argument continues unabated. Evolutionary biologists continue to uphold homology as evidence of common ancestry.

However, because some organisms have similar structures doesn't mean that the organisms had a common ancestor. For example, the structure of an octopus eye is somewhat similar to the structure of a human eye; but when structures appear homologous, they should have developed from homologous genes. The evolutionary basis of homology is even more severely damaged by the discovery of apparently homologous structures specified by quite different genes in different species.[6] It is clear that homologous structures can be produced by different genes and indeed have different developmental pathways. For example, the adult body segments of the wasp and the fruit fly are homologous but have different developmental pathways.[7] Evolutionary biologists have also discovered that the same gene can produce different anatomical structures. The facts of comparative anatomy provide no evidence for evolution in the way that Darwin described.[8]

According to neo-Darwinism, a genetic programme coded in the DNA controls the developmental pathways of the embryo. This genetic information is transmitted from generation to generation. Anthony Latham writes, 'We should definitely expect, if Darwin is correct, that the genes for a homology such as limb structure of vertebrates, should themselves be homologous'.[9] However, detailed studies at a molecular level have failed to demonstrate the expected correspondence between the change in the gene products and the organismal changes in the phenotype. Some

---

A. Nelson, *Explore Evolution: The Arguments for and against Neo-Darwinianism* (Melbourne and London: Hill House Publishers, 2007), p. 49.

6. Michael Denton, *Evolution: A Theory in Crisis* (Chevy Chase: Adler & Adler, 1985), p. 149.

7. Meyer *et al.*, *Explore Evolution*, p. 44.

8. Denton, *Evolution*, p. 155.

9. A. Latham, *The Naked Emperor: Darwinism Exposed* (London: Janus Publishing Company, London 2005), p. 175.

biologists consider that homologous features are programmed by similar genes. However, not only are non-homologous structures produced by organisms with supposedly homologous genes but different genes in organisms can produce similar structures.

The assumption that a genetic programme directs embryonic development has been questioned. Efforts to correlate homology with developmental pathways have been unsuccessful. Firstly, similar developmental pathways may produce dissimilar features. Second, similar features are often produced by very different developmental pathways. For example, the neural tube, the embryonic precursor of the spinal cord, is homologous throughout the chordates, yet in some its formation depends on induction by the underlying notochord while in others it does not.[10] Production of homologous forms from dissimilar pathways is frequent. Frogs may develop indirectly from a tadpole stage to adult frog whereas others develop directly, bypassing the tadpole stage. The adult frogs, whether they have developed directly or indirectly, are indistinguishable from each other.[11] The fore- and hind-limb development in vertebrates also shows that homology cannot be explained by similarities in developmental pathways. The pattern of the limb bones is laid down in cartilage and later ossified into bone. Similar bone patterns in different species arise from different sequences of cartilage condensation.[12] Thus the case for a Darwinian explanation for homology is not supported by the evidence.

Michael Denton raises a further problem with homology. He writes: 'The evolutionary interpretation of homology is clouded even further by the uncomfortable fact that there are many cases

10. S. F. Gilbert, *Developmental Biology* (Sunderland MA: Sinauer Associates, ⁴1994).

11. R. A. Raff, *The Shape of Life: Genes, Development and the Evolution of Animal Form* (Chicago: University Press of Chicago, 1996).

12. N. H. Shubin, 'The Implications of the "The Bauplan" for Development and Evolution of the Tetrapod Limb', in J. R. Hinchliffe, J M. Hurle and D. Summerbell (eds.), *Developmental Patterning of the Vertebrate Limb: Workshop Proceedings* (NATO Science Series A: Life Sciences; New York: Kluwer Academic / Plenum Publishers, 1991), pp. 411–421.

of "homologous like" resemblances which cannot by any stretch of imagination be explained by descent from a common ancestor.' He goes on to elaborate:

> [the] similar pentadactyl design of vertebrate fore- and hindlimbs provides the classic example . . . this is attributed by evolutionary biologists as showing that all have been derived from a common ancestral source. But the *hindlimbs* . . . are strikingly similar to the forelimbs in bone structure and in their detailed embryological development. Yet no evolutionist claims that the hindlimb evolved from the forelimb, or that hindlimbs and forelimbs evolved from a common source.[13]

Molecular homology

Evolutionary scientists consider that homologous structures must be under the control of similar genes. The DNA is essentially the same in all living organisms. The United States National Academy of Science on the role of DNA states that 'unity of composition and function is a powerful argument in favour of common descent'.[14] Denton argues that in order for homology to be evidence of evolution, similar structures should be controlled by similar genes and similar organs demonstrate similar embryological pathways. He writes:

> [the] validity of evolutionary interpretation of homology would have been greatly strengthened if embryological and genetic research could have shown that homologous structures were specified by homologous genes and followed homologous patterns of embryological development. Such homology would indeed be strongly suggestive of 'true relationship of inheritance from a common ancestor.'[15]

---

13. Denton, *Evolution*, p. 151.
14. US National Academy of Science, *Science and Creationism: A View from the National Academy of Sciences* (Washington: National Academy Press, ²1999), p. 17.
15. Denton, *Evolution*, p. 145.

However, it turns out that the genetic code is not universal. A variety of genetic codes which differ significantly from the standard genetic code have been found in several species.[16] Genome sequencing is now commonplace, leading to a further puzzle facing geneticists in the recognition of numerous genes coding for proteins whose function is not understood. These are called ORFan genes and their origin is uncertain. According to evolutionary theory, new genes are derived from old genes by mutation. However, ORFan genes do not match any DNA sequence that codes for a known protein.[17]

There is now evidence that often homologies are not based on common inherited genes or embryological pathways. The underlying mechanism(s) for homologies remains uncertain.

The concept of homology remains under attack. Milton notes that 'it is homology that provided the greatest stumbling block to Darwinian Theory, for at the final and most crucial hurdle homology has fallen'.[18] The facts of comparative anatomy provide no support for evolution in the way conceived by Darwin and research at the molecular level has not demonstrated a correspondence between the structure of the gene and the structural and physical homology.

© Norman C. Nevin, 2009

---

16. Meyer *et al.*, *Explore Evolution*, p. 58.

17. R. F. Doolittle, 'Microbial Genomes Multiply', *Nature* 416 (2002), p. 689.

18. R. Milton, *Shattering the Myths of Darwinism* (Rochester: Park Street Press, 1997), p. 179.

9B. THE NATURE OF THE FOSSIL RECORD

Norman C. Nevin

Fossils are the mineralized remains or imprints of past plants and organisms in sedimentary rock. Darwinists claim that the fossil record represents the history of life on earth written in the rocks, perhaps 'a history book torn and twisted with remnants of pages scattered about, but it is there, and significant portions are still legible'.[1] Palaeontologists, scientists who study the fossil remains of life forms and plants, endeavour to reconstruct past events and to infer a reasonable explanation from their observations. To such scientists fossils are invaluable for 'without them, we'd have only a sketchy outline of evolution'.[2] It is clear that preconceptions play an enormous role in the interpretation of the fossil record. Obviously if starting with the assumption that Darwinism is true then the fossil record will be interpreted 'as the account of blind material forces

---

1. Jerry A. Coyne, *Why Evolution Is True* (Oxford: Oxford University Press, 2009), p. 21.
2. Ibid., p. 22.

operating without an overarching purpose'.[3] This assumption may be mistaken, in which case the interpretation is likely to be false.

Darwin considered that fossils revealed much about the history of living organisms and considered that the sequence of fossils in the sedimentary rocks was support for his concept of common descent, namely that all living things are descendants of a common ancestor, modified by natural processes. He also observed that there was a progression of fossils from simple to complex and posited that every life form was ultimately linked to a common ancestor, the root of the so-called Tree of Life. Later, it was argued that the tree of life was a fact of nature and central to the theory. At the root of the tree was the last universal common ancestor (LUCA) and although most of the branches come to a dead end as species become extinct, some reach to the top, the living species of today. Between a branch of the tree and another, Darwin suggested that there are numerous intermediates of transitional fossils. As to the absence of transitional fossils, he indicated that the fossil record was imperfect and that in the future many of these gaps would be filled.

Recently, a number of scientists have felt that the concept of a tree of life has outlived its usefulness. Graham Lawton writes, 'it is clear that the Darwinian Tree is no longer an adequate description of how evolution in general works'.[4] Most biologists now accept that the tree of life, which Darwin used as an organizing principle and which has been a central tenet in biology, is not a fact of nature.[5] Others disagree. According to Denis Alexander the fossil record 'is consistent with evolutionary history involving common descent' and goes on to state that 'every twig and branch of the great bush of life can be traced

---

3. William A. Dembski and Sean McDowell, *Understanding Intelligent Design* (Eugene: Harvest House Publishers, 2008), p. 66.

4. Graham Lawton, 'Uprooting Darwin's Tree', *New Scientist* (24 January 2009), pp. 34–39.

5. Editorial, 'The Future of Life, But Not as We Know It', *New Scientist* (24 January 2009), p. 15.

back in time to the trunk and the roots from which the whole bush originates'.[6]

What constitutes evidence in the fossil record for evolution? According to the Darwinist there are a number of strands of evidence. First, the sequence of rock strata should show simple fossils in the earlier stratum with more complex fossils in later layers of rock. Further, there should be evidence of change within the lineage of fossils – that is, one species of an organism changing into something different over time. In addition the fossil record should show evidence of splitting of species from common ancestors.[7] However, scientists still claim that it will not be possible to document all such evidence as the fossil record is incomplete.

Darwin's theory implies that the fossil record should show a gradual continuous sequence of life forms blending into one another with numerous transitional forms. Many prominent palaeontologists of his day were opposed to the idea of gradualist change in the fossil record. Darwin acknowledged that there was an absence of transitional fossils or 'missing links' between major organisms that could document evolutionary change. However, he was convinced that palaeontologists would eventually find the missing transitional fossils which would vindicate his theory. However, the fossil record does not show a continuous gradual evolution, but rather an abrupt and sudden emergence of new life forms. Many organisms appear without known ancestors. Indeed, some life forms persist in the fossil record virtually unchanged throughout geological history. Some organisms suddenly appear and after some time disappear completely, as the trilobite, while other fossils may persist totally unchanged, as the horseshoe crab. What is characteristic of the fossil record is long periods of stasis interspersed with the sudden appearance and then disappearance of new life forms.

Despite Alexander's claim that we 'now have some clear and detailed step-by-step transitional fossil records illustrating

6. Denis Alexander, *Creation or Evolution: Do We Have to Choose?*
(Oxford: Monarch Books, 2008), p. 125.

7. Coyne, *Evolution*, p. 27.

evolution of one life form into something quite different',[8] the thousands of transitional forms predicted by Darwin have not been found. The most famous so-called transitional fossil between birds and reptiles is *Archaeopteryx*, discovered in a limestone quarry in Germany. The fossil shows reptilian features such as a jaw with teeth, a long bony tail, separate digits on the wing, and a neck attached to the skull from behind. It also has bird-like traits including large well-developed feathers and opposable great toe. Rather than a transitional fossil between reptiles and birds, most palaeontologists consider that it is a unique species of bird now extinct.

It is also claimed that a chronologically ordered series of fossils demonstrates the movement of animals from land to water.[9] The series begins with *Indohyus*, a racoon-sized animal, and *Pakicetus*, the ancestor of the whale. James Le Fanu concludes,

> There is, in short, neither the time nor the mechanism that could begin to account for so rapid and dramatic an evolutionary transformation from that small mammal to the extraordinary whale in so (relatively) short a period as twelve million years – or indeed to account for why it should have taken to the air and acquired the equally great number of unique physical characteristics to become a bat.[10]

The lack of transitional fossils remains a major problem for neo-Darwinism. Several reasons have been suggested. Some scientists consider that the fossil record is imperfect and that with time the 'gaps' will be filled giving a more complete record. On the other hand, according to Denis Alexander 'despite the gaps in the fossil record, the well attested evolutionary sequence that we do have is impressive and from time to time further discovery of new fossils are helping to make the story more complete'.[11]

---

8. Alexander, *Creation or Evolution*, p. 126.

9. Coyne, *Evolution*, p. 52.

10. James Le Fanu, *Why Us? How Science Rediscovers the Mystery of Ourselves* (London: Harper Press 2009), p. 120.

11. Alexander, *Creation or Evolution*, p. 129.

The theory of gradual evolution over long time periods finds no support in the fossil record, which fails to support common descent. The discontinuous nature of this record, with its long periods of stasis and sudden appearance of new life forms led to some scientists positing a modified version of Darwin's theory, punctuated equilibrium.[12] It describes the fossil record more accurately than Darwinism and answers the question of the absence of transitional fossils. However, no new underlying mechanism has been suggested other than natural selection acting on novel change.[13] No sequence of fossils provides evidence for the Darwinian theory of descent with modification. To take a series of fossils and claim that they represent a lineage cannot be tested scientifically.

One of the major events in the fossil record is the Cambrian explosion, during which many animal forms and body plans (representing new phyla, subphyla and classes) arose in a brief geological period. The evidence points to the appearance of many new animal forms and body plans in fossils, without transitional fossils or common ancestors, in early Cambrian rocks. As many as thirty-five phyla, and between thirty-two to forty-eight new subphyla and classes of animals[14] appeared abruptly, apparently from nowhere at all, fully formed, with no fossil evidence that they branched off from common ancestors. This Cambrian explosion, which marked a major event in morphogenesis, was very sudden. The question arises: what significance does the Cambrian explosion have for evaluating Darwin's theory that all animals are modified descents of a common ancestor?

12. Niles Eldredge and Stephen Jay Gould, 'Punctuated Equilibria: An Alternative to Phyletic Gradualism', (1972), repr. in N. Eldredge, *Time Frames* (Princeton: Princeton Univ. Press, 1985).

13. Stephen C. Meyer, Scott Minnich, Jonathan Moneymaker and Paul A. Nelson, *Explore Evolution: The Arguments for and Against Neo-Darwinianism* (Melbourne and London: Hill House Publishers, 2007), p. 33.

14. Stephen C. Meyer, 'The origin of biological information and higher taxonomic categories', *Proceedings of the Biological Society of Washington* 117 (2004), pp. 213–239.

Darwin was well aware of the problems that the fossil record posed for his theory. Two chapters in *On the Origin of Species* were devoted to discussing the fossil record as to why it did not fit with the idea of common descent and the lack of transitional fossils.

The evolutionary theory has a major difficulty in this lack of evidence for the 'inconceivably great' number of transitional fossils needed to support a process of evolutionary transformation. One hundred and fifty years on since the publication of *On the Origin of Species*, the fossil record does not support the theory of evolution. David Raup of the Natural History Museum, Chicago, summarizes the current understanding: 'Most people assume that fossils provide important [evidence] in favour of the Darwinian interpretation of the history of life. Unfortunately this is not strictly true. Rather than gradual unfolding of life . . . species appear in the sequence very suddenly, show little or no change during their existence in the record, then abruptly [disappear].'[15]

Genetic fossils

Alexander points out that 'the study of the fossil record was critical in getting evolutionary theory off the ground in the first place' but 'if there were no fossils at all, we would still be able to construct much of evolutionary history just from genetics'.[16]

In 2001 the first draft of the human genome was published. Since that time the genomic sequences of many other living organisms have been published. And Alexander explains that

All genomes of organisms that have evolved recently are littered
with ancient genes . . . that we can identify as going deep back into
evolutionary time. But in addition they are replete with the relics of

---

15. David Raup, 'Conflicts between Darwin and Palaeontology', *Field
    Museum of Natural History Bulletin* 50 (1979), pp. 22–29.
16. Alexander, *Creation or Evolution*, p. 119.

genes no longer in use and additionally with stretches of non-functional DNA . . . providing indelible signatures of evolutionary history.[17]

The record of our evolutionary past is indelibly inscribed within the DNA of every cell of our bodies. We are all walking genetic fossil museums.[18]

Long sequences of the human genome resemble protein coding genes, but they are not transcribed to a messenger RNA in a manner that they could be translated into a protein. Around 97% of the human genome consists of DNA sequences that do not code for protein. They have been classified as 'junk' (non-protein coding) DNA. Scientists have considered that the non-protein coding DNA consists of random sequences that have lost their coding ability, such as pseudogenes (processed and unprocessed), retrotransposons, long interspersed repeat sequences (LINEs), short interspersed repeat sequences (SINEs) and retroviral insertions. Neo-Darwinists have long argued that the non-protein coding DNA is powerful evidence of the 'fossil' remains of the evolutionary history of the organism that take us back to the dawn of life. Francis Collins, head of the Human Genome Project, considers that many of these vast stretches of 'junk' DNA are scattered throughout the genomes of all higher organisms and in the same location in the genomes that is consistent with them having location in the genome from a common ancestor. They have been carried along ever since.[19] Similarly Kenneth Miller states: 'The problem is the genome itself: It's not perfect. In fact it's riddled with useless information, mistakes and broken genes. And there is a more serious problem: it looks as though our genome was copied from somebody else's.'[20] Of course the 'somebody else' is the so-called common ancestor of the organisms.

---

17. Ibid., pp. 108–109.

18. Ibid., p. 200.

19. Francis S. Collins, *The Language of God* (New York: Free Press, 2006), p. 136.

20. K. R. Miller, *Only a Theory: Evolution and the Battle for America's Soul* (New York: Viking, 2008), p. 244.

Recent research has reversed previous scientific thought, confirming that non-coding sequences of the genome, far from being inactive, have important biological roles in the genome. The ENCODE Project[21] identified functional roles in the genome which included genes that may code for proteins, regulatory elements that control the transcription of genes, RNAs and sequences that maintain the structure of chromosomes. The main finding of the project is the discovery that most of the supposedly useless DNA now appears to perform important biological functions. These results have implications for evolutionary theory. The non-protein coding DNA was described by the now redundant term 'junk' DNA. It would now be incorrect to suggest that 'fossil genes' represent evidence of evolutionary history. Publications describing biological roles for the non-protein coding DNA are appearing regularly in scientific literature.

© Norman C. Nevin, 2009

---

21. The ENCODE Project Consortium, 'Identification and Analysis of
    Functional Elements in 1% of the Human Genome by the ENCODE
    Pilot Project', *Nature* 447 (2007), pp. 799–816.

9C. CHROMOSOMAL FUSION AND COMMON ANCESTRY

Geoff Barnard

According to Denis Alexander,[1] there is now incontrovertible genetic evidence that humans and chimpanzees have descended from the same common hominid ancestor. Apart from the presence of similar pseudogenes, he supports his argument by reference to chromosomal fusion. Human have forty-six chromosomes, while the great apes have forty-eight. The human chromosomes comprise twenty-two pairs of autosomes and one pair of sex chromosomes. In the case of the great apes (chimpanzees, gorillas and orang-utans) there are twenty-three pairs of autosomes and one pair of sex chromosomes. A comparison of chromosomes in male humans (H) and chimpanzees (C) is shown in Figure 1.

The most significant difference is chromosome 2. In the human, this is a single chromosome but in the chimpanzee it is represented by two chromosomes (chromosomes 12 and 13). It is now generally believed that there was an ancestral fusion of the two

---

1. Denis Alexander, *Creation or Evolution: Do We Have to Choose?* (Oxford: Monarch Books, 2008).

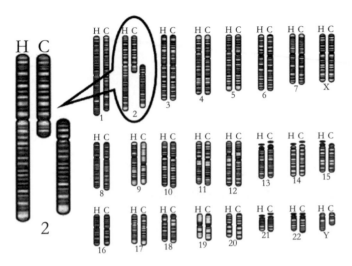

Figure 1: *Comparison between human and chimpanzee chromosomes*

chromosomes. The ape chromosomes 12 and 13 have been re-designated as chromosomes 2p and 2q.

Alexander states:

> The story of our 'missing pair' provides another great piece of historical sleuthing that reveals our shared ancestry with the apes . . . What happened during evolution is that two separate ape chromosomes (known as 2p and 2q) fused to form our human chromosome 2, the second largest of our chromosomes.[2]

What evidence is there that a fusion of chromosomes has indeed taken place? Remarkably, there does appear to be some convincing evidence. Figure 2 illustrates the generalized structure of a chromosome. The ends of the chromosomes are termed telomeres, which are repetitive stretches of DNA. Subsequently, the single chromosome is replicated into identical sister chromatids which are held together by specific DNA present within the central region of each chromosome (the centromere).

---

2. Ibid., p. 211.

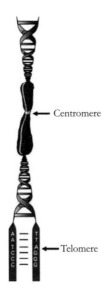

Centromere

Telomere

Figure 2: Generalized structure of a chromosome

The evidence for chromosomal fusion

The first evidence that the human chromosome 2 might be a fusion product of two smaller chromosomes, not dissimilar to those found in the great apes, was provided by Yunis and Prakash in 1982.[3] They reached their conclusions by aligning high-resolution banding patterns of human, chimpanzee, gorilla and orang-utan chromosomes. More substantial evidence came when human chromosome 2-specific DNA was observed to 'paint' (fluorescence in-situ hybridization) chimpanzee chromosomes 12 and 13.[4] What does this tell us?

First, we can infer from the findings that there are very similar DNA sequences in human chromosome 2 and in the two cor-

3. J. J. Yunis and O. Prakash, 'The Origin of Man: A Chromosomal Pictorial Legacy', *Science* 215 (1982), pp. 1525–1530.

4. J. Wienberg, *et al.,* 'The Origin of Human Chromosome 2 Analyzed by Comparative Chromosome Mapping with a DNA Microlibrary', *Chromosome Research* 2 (1994), pp. 405–410.

responding chimpanzee chromosomes. Secondly, if there was a fusion of ancestral chromosomes, it must have taken place *after* the supposed evolutionary split of the chimpanzee from the human lineage. Exactly when this might have taken place is unknown, as the 'fused' chromosome is unique to humans.

Further research demonstrated that a fusion event did take place. It was identified that a central genomic region in human chromosome 2 contained repeating DNA sequence TTAGG running 'head to head' with the repeating complementary sequence CCTAA, a motif characteristic of telomeres found primarily at the ends of chromosomes.[5] Furthermore, the sequences flanking these telomeric repeats within the centralized region of human chromosome 2 are characteristic of human pre-telomeres which flank the telomeres.

As well as telomeres, centromeres also have a characteristic DNA, termed alphoid sequences. If a fusion event has taken place between two ancestral chromosomes, one would expect to find the evidence of more than one centromere in the fused product. Scientists have claimed to find such evidence.[6] Since the centromere is intimately involved with the replication of DNA and cell division, one could argue that any chromosome will only have one active centromere. Accordingly, secondary alphoid DNA in a chromosome might be seen as a genetic residue from a previously functioning centromere on a separate chromosome. However, the situation has become more difficult to interpret.

It was reported that the presence of secondary alphoid DNA was not just in human chromosome 2 but also in human

---

5. J. W. Ijdo, *et al.*, 'Improved Telomere Detection Using a Telomere Repeat Probe (TTAGGG)n Generated by PCR', *Nucleic Acids Research* 19 (1991), p. 4780; J. Ijdo, 'Origin of Human Chromosome 2: An Ancestral Telomere-Telomere Fusion', *Proceedings of the US National Academy of Science* 88 (1991), pp. 9051–9055.

6. R. Avarello, *et al.*, 'Evidence for an Ancestral Alphoid Domain on the Long Arm of Human Chromosome 2', *Human Genetics* 89 (1992), pp. 247–249.

chromosome 9.[7] To complicate matters further, others reported finding secondary alphoid DNA in all primates.[8] Subsequently, other scientists hybridized twenty-one different chromosome-specific human alphoid DNA probes to the full complement of chromosomes from chimpanzee, gorilla and orang-utan. They found that the majority of the human probes did not hybridize to their corresponding equivalent ape chromosome but rather gave positive signals on non-corresponding chromosomes. They concluded that alphoid DNA sequences showed little conservation in the primates.[9]

It was found that the telomeric repeat structure within the chromosome around the proposed fusion site of human chromosome 2 was highly degenerate (14%) when compared with the normal telomere repeats at the ends of the chromosome. On the other hand, general non-coding sequences were much more highly conserved, showing less than 1.5% difference. In addition, it was also demonstrated that human chromosome 9 has sequences which are very similar to the human chromosome 2 fusion region. Many genes were identified in close proximity to the proposed fusion site on the human chromosome, including twenty-four potentially functional genes and sixteen pseudogenes which were also found 'scattered' throughout the human genome and, in many cases, were transcriptionally active on other chromosomes.[10] It will be very

7. A. Baldini, et al., 'An Alphoid DNA Sequence Conserved in All Human and Great Ape Chromosomes: Evidence for Ancient Centromeric Sequences at Human Chromosomal Regions 2q21 and 9q13', *Human Genetics* 90 (1993), pp. 577–583.

8. S. Luke and R. S. Verma, 'Human (*Homo sapiens*) and Chimpanzee (*Pan troglodytes*) Share Similar Ancestral Centromeric Alpha Satellite DNA Sequences but Other Fractions of Heterochromatin Differ Considerably,' *American Journal of Physical Anthropolology* 96 (1995), pp. 63–71.

9. R. V. Samonte, K. H. Ramesh and R. S. Verma, 'Comparative Mapping of Human Alphoid Satellite DNA Repeat Sequences in the Great Apes', *Genetica* 101 (1997), pp. 97–104.

10. Y. Fan, et al., 'Gene Content and Function of the Ancestral Chromosome Fusion Site in Human Chromosome 2q13–2q14.1 and Paralogous

interesting to discover if any of these particular genes are unique to humans and whether any homologues are actually present towards the terminal regions of chimpanzee chromosomes 2q and 2p.

Alexander writes:

> The functional centromere in chromosome 2 lines up with the chimpanzee chromosome 2p chromosomal centromere. The remains of the redundant centromere from one of the ancestral ape chromosomes can also be found . . . The DNA sequence of the rest of human chromosome 2 matches very precisely the sequences of the two separate chimpanzee chromosomes 2p and 2q that were involved in the fusion. Taken together these data make it overwhelmingly likely that human chromosome 2 was derived by the fusion of two ancestral ape chromosomes, providing further compelling evidence for our shared ancestry with the apes.[11]

However, scientists now are able to make a direct genetic comparison between the two species. A very recent review summarizes the significant differences between the two species.[12] Apart from chromosomal numbers, it describes the major human-specific inversions (e.g. chromosomes 1 and 18). Furthermore, the authors catalogue lineage-specific segmental duplications which are at least threefold greater than anything due to nucleotide substitutions. In their own words: 'Interspecies comparisons have revealed numerous human-specific gains and losses of genes as well as changes in gene expression.' The somewhat simplistic views of Alexander fail to mention any of these details.

Footnote 10 (*cont.*)

   Regions', *Genome Research* 12 (2002), pp. 1663–1672; Y. Fan, *et al.*, 'Genomic Structure and Evolution of the Ancestral Chromosome Fusion Site in 2q13–2q14.1 and Paralogous Regions on Other Human Chromosomes', *Genome Research* 12 (2002), pp. 1651–1662.

11. Alexander, *Creation or Evolution*, pp. 212–213.

12. H. Kehrer-Sawatzki and D. N. Cooper, 'Understanding the Recent Evolution of the Human Genome: Insights From Human-Chimpanzee Genome Comparisons', *Human Mutation* 28 (2007), pp. 99–130.

Has there been a chromosomal fusion event in human history?

The answer could be 'yes'. The telomeric DNA sequence around the proposed fusion site on human chromosome 2 is compelling evidence. The presence of secondary alphoid DNA in the same chromosome might add weight to the argument although its true significance remains uncertain. However, to suggest that all this is clear evidence of common descent from hominid ancestry is unjustified as the fused chromosome (if indeed that is what it is) is unique to the human. None of the great apes possess such a chromosome. The fusion has occurred within the human lineage and the discrepancy of degeneration between telomeric regions at the fusion point and the usual non-coding DNA makes it impossible to date when this fusion might have taken place.

In addition, there are other examples of chromosomal fusion within individual species? In addition, there are other examples of chromosomal fusion within individual species. Perhaps the most remarkable is the Muntjac deer. The Indian Muntjac (*Muntiacus muntjak*) possesses the lowest chromosomal number in mammals (six chromosomes in the female, seven in the male) whereas the Chinese Muntjac (*Muntiacus reevesi*) has twenty-three pairs of chromosomes in both sexes. They look identical and can interbreed. Variations in chromosomal numbers have also been reported in other mammals including the humble house mouse. So what is clear is that chromosomal number reduction *within a specific lineage* can be tolerated in some circumstances.

We have considered the argument of chromosomal fusion presented by Alexander. It is probable that a chromosomal fusion event has taken place within the human lineage, possibly when the human population was very small. Furthermore, it is self-evident that if such an event has taken place, it has been tolerated and passed on to subsequent generations.

What is certain, however, is that the wide variety of chromosomal variations that clearly exist between the human and chimpanzee, dictate against the thesis that these species have common ancestry.

9D. INFORMATION AND THERMODYNAMICS

Andy McIntosh

In this chapter[1] we focus primarily on thermodynamics and information but it should be recognized that much is intertwined with the discussion on genetics.

Creation by the word of God

Creation occurred by the spoken word of God – a fact which Denis Alexander skilfully sidesteps in the opening chapters of his book.[2] Christ is the pre-eminent person of the Trinity involved in

---

1. This chapter is based on two previously published articles: 'The Downgrade Controversy of the 21st Century', *Evangelical Times* (Oct. 2008), and 'Standing firm on Creation', *Evangelicals Now* (Dec. 2008). We are grateful for permission to use them in revised form here. The author is Professor of Thermodynamics at the University of Leeds and writes this in a private capacity.
2. *Creation or Evolution: Do We Have to Choose?* (Oxford: Monarch Books, 2008).

creation (John 1:3; Col. 1:16; Heb. 1:2–3) and elsewhere uses the same agency (his spoken word) to heal the sick, calm the storm and raise the dead.

These miracles occurred immediately he spoke – no prolonged process was involved. Why, therefore, should we not accept that the miraculous creative acts of Genesis 1 were similarly expedited? It is as written – God spoke and it was so. Indeed the prologue of John's Gospel has a very deep and profound implication, which is that in a very real sense Christ the Word of God has left his imprint as it were on all living systems through the information-rich biochemistry of the natural world.

Such concepts have been addressed by authors of great scientific standing, whom significantly Alexander ignores – scientists such as A. E. Wilder-Smith who wrote *The Natural Sciences Know Nothing of Evolution*[3] and whose books laid the foundation for understanding biochemistry within the context of a coherent creation paradigm. Alexander even fails to engage with creationist literature in his own field of genetics, there being no reference to John Sanford's masterful book *Genetic Entropy and the Mystery of the Genome*.[4]

According to neo-Darwinian theory, random mutations are the source of variety on which natural selection works to select those that are advantageous, thereby gradually transforming a species. But Sanford argues that the vast majority of mutations are deleterious and that the human genome is fast acquiring serious deficiencies which affect the phenotype negatively rather than positively.

Far from being an engine for beneficial change, mutations are a downhill slope. There are also implications in my own discipline of thermodynamics which (contrary to Alexander's assertions[5]) also shows that new biological machinery cannot simply arise by mutations.

---

3. Green Forest: Master Books, 1981.

4. Lima, NY: Elim Publishing, ²2005.

5. *Creation or Evolution*, pp. 138–139.

Information in living systems

Where neo-Darwinists are at their weakest is concerning the very nature of information in living systems. Walter Remine's *The Biotic Message*,[6] Thaxton, Bradley and Olsen's *The Mystery of Life's Origin*[7] and the classic volume by Werner Gitt, *In the Beginning Was Information*,[8] deal with this issue from a creation perspective. It is notable that Alexander avoids addressing the issue entirely. Gitt's work shows that information has five levels of operation, all of which indicate that information is essentially non-material and yet no less real. Here we just stress two levels which make the basic point.

Information uses a language or code to transmit a message. The code can be any consistent set of noises for verbal communication, or letters, alphabet or symbols for a written language. Whatever the code used, the code is *not* defined by the material on which it is written or the medium through which the communication is made. The air through which verbal communication passes does not define the information. Neither does the tympanic membrane of the ear or the tongue or larynx of the speaker. The paper and ink do not define the code used in a book and neither do the computer and electronic disk define the coded information contained within them. Furthermore the message expressed using a language or code is *not* defined by the code used. The English code is being used for this chapter, but if I was proficient in French, the same thoughts could have been expressed in that rich language. It could have been expressed in Chinese, where the alphabet itself bears no resemblance to the

---

6. *The Biotic Message: Evolution Versus Message Theory* (Saint Paul: St Paul Science, 1993).

7. Charles Thaxton, Walter L. Bradley and Roger L. Olsen, *The Mystery of Life's Origin: Reassessing Current Theories* (New York: Philosophical Library, 1984).

8. *In the Beginning was Information: A Scientist Explains the Incredible Design in Nature*, transl. Jaap Kies (Bielefeld: Christliche Literatur-Verbreitung, 2000).

English or French. Would that have affected the message? Not in principle. The message transcends the code or language used.

This is profoundly the case for the DNA encoded message in every living cell of our bodies. The very presence of message at the lowest level shows that there is a non-material aspect to all living systems. It is at this point that Crick and Watson in their brilliant discovery in 1953 failed to follow through the implications, since as Paul states, 'For since the creation of the world God's invisible qualities – his eternal power and divine nature – have been clearly seen, being understood from what has been made, so that men are without excuse' (Rom. 1:20).

The intelligent design and creation position which Alexander rejects is based on the science not of what we don't know (Alexander often tries to caricature the position as 'God of the gaps') but on what we do know. When one considers the DNA system of communication, it profoundly demonstrates that there must be intelligence involved in such a system.

The irony is that Michael Faraday, after whom Alexander named the Faraday Institute at Cambridge, referred to exactly the same point, granted not in living systems but to his brilliant research in electromagnetism. Speaking at a lecture in 1847 he said,

> . . .And therefore our philosophy [here used as we would now say 'our science'], whilst it shows us these things, should lead us to think of Him who hath wrought them; for it is said by an authority far above even that which these works present, that 'the invisible things of Him from the creation of the world are clearly seen, being understood by the things that are made, even His eternal power and Godhead'.[9]

This shows that intelligent design, far from being non-science as Alexander advocates, is very much at the heart of mainstream science, and has been for many centuries of prestigious societies such as the Royal Society where men like Boyle and Newton were driven by exactly the same philosophy.

---

9. W. L. Randell, *Michael Faraday* (London: Leonard Parsons and Boston: Small, Maynard & Co. 1924), pp. 132–133.

Thermodynamics

Information is closely related to the discipline of thermodynamics. Alexander's sweeping statements that the biological machinery of life could arise by natural selection operating on mutations[10] shows that he has not grasped the fundamental nature of these laws.

The experimental findings of science are that natural selection has no power to create new functional structures. Natural selection, as the name suggests, acts on devices which are already inherently in a system; there is no possibility of producing new systems or obtaining new information for such systems. In summary, natural selection does not increase information and does not build new machines (either as sub-machines or in embryonic form).

The reason for this is that the principles of thermodynamics do not allow a new functional biological structure to be achieved without such machinery in some generic form already being in place. The first law of thermodynamics is the principle of conservation of energy, which means that no energy is either created or destroyed. The second law states that in an isolated system the entropy will always increase in any non-equilibrium process. Entropy is dissipated energy (measured as energy per unit degree of temperature) which is no longer available to do work. This then is energy 'lost' to the system and means that in an isolated system the energy available to do useful work is always running down. However, the principle of energy loss for useful work still applies to closed systems (where energy transfer to the outside is allowed), and even to open systems (where mass transfer is allowed as well).

In order to make new machinery as advocated by the neo-Darwinists, it is vital to have energy available to do work in a series of precise actions – the author has written more extensively on this subject.[11] Many have suggested that by just adding energy from the

10. *Creation or Evolution*, pp. 138–139.

11. A. C. McIntosh, 'Functional Information and Entropy in living systems', in C. A. Brebbia (ed.), *Design and Nature III: Comparing Design in Nature*

sun, new machines can readily be made and that as soon as one moves into the notion of non-isolated systems, thermodynamics is in favour of evolutionary thinking. However just appealing to the notion of adding energy from the sun solves nothing, since there is no benefit unless there is a machine to use the energy added. Boeing 777s cannot be made in a car factory by adding loads of sunlight or electricity unless the machinery is available to use that energy to build Boeing 777s. Similarly the human brain cannot be formed from simpler machines just by adding energy if there is no machinery available to do this. The spontaneous formation of such machinery will not happen.

In this discussion the term 'machine' refers very precisely to a device using energy to do work of some kind. Energy without machines just dissipates (the sun's energy would be typical). But a machine in this definition harnesses energy to advantage: so a solar cell turns the suns rays into electricity; a Rolls Royce Trent gas turbine turns chemical energy into thrust to power aircraft; the chlorophyll reaction in a plant leaf uses sunlight to enable the plant to grow and absorb carbon dioxide while emitting oxygen; the adenosine triphosphate (ATP) motor in living organisms transfers energy from food and respiration into useable energy to drive the cell machinery of DNA, ribosomes, amino acids and protein building, etc. In this sense all machines are entropy-lowering devices. But, unlike macro machines, chemical machinery at the molecular level involves setting up proteins of hundreds and usually thousands of polypeptide bonds linking a string of amino acids. And each of these bonds is in a raised free-energy state such that left to itself, it would break down. To suggest, as some are saying, that the raised free-energy state would be maintained while natural selection favoured, over many generations, single random mutations, one by one, to finally bring together the full complement of necessary amino acids is, frankly, thermodynamically absurd. This

with Science and Engineering, Third International Conference on Design & Nature, 24th–26th May 2006: (WIT Transactions on Ecology and the Environment, vol. 87; New Forest: Wessex Institute of Technology Press, 2006), pp. 115–126.

would mean a suite of multiple chemical bonds all being kept in an unnatural non-equilibrium state. This is never observed and is contrary to all thermodynamic principles of energy transfer.

New machines are not made by simply adding energy to existing machines. Intelligence is needed. And this thesis is falsifiable: if anyone was to take an existing chemical machine and produce a different chemical machine which was not there before (either as a sub-part or latently coded for in the DNA template), then this argument would have been falsified. No one has ever achieved this.

Wilder-Smith summarizes the argument from thermodynamics:

> Today it is simply unscientific to claim that the fantastically reduced entropy of the human brain, of the dolphin's sound lens, and of the eye of a fossilised trilobite simply 'happened', for experimental experience has shown that such miracles just do not 'happen'.[12]

No one has ever gainsaid the wisdom of Wilder-Smith in this regard.

Conclusion

In natural biological systems there is a link between thermodynamics and information. As already stated, information is non-material. It is defined by the arrangement of letters, or, in the case of DNA, by the order of triplets of nucleotides, and not by the molecules themselves. But often missed is the deeper second matter; that all coding in living systems sits on chemical bonds which are in a raised free-energy state. The implications are profound. All the indications are that logical arrangement drives the non-equilibrium dynamics and not the other way around. This fits with Christ as the Word, the Logos, and the sustainer of all things (John 1:1; Rom. 11:36; Col 1:17; Heb. 1:3).

---

12. Wilder-Smith, *Natural Sciences*, p. 146.

Alexander turns the intelligent design argument into a straw man, claiming that it simply amounts to a 'God of the gaps' hypothesis. But he fails to understand the design position. Evolution is a *paradigm* within which evolutionary biologists seek to explain their findings. Contrary to Alexander's assertions, the design position is also a paradigm – an alternative to the evolutionary framework and one which often provides superior descriptions of biological systems.

The design argument cannot be a god-of-the-gaps argument because it is based on what we *know*, not what we don't know. To repeat Romans 1:20: 'God's invisible qualities – his eternal power and divine nature – [are] clearly seen, being understood from what has been made. . .'

The design thesis now gaining ground in the scientific world is precisely the reverse of Alexander's perception – the gaps arise in the just-so stories of the evolutionary camp. What can be understood from 'the things that are made' testifies to the awesome power of the Creator.

He is right in saying that true science can never disagree with the Bible, but he has failed to realize that there is much that claims to be science that is actually speculation. When one separates out the scientific facts from their interpretation, there is nothing in the science that contradicts the straightforward statements of Genesis – special *ex-nihilo* creation; the creation of animals and man without common descent; a real garden of Eden; followed by the fall of a real Adam and Eve; which coherently explains the origin of death and disease due to the sin of man. Genesis is far, far more than a 'theological essay'.

10. DOES THE GENOME PROVIDE EVIDENCE FOR COMMON ANCESTRY?

Geoff Barnard

In February 2001, the first draft of the human genome was published and since then more complete sequences of the entire human chromosomes have become available.[1] The most significant DNA sequence other than the human is that of the chimpanzee genome[2] and, with its publication, it became possible to search for sequence homologies (similarities) which could provide incontrovertible evidence for the common ancestry of the two species.

The major dispute over Darwinism is about common descent. It is now argued that genomic evidence has settled the case, once and for all. A recent book written from a Christian perspective

---

1. J. D. McPherson, *et al.*, 'A Physical Map of the Human Genome', *Nature* 409 (2001), pp. 934–941; J. C. Venter, *et al.*, 'The Sequence of the Human Genome', *Science* 291 (2001), pp. 1304–1351.

2. The Chimpanzee Sequencing and Analysis Consortium, 'Initial sequence of the chimpanzee genome and comparison with the human genome', *Nature* 437 (2005), pp. 69–87.

seeks to adopt all that neo-Darwinism has to offer. In other words, the author subsumes evolutionary thinking into his theology. Denis Alexander, director of the Faraday Institute for Science and Religion and an evangelical Christian, writes in *Creation or Evolution: Do We Have to Choose?*:

> First it should be emphasised that our shared inheritance with the apes is one of the most certain conclusions of contemporary biology. The reason for being so sure is because of . . . comparative genomics . . . We are all walking genetic fossil museums! I find it ironic that people who deny our shared inheritance with the apes are carrying around in their bodies about 10 million million (10^{13}) copies (the DNA content of each cell) of their evolutionary history . . . all this means that we once shared a common ancestor with the apes.[3]

In this chapter, we consider some of the genetic arguments that he presents. The most significant include the presence of pseudogenes. The two examples given are (1) the missing enzyme in vitamin C biosynthesis and (2) non-functional olfactory receptor genes. Alexander also considers the significance of mobile genomic elements such as *Alu* sequences and endogenous retroviruses as evidence for common ancestry.

Pseudogenes

Pseudogenes are DNA sequences that resemble protein-coding genes but they are not transcribed to messenger RNA (mRNA) in a way that could then be translated into some functional protein. Many have suggested that pseudogenes are simply molecular fossils that provide evidence for evolutionary history. Implicit in this argument is that pseudogenes are genetic relics that have lost the original protein-coding function which had been possessed by some ancestral creature. In support of this argument, evolutionary

---

3. Denis Alexander, *Creation or Evolution: Do We Have to Choose?* (Oxford: Monarch Books, 2008), pp. 200–201.

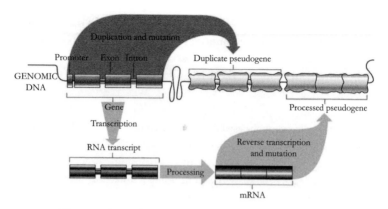

Figure 1: *Formation of processed and unprocessed pseudogenes.*[4]

scientists point to the fact that pseudogenes are scattered through-out the genomes of all higher species (animals and plants) and, in particular, many similar pseudogenes are found in all primates.

There are two distinct types of pseudogene, which are described as 'processed' and 'unprocessed'. This is illustrated in Figure 1, which shows the parent-coding gene as having a promoter region together with exons and introns. The promoter is not transcribed (copied) into mRNA but actually controls the production of mRNA. The initial mRNA transcript (the complementary copy of DNA) comprises both exons and introns. Before the mRNA is translated into protein, the introns are cut out of the final mRNA by specific enzymes.

As a general rule, processed pseudogenes are usually located on different chromosomes from their corresponding functional pro-tein-coding gene. Most biologists believe that such pseudogenes were created by the retro-transposition of mRNA transcripts from the parent gene. The evidence for this is that pseudogenes lack introns. Processed pseudogenes also lack regulatory sequences, including promoters and specific DNA sequences, which bind to enhancers and inhibitors. All this evidence is very suggestive of the processed pseudogene being derived from the mRNA which has been relocated and reversed transcribed back into the DNA.

---

4. Redrawn after M. Gerstein and D. Zheng, 'The Real Life of Pseudogenes', *Scientific American* 295 (2006), pp. 48–55.

Unprocessed pseudogenes, however, are usually found in close proximity to their corresponding protein-coding gene, usually on the same chromosome. Unlike processed pseudogenes, they possess introns and other associated upstream regulatory sequences. Nevertheless, it is widely believed that the expression of these 'genes' is prevented by genetic changes which lead to premature termination or may introduce 'frameshifts' that render the message meaningless.

It is also suggested that unprocessed pseudogenes might arise simply by gene duplication. Inevitably, the duplicated gene would be in close proximity to the parent but would then be free to accumulate random mutations without actually harming the organism, as it would still possess the original functional copy.

Are some pseudogenes functional?

Conservation of similar genetic sequences between species may indicate that pseudogenes (or any other non-protein coding sequence) could possess an important biological function, even though that function might be unknown. Genetic sequences are conserved and maintained when any mutation would render them non-functional (or less functional) and when any loss of activity is damaging the organism's prospects of survival. Such sequences are said to be under purifying (or stabilizing) selection which means that deleterious mutations are removed from the gene pool, restricting genetic diversity. It is probably the most common mechanism of action for natural selection and leads to the maintenance of genetic integrity. It is certainly not the driving force behind evolutionary change.

Two recent reviews[5] on the potential functions of pseudogenes describe examples of pseudogenes that are involved in gene expression, gene regulation and generation of genetic (antibody, antigenic and other) diversity. One of the great surprises of the large-scale

---

5. E. S. Balakirev and F. J. Ayala, 'Pseudogenes: Are They "Junk" or Functional DNA?', *Annual Review of Genetics* 37 (2003), pp. 123–151; idem, 'Pseudogenes: Structure Conservation, Expression, and functions', *Zhurnal Obshchei Biologii* 65 (2004), pp. 306–321.

study of 1% of the human genome (ENCODE) was the remarkable and unexpected finding that vast regions of non-coding
DNA (formerly known as junk) were transcribed into RNA,[6] This
included a significant number of pseudogenes.[7] Scientific publications describing functional pseudogenes are now appearing at very
regular intervals.

Vitamin C and pseudogenes

In the days of maritime exploration, sailors were often deprived
of fresh fruit and vegetables for extended periods. As a result,
they commonly developed a debilitating sickness called scurvy.
The availability of citrus fruit, which provides ascorbic acid or
vitamin C, cured the disease. Most plants and many animals can
synthesize ascorbic acid from glucose or galactose. Some animals
are unable to synthesize ascorbic acid and rely on dietary sources
for what becomes for them an essential vitamin. This inability to
synthesize ascorbic acid is due to non-activity of the final enzyme
in the biosynthetic pathway, namely, L-gulonolactone oxidase
(GULO). Non-activity of GULO also results in the formation of
hydrogen peroxide,[8] which is highly toxic to cells.

GULO and its pseudogene

Many animals cannot synthesize vitamin C because of the lack of
a functioning GULO. A Japanese research group demonstrated
that the inability of humans to synthesize L-ascorbic acid was

6. E. Birney, et al., 'Identification and Analysis of Functional Elements
   in 1% of the Human Genome by the ENCODE Pilot Project', Nature 447
   (2007), pp. 799–816.

7. D. Zheng, et al., 'Pseudogenes in the ENCODE Regions:
   Consensus Annotation, Analysis of Transcription, and Evolution', Genome
   Research 17 (2007), pp. 839–851.

8. G. Banhegyi, et al., 'Ascorbate Metabolism and its Regulation in
   Animals', Free Radical Biology & Medicine 23 (1997), pp. 793–803; F. Puskas,
   et al., 'Gulonolactone Oxidase Activity-Dependent Intra Vesicular
   Glutathione Oxidation in Rat Liver Microsomes', FEBS Letters 430
   (1998), pp. 293–296.

due to a lack of functional GULO.[9] They isolated the genetic sequence coding for a fragment of human GULO by comparing it to the complete genetic sequence of the fully functional rat enzyme. They concluded that the human enzyme had accumulated a large number of mutations and deletions and that it now exists as a pseudogene in the human genome.[10] Later they published the structure of the human gene homologue for this enzyme obtained by computer-assisted search.[11] This is shown in Figure 2. The fully functional rat GULO comprises 12 exons (numbered I to XII) interspersed by introns.

The GULO fragment in the human genome revealed that regions equivalent to rat exons I to VI and exon XI were completely missing.

Thus the genetic fragment of human GULO comprises only five exons as compared to the twelve in the rat. In particular, the research group identified two single nucleotide deletions, one triple nucleotide deletion, and one single nucleotide insertion in the human sequence. When compared in terms of potential amino acid composition, the human sequence demonstrated a single amino acid deletion and several amino acid substitutions. The human genetic sequence also had additional stop signals. Some of these differences were also reflected in the genetic sequence of the

9. M. Nishikimi and K. Yagi, 'Molecular Basis for the Deficiency in Humans of Gulonolactone Oxidase, a Key Enzyme for Ascorbic Acid Biosynthesis', *American Journal of Clinical Nutrition* 54 (1991), pp. 1203S–1208S.

10. M. Nishikimi, *et al.*, 'Cloning and Chromosomal Mapping of the Human Nonfunctional Gene for L-gulono-gamma-lactone Oxidase, the Enzyme for L-ascorbic Acid Biosynthesis Missing in Man', *Journal of Biological Chemistry* 269 (1994), pp. 13685–13688.

11. Y. Inai, Y. Ohta and M. Nishikimi, 'The Whole Structure of the Human Nonfunctional L-gulono-gamma-lactone oxidase Gene – the Gene Responsible for Scurvy – and the Evolution of Repetitive Sequences Thereon', *Journal of Nutritional Science and Vitaminology (Tokyo)* 49 (2003), pp. 315–319.

Rat GULO gene

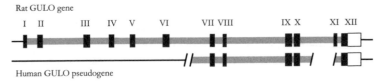

Human GULO pseudogene

Figure 2: *A comparison between the rat gene and human pseudogene.*[12]

corresponding GULO in the guinea pig, which is also unable to synthesize the vitamin.

Remarkably, similar deletions and substitutions were found in the chimpanzee, orang-utan and macaque.[13] A 330 base pair fragment was obtained for human, chimpanzee and macaque and a 410 base pair fragment was obtained for orang-utan. One hundred and sixty-four (164) nucleotides were common in all primate species but different from the rat sequence. It was also noted that the nucleotide at position 97 (of the rat sequence) was deleted in all the corresponding primate sequences, causing a frameshift and deletion of part of exon X.

Evolutionary significance

It has been suggested that the similarity of nucleotide sequence and, in particular, the identical nucleotide deletion at position 97 in exon X of the GULO pseudogene in primates, is clear indication of common ancestry.[14]

---

12. Redrawn and modified from figure at http://www.detectingdesign.com/peudogenes.html.

13. Y. Ohta and M. Nishikimi, 'Random Nucleotide Substitutions in Primate Nonfunctional Gene for L-gulono-gamma-lactone oxidase, the Missing Enzyme in L-ascorbic Acid Biosynthesis', *Biochimica Biophysica Acta* 1472 (1999), pp. 408–411.

14. Ibid.; A. Nandi, *et al.*, 'Evolutionary Significance of Vitamin C Biosynthesis in Terrestrial Vertebrates,' *Free Radical Biology & Medicine* 22 (1997), pp. 1047–1054; J. J. Challem and E. W. Taylor, 'Retro viruses, ascorbate, and mutations, in the evolution of *Homo sapiens*', *Free Radical Biology & Medicine* 25 (1998), pp. 130–132; Z. Zhang, *et al.*, 'Millions of Years of Evolution Preserved: A Comprehensive Catalog of the

Recently the Japanese group reported a more extensive comparison of the complete guinea pig and human GULO pseudogene against the fully functional rat gene.[15] They found 129 and 96 substitutions in humans and guinea pigs, respectively, when compared with the corresponding rat sequence. Furthermore, of the 129 substitutions of the human sequence, 47 were identical in the guinea pig pseudogene. This high degree of conservation between distantly related species is unexpected and may point more to pseudogene functionality rather than any evolutionary relationship.

Does the GULO pseudogene have any function?

It is becoming increasingly apparent that many pseudogenes have various functions, such as mRNA silencing. Thus an important question to consider is whether the pseudogene of GULO is just an evolutionary relic or does it point to any physiological significance? Can it ever be demonstrated that humans had or indeed have the capability to synthesize ascorbic acid in their life cycle? Remarkably, there is evidence that indicates that ascorbic acid concentrations in the foetus and in the neonate cannot be explained on the basis of maternal dietary intake of vitamin C.

In 1955, Andersson and her colleagues reported an investigation into the rarity of infantile scurvy in malnourished South African Bantu children.[16] In a five-year period, only two cases of scurvy were reported even though it could be demonstrated that many of the infants had been weaned onto an almost exclusive diet of cereal 'paps' containing negligible amounts of vitamin C. However, plasma levels of vitamin C were similar to well nourished infants. The authors postulated that the only explanation was endogenous production of the vitamin.

Processed Pseudo Genes in the Human Genome,' *Genome Research* 13 (2003), pp. 2541–2558.

15. Inai, Ohta and Nishikimi, 'Whole Structure of the Human Nonfunctional L-gulono-gamma-lactone oxidase Gene'.

16. M. Andersson, A. R. Walker and H. C. Falcke, 'An Investigation of the Rarity of Infantile Scurvy Among the South African Bantu', *British Journal of Nutrition* 10 (1956), pp. 101–105.

Furthermore, in 1974 it was reported that ascorbic acid levels in foetal human brain could be more than tenfold higher than in adult brain (and at least 100-fold higher than in maternal plasma) and that those levels fell progressively with increasing gestational age. Cord blood concentrations of the vitamin were approximately four times higher than in the maternal circulation. It also was demonstrated at post-mortem that ascorbic acid levels were still at least threefold higher in neonatal brain that in adults.[17]

Others have reported that exclusively breast-fed infants were able to maintain their plasma vitamin C concentration at the same or a higher concentration than vitamin C-supplemented controls. Their plasma concentration of vitamin C was about twofold compared with the maternal concentration.[18] According to the same author: 'Surprisingly, the infantile plasma concentration [of vitamin C], which was already high compared with maternal concentration, continued to rise despite the decreasing concentration in milk . . . the significance of this phenomenon is unknown.'

This circumstantial evidence is highly suggestive that humans might be able to synthesize vitamin C in certain physiological situations. In particular, the role of endogenous ascorbic acid biosynthesis may be vital *in utero* where the developing embryo/foetus is rapidly growing. The need for vitamin C biosynthesis, however, will rapidly diminish after birth and there may be very good biochemical reasons why the expression of a functioning GULO might be suppressed in the presence of an adequate dietary intake.

The by-product of ascorbic acid synthesis is hydrogen peroxide. This is potentially highly toxic to cells and it has been suggested by several authors that the loss of a functional GULO might confer some advantage.[19] Of course, this is most often seen in evolution-

---

17. B. P. Adlard, S. W. De Souza and S. Moon, 'Ascorbic Acid in Fetal Human Brain', *Archives of Disease in Childhood* 49 (1974), pp. 278–282.

18. L. Salmenpera, 'Vitamin C Nutrition During Prolonged Lactation: Optimal in Infants while Marginal in Some Mothers', *American Journal of Clinical Nutrition* 40 (1984), pp. 1050–1056.

19. Banhegyi, *et al.*, 'Ascorbate Metabolism'; C. L. Linster, and E. Van Schaftingen, 'Vitamin C. Biosynthesis, Recycling and Degradation

ary terms but might it be seen in a physiological context? There is no doubt that adult humans have lost the ability to synthesize ascorbic acid. Nevertheless, there is circumstantial evidence that the developing foetus and the neonate may still have this capability. If this is the case, we have been misled in believing that the GULO pseudogene is solely an evolutionary artefact, a molecular fossil. Moreover, if evidence is found that clearly demonstrates that humans (and, for that matter, chimpanzees) can synthesize ascorbic acid in the early stages of life, it will provide more direct evidence that pseudogenes have important biological functions.

Olfactory receptor genes

For most species, the ability to detect odour is essential for the location of food, for sexual attraction and, therefore, reproduction, as well as for an advance warning of the proximity of predators. When compared to rodents and dogs, however, humans possess a greatly reduced sense of smell and this reduction may be correlated with a high percentage of non-functional olfactory receptors (ORs) which have been designated as pseudogenes. For example, it has been estimated that the human OR repertoire contains some 1,000 genes, of which approximately 50% are pseudogenes, whereas the mouse has some 1,500 OR genes, of which approximately only 20% are pseudogenes. In other words, the mouse genome has up to three times more functional OR genes than humans.[20] In mammals, ORs are located within two different nasal organs: the nasal olfactory epithelium and vomeronasal organ.

The nasal olfactory epithelium is responsible for the perception of odours, and the vomeronasal organ which binds pheromones is responsible for various neuroendocrine responses between

---

in Mammals', *FEBS Journal* 274 (2007), pp. 1–22; E. J. Calabrese, 'Evolutionary Loss of Ascorbic Acid Synthesis: How it May Have Enhanced the Survival Interests of Man', *Medical Hypotheses* 8 (1982), pp. 173–175.

20. J. M. Young, *et al.*, 'Different Evolutionary Processes Shaped the Mouse and Human Olfactory Receptor Gene Families', *Human Molecular Genetics* 11 (2002), pp. 535–546.

individuals of the same species. Both odorants and pheromones bind to ORs, which are G-protein-coupled receptors containing seven trans-membrane domains encoded by large multigene families.[21]

Over the last few years, entire repertoires of OR genes from various species have been identified, including humans, mice, dogs, fish and other vertebrates. These studies have revealed wide variations in the numbers of OR genes and pseudogenes among the different species.

Rouquier and her colleagues reported the discovery of a new mammalian OR gene which they designated 912–93.[22] The human gene is apparently non-functional. They also reported a second frameshift mutation which was present in the gorilla ortholog. It is this gene that Alexander suggests is 'fully active in chimpanzees, orangutans and gibbons'[23] but this is only partly true. More recently, Gaillard *et al.* studied changes in the specificity of this receptor in six primate species including the squirrel monkey.[24] They used a novel *in vitro* system to detect receptor responses to specific odorants, the ketones 2- and 3-heptanone. Of the five species mentioned by Alexander, only two are functional in this assay system and these are chimpanzee and gibbon, which from an evolutionary perspective is counter-intuitive. The human, gorilla and orang-utan 912–93 OR genes are all non-functional, but for different reasons. Furthermore, squirrel-monkey OR only responded to one of the ketone stimuli, namely, 3-heptanone.

More recently, scientists have re-investigated OR gene and pseudogene distribution in the human, chimpanzee and macaque

21. I. Gaillard, S. Rouquier and D. Giorgi, 'Olfactory Receptors', *Cellular and Molecular Life Sciences* 61 (2004), pp. 456–469.

22. S. Rouquier, *et al.*, 'A Gene Recently Inactivated in Human Defines a New Olfactory Receptor Family in Mammals', *Human Molecular Genetics* 7 (1998), pp. 1337–1345.

23. Alexander, *Creation or Evolution*, p. 206.

24. I. Gaillard, *et al.*, 'Amino-acid Changes Acquired During Evolution by Olfactory Receptor 912–93 Modify the Specificity of Odorant Recognition,' *Human Molecular Genetics* 13 (2004), pp. 771–780.

genomes using the very latest sequences.[25] In contrast to previous studies, they showed that the number of OR genes (810) and the fraction of pseudogenes (51%) in chimpanzees are very similar to those in humans, though macaques have considerably fewer OR genes. In addition, they identified that approximately 25% of the functional repertoires of human and chimpanzee OR genes are 'species specific due to massive gene losses'. Thus, according to these authors, the ancestors of both humans and chimpanzees possessed more functional OR genes and fewer pseudogenes, suggesting to them that both lineages are in a phase of deterioration.

Summary of pseudogenes

The non-protein coding genome was once described by the now redundant term 'junk DNA'. Nevertheless, it is becoming increasingly apparent that non-protein coding DNA, including the pseudogenes, may perform important biological roles. Thus, it has been somewhat premature to suggest that pseudogenes are simply genetic fossils. This is not to say, however, that there will never be an example of a pseudogene that is a defunct copy of protein-coding gene which has lost its activity due to mutational damage. Eventually, it may be necessary to redefine the term 'pseudogene' to distinguish between those genes that are truly broken from those genomic elements that possess important roles in gene regulation.

Mobile genetic elements

According to Alexander:

> Transposable elements or jumping genes comprise nearly half our
> genomes. These are those 'copy-and-paste' sequences of DNA that
> have no function, but which provide further valuable genetic fossils for

---

25. Y. Go and Y. Niimura, 'Similar Numbers But Different Repertoires of Olfactory Receptor Genes in Humans and Chimpanzees', *Molecular Biology and Evolution* 25 (2008), pp. 1897–1907.

tracking our own evolutionary history. If one of these sequences has
been inserted at a particular specific location in the genomes of different
species, then this demonstrates unequivocally that these species must all
have descended from the same common ancestor.[26]

Transposable elements are generally known as transposons:
sequences of DNA that can move from one position in the
genome to another. There are several types of transposons (also
known as mobile genetic elements) and they are classified according to their mechanism of transposition.

An example of a class I transposons is quite similar to the processed pseudogene. The DNA sequence is first transcribed into
RNA and then transcribed back into DNA at another location by
the enzyme reverse transcriptase. These mobile genetic elements
are also called retrotransposons. Class II transposons are similar
to unprocessed pseudogenes which are simply duplicated (copied)
and pasted from one genomic position to another using another
type of enzyme called a transposase.

Retrotransposons

Most retrotransposed genomic elements are DNA sequences
known as either short interspersed repeated sequences (SINEs) or
long interspersed repeated sequences (LINEs). Both types are replicated via RNA intermediates. The majority of the SINEs are the
so-called 'Alu sequences' which are about 300 base-pairs long, and
there are over one million of these in the human genome.

Denis Alexander gives us just one example of an Alu insert that
is common in the human, chimpanzee and gorilla although it is not
present in the orang-utan. According to Alexander:

> In this example the 'jumping gene' is known as an 'Alu insert'. It is
> hundreds of nucleotide base-pairs long. It has inserted into a non-
> protein coding region of the genome of the common ancestor of human,
> chimp and gorilla, but is not present in the DNA of the orangutan. This
> tells us immediately that the insertional event must have taken place after

---

26. Alexander, *Creation or Evolution*, p. 208.

our lineage split off from the orangutan about 12–15 million years ago . . .Anybody can read the evidence![27]

One problem is that there is no indication as to what this example actually is. No reference is given that will help us to identify and verify his statement. We need to remember that there are over one million *Alu* sequences scattered throughout the human genome. Hedges *et al.* reported the first chromosomal-level comparison of *Alu* sequences in humans and chimpanzees.[28] They found a twofold increase in *Alu* insertions in humans in comparison to the common chimpanzee, but also that the level of chimpanzee *Alu* diversity was approximately 1.7 times higher than that of humans. They concluded that *Alu* subfamily structure differed markedly between the human and chimpanzee lineages, with the major human subfamilies remaining largely inactive in the chimpanzee lineage. In particular, they give a specific example of an *Alu* insertion in human, chimpanzee, gorilla and orang-utan (HS6) which is totally contrary to that given by Alexander. This is shown in Figure 3. Anybody can read the evidence!

Furthermore, there is a considerable number of *Alu* sequences that are unique to the human and which are not present in the great apes.[29] Likewise each species has its own unique complement as well as sharing *Alu* sequences with other primates. This unique species distribution of *Alu* sequences renders Alexander's words meaningless.

Recently, Han *et al.* have identified 663 deletions of *Alu* sequences in the chimpanzee that are present in the human genome.[30] Technically,

---

27. Ibid., p. 209.
28. D. J. Hedges, *et al.,* 'Differential Alu mobilization and polymorphism among the human and chimpanzee lineages', *Genome Research* 14 (2004), pp. 1068–1075.
29. A. H. Salem, *et al.,* 'Recently Integrated Alu Elements and Human Genomic Diversity', *Molecular Biology and Evolution* 20 (2003), pp. 1349–1361.
30. K. Han, *et al.,* 'Alu Recombination-Mediated Structural Deletions in the Chimpanzee Genome', *PLoS Genetics* 3 (2007), pp. 1939–1949.

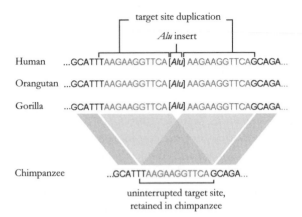

Figure 3: Reconstructed Alu HS6 insertion sites in human and nonhuman primates.[31]

these species-specific deletions are known as *Alu* recombination-mediated genomic deletion (ARMD). The authors write:

> Despite the high level of overall similarity between their genomes, humans and chimpanzees have subtly different genomic landscapes because of alterations such as insertions, deletions, inversions, and duplications after their divergence from a common ancestral primate. Although from a mechanistic viewpoint, the chimpanzee-specific ARMD events are similar to the human-specific ones, the total number and size of deletions are substantially different between the two lineages.[32]

In the light of these species-specific 'genomic landscapes', what do we make of Alexander's suggestion that 'anybody can read the evidence'? For example, how can we ever be certain that the absence of any particular *Alu* sequence in the orangutan (or any other primate) is not the result of an ARMD event?

---

31. After Hedges *et al.*, ibid., p. 1070, drawn after the style of Alexander, *Creation or Evolution,* p. 209.

32. Ibid., p. 1944.

Do Alu *sequences have any function?*

It is also very premature to conclude that *Alu* sequences are just 'genetic fossils' as Alexander would like to maintain. Not surprisingly, there have been several recent publications that indicate that *Alu* sequences may have very important genomic roles. Britten described the sequence analysis of 1,500 interspersed *Alu* repeats of human DNA containing defined mutations.[33] He discovered that there were specific regions in the *Alu* sequence where mutations rarely occurred. Furthermore, he suggested that these highly conserved regions occurred in positions which appeared to be sites for protein binding. He concluded that 'the implication is that hundreds of thousands of Alu sequences have sequence-dependent functions in the genome that are selectively important for primates'.

Current knowledge about *Alu* sequences and their possible functions was reviewed in 1997.[34] Although *Alu* sequences are rare in protein-coding exons, where they would be totally disruptive, they are relatively common in introns where they can have a dramatic impact on gene expression. In particular, normal mRNA processing which involves the removal of introns can be disrupted by point mutation in an *Alu* element and this can lead to clinical diseases such as Alport syndrome.[35] Furthermore, normal mRNA splicing can also be disrupted by retrotransposition of an *Alu* element into an intron, with formation of a truncated, abnormal protein, as in a case of neurofibromatosis.[36] *Alu* sequences can influence normal gene expression. For example, *Alu* sequences

33. R. J. Britten, 'Evolutionary Selection Against Change in Many Alu Repeat Sequences Interspersed Through Primate Genomes', *Proceedings of the National Academy of Science USA* 91 (1994), pp. 5992–5996.

34. A. J. Mighell, A. F. Markham and P. A. Robinson, 'Alu Sequences', *FEBS Letter* 417 (1997), pp. 1–5.

35. B. Knebelmann, *et al.*, 'Splice-Mediated Insertion of an Alu Sequence in the COL4A3 mRNA Causing Autosomal Recessive Alport Syndrome', *Human Molecular Genetics* 4 (1995), pp. 675–679.

36. M. R. Wallace, *et al.*, 'A de novo Alu Insertion Results in Neurofibromatosis Type 1', *Nature* 353 (1991), pp. 864–866.

within introns of several reported genes include transcription factor binding sites, presumably exerting an effect on transcriptional regulation.[37]

As a general rule, the various roles for *Alu* sequences are being discovered by what goes wrong when there is a mutation or inappropriate duplication or deletion. For example, both familial hypercholesterolaemia[38] and angioedema[39] are associated with *Alu-Alu* recombinations. Complex events, such as inversion or deletions between *Alu* elements, have also been identified which lead to various genetic disorders such as α-thalassaemia[40] and even the increased risk of myocardial infarction.[41] These findings are suggestive evidence that normal *Alu* sequences have important roles.

None of this clinical, comparative genomic and functional data finds its way into Alexander's argument. He is willing to conclude from his superficial analysis of one *Alu* sequence that there is clear evidence for common ancestry, where recent publications would indicate that there is actually a radical difference between the *Alu* sequences in humans and chimpanzees. Nevertheless, in spite of all the evidence to the contrary, Alexander maintains:

---

37. S. L. Oei, *et al.*, 'Clusters of Regulatory Signals for RNA Polymerase II Transcription Associated with Alu Family Repeats and CpG Islands in Human Promoters', *Genomics* 83 (2004), pp. 873–882.

38. M. A. Lehrman, *et al.*, 'Duplication of Seven Exons in LDL Receptor Gene Caused by Alu-Alu Recombination in a Subject with Familial Hypercholesterolemia', *Cell* 48 (1987), pp. 827–835.

39. T. Ariga, P. E. Carter and A. E. Davis, 'Recombinations Between Alu Repeat Sequences that Result in Partial Deletions Within the C1 Inhibitor Gene', *Genomics* 8 (1990), pp. 607–613.

40. K. L. Harteveld, *et al.*, 'The Involvement of Alu Repeats in Recombination Events at the Alpha-globin Gene Cluster: Characterization of two Alphazero-thalassaemia Deletion Breakpoints', *Human Genetics* 99 (1997), pp. 528–534.

41. P. M. Ridker, *et al.*, 'Alu-repeat Polymorphism in the Gene Coding for Tissue-type Plasminogen Activator (t-PA) and Risks of Myocardial Infarction Among Middle-aged Men', *Arteriosclerosis, Thrombosis, and Vasculariology* 17 (1997), pp. 1687–1690.

If one of these sequences has been inserted at a particular specific location in the genomes of different species, then this *demonstrates unequivocally that these species must all have descended from the same common ancestor.* We share nearly all (99%) of these fossilised inserts into our genomes in common with chimpanzees, most with macaques, and many with distantly related mammals.[42]

These statements are just not borne out by the facts. Alexander appears to have used one or two examples to justify his evolutionary philosophy.

Retroviral insertions

Retroviruses carry their genetic material as RNA rather than DNA. They possess a relatively small number of genes and cannot survive (i.e. replicate) without 'hijacking' the genetic machinery of the host cell of a higher organism. Retroviruses exploit the enzyme reverse transcriptase to copy their RNA genome into DNA which is then integrated into the host's DNA genome. From that moment on, the virus replicates as part of the host cell cycle.

Many retroviruses are benign but some produce disease. The classic example is HIV, which specifically targets cells in the immune system. Under normal circumstances, these cells would be involved in eradicating the viral threat but because the cells, known as T-cells, are taken over by the virus, AIDS has become a devastating disease. The other problem is the fact that the structural proteins on the surface of the viral particle are constantly mutating. Consequently, it has become very difficult to come up with a universal vaccine. According to Alexander:

In many cases retroviruses incorporate their DNA message into genomes without any harm to the individual, and in some cases this infection occurs in germ line cells, meaning that the inserted DNA becomes a permanent part of the genome of all the descendants of that

42. Alexander, *Creation or Evolution*, p. 208, emphasis added.

single individual. So once again our cells are like little history books, faithfully reproducing for our interest evolutionary histories that go back millions of years.[43]

It is generally assumed that these genetic insertions have entered the human genome over time and have been passed on from one generation to another. In the human genome, these insertions are known as human endogenous retroviruses (HERVs) and they make up between 5% and 8% of the total genome. Most insertions have no known function but we now understand that at least some HERVs play important roles in host biology such as the control of gene expression[44] and reproduction (e.g. placental function and spermatogenesis)[45] as well as enhancing resistance to exogenous pathogenic retroviral infection.[46]

One family of HERVs that has been well studied is human endogenous retrovirus K (HERV-K), which is thought to be related to the mouse mammary tumour virus. This family is represented in the genomes of humans, apes and the Old World monkeys.[47]

---

43. Ibid., p. 210.

44. H. S. Sin, *et al.*, 'Transcriptional Control of the HER V-H LTR Element of the GSDML Gene in Human Tissues and Cancer Cells', *Archives of Virology* 151 (2006), pp. 1985–1994.

45. A. Muir, A. Lever and A. Moffett, 'Expression and Functions of Human Endogenous Retro Viruses in the Placenta: An Update', *Placenta* 25 Suppl A (2004), pp. S16–25; E. Larsson, A. C. Andersson and B. O. Nilsson, 'Expression of an Endogenous Retro Virus (ERV3 HERV-R) in Human Reproductive and Embryonic Tissues – Evidence for a Function for Envelope Gene Products', *Upsala Journal of Medical Sciences* 99 (1994), pp. 113–120.

46. V. G. Ponferrada, B. S. Mauck and D. P. Wooley, 'The Envelope Glycoprotein of Human Endogenous Retro Virus HERV-W Induces Cellular Resistance to Spleen Necrosis Virus', *Archives of Virology* 148 (2003), pp. 659–675.

47. M. Mack, K. Bender and P. M. Schneider, 'Detection of Retroviral Antisense Transcripts and Promoter Activity of the HER V-K(C4) Insertion in the MHC Class III Region', *Immunogenetics* 56 (2004), pp. 321–332.

Recently,[48] ten different HERV-Ks in the human genome were identified, of which eight were unique to the human lineage even though intact pre-integration sites for each were present in the apes. A ninth HERV-K was detected in the human, chimpanzee, bonobo and gorilla genomes, but not in the orang-utan genome. The tenth was found only in humans, chimpanzees and bonobos,[49] presumably the example used by Alexander:[50]

human	CTCTGGAATTC[HERVIGAATTCTATGT
chimpanzee	CTCTGGAATTC[HERV]GAATTCTATGT
bonobo	CTCTGGAATTC[HERV]GAATTCTATGT

Figure 4: Insertion site for K10 retrovirus sequence in the human, chimpanzee and bonobo.

We should not be surprised that the HERV is located in exactly the same sequence in all three species. This is indicative of the specificity of the 'pre-integration site'. In other words, HERVs are not distributed in haphazard manner; their location is very precise. The above findings are all the more remarkable since, in eight cases, the great apes have identical pre-integration sites to humans but no HERV-K. If the infectious origin of the HERV is correct, it raises a major problem as to why the great apes do not have these particular HERV-Ks inserted.

It also raises the possibility that maybe the infectious origin of HERVs is only partly true. Is it not possible that many HERVs are actually important functional genetic components which have, as yet, an unknown function? The objection to this argument, of course, would be the similarity of the protein-coding regions of the HERV to exogenous retroviruses. However, an alternative hypothesis is that retroviruses themselves might have their origin

---

48. M. Barbulescu, *et al.*, 'A HERV-K Provirus in Chimpanzees, Bonobos and Gorillas, But Not in Humans', *Current Biology* 11 (2001), pp. 779–783.
49. Mack, Bender and Schneider, 'Detection of Retroviral Antisense Transcripts'.
50. Alexander, *Creation or Evolution*, p. 210.

as conventional genomic components. Only time will tell if there is any substance to this suggestion.

Alexander concludes his section on retroviruses by suggesting:

> . . . in other words on a particular day of a particular week in a particular year, millions of years ago, that particular retroviral DNA sequence was inserted into a particular germ cell of one of our ancestors, and it has been there ever since; we all continue to make millions of copies of it, very precisely, every day of our lives. That is an amazing thought.[51]

The arguments presented by Alexander are quite fallacious. If the infectious origin of HERVs is substantiated, there is no way of knowing whether the presence of common HERVs in humans and great apes could not be interpreted simply on the basis of independent species infection. One can only infer common ancestry if one assumes common ancestry in the first place. However, if HERVs are an integral part of the functional genome, then one would expect to discover species-specific commonality and discontinuity, which is indeed the case.

Conclusion

The claim that there is overwhelming evidence that humans and chimpanzees have common ancestry is an overstatement. We have considered the issue of pseudogenes, using the examples presented by Alexander, and the significance of mobile genetic elements. The selective arguments of Alexander do not hold up when counter-arguments in the wider academic literature are considered.

With increasing frequency, papers are being published describing the complexity and information-bearing properties of non-coding regions of the genome, once dismissed as 'junk' DNA. It is here that the profound limitations of Darwinism, with its assumed common ancestry, will be clearly demonstrated.

© Geoff Barnard, 2009

---

51. Ibid., pp. 210–211.

11. THE ORIGIN OF LIFE: SCIENTISTS PLAY DICE

John C. Walton

No place for natural selection in explanations of the origin of life

In the present-day world, inanimate things like rocks, mountains, clouds, atmosphere and seas are clearly distinct from living things like animals, birds, fish and micro-organisms; although the two domains are in constant interaction. The extreme diversity of the living kingdom is very striking, extending from venerable bristle-cone pines, which have graced the White Mountains of eastern California for nearly 5,000 years, to the ubiquitous *Escherichia coli*, which live only a few minutes before cell division. Despite life's huge variegation, sophisticated organization and cooperation are evident at all levels. Curiosity about how all this came into being is as old as history. The currently popular chemical evolutionary scenario claims that the inanimate mineral backdrop preceded the biological action-play, *and gave rise to it,* in a long drawn out step-by-step process. On the other hand, the creationist/interventionist worldview, deriving from Scripture, affirms that the inanimate environment was specifically tuned to support living things which were also designed and made by God. The conceptual and physical evidence relating to these two claims will be evaluated in this chapter.

It is widely acknowledged that the principal features characteristic of living things are: organization, metabolism, adaptation, response to stimuli and, particularly, reproduction. Viruses, which are intricate assemblages of proteins and DNA, are clearly excluded by these criteria, leaving single cell micro-organisms, lacking nuclei (i.e. bacteria and archaea) as the simplest forms of life.

To explain the origin of new organisms in the biological kingdom biologists regularly appeal to neo-Darwinian evolution. However, the evolutionary mechanism cannot be invoked to explain how the first living organism came into being during a postulated era of chemical evolution. The operation of neo-Darwinian natural selection depends on the *prior existence of entities capable of self-replication*. Variants are produced in their genetic material by mutations, the variants are copied by the organism's biochemical machinery, and then natural selection ensures the most 'fit' survive. Before the arrival of organisms capable of reproduction this process could not operate. In the words of eminent evolutionist Theodosius Dobzhansky: 'Prebiological natural selection is a contradiction in terms.'[1] It follows that, even in principle, some quite different explanation is required to account for the origin of life.

The smallest autonomous living organism

Discoveries in the last half century have shown that single-celled organisms are anything but simple. Their complex lipopolysaccharide membranes are furnished with various specialized proteins and enclose a system of sophisticated organelles, including ribosomes, carboxysomes and plasmids, together with information-loaded DNA in their nucleoids. Each of these organelles is composed

---

1. T. Dobzhansky, in S. W. Fox (ed.), *The Origins of Prebiological Systems and Their Molecular Matrices* (New York: Academic Press, 1965), p. 310.

of many specialized proteins that are organized like machines in a factory. In many bacteria mobility is made possible by means of amazing nano-scale molecular machines called flagella that are composed of about twenty proteins and are dependent on a further thirty proteins for regulation and assembly.[2] No wonder there has been much discussion about just how small, or rather how large, the first fully reproductive organism would have had to be, and whether it started from proteins or from nucleic acids. The 'minimal genome project' currently underway at the J. Craig Venter Institute aims to find the minimal set of genes that can sustain life.[3]

The smallest known bacterium is *Carsonella ruddii* which lives in a symbiotic relationship with sap-feeding insects called psyllids.[4] The genomic DNA of *Carsonella ruddii* contains about 160,000 base pairs (pairs of nucleotides). This species cannot reproduce on its own but is dependent on its host psyllid for many enzymes. The smallest known free-living organism, *Mycoplasma genitalium*, has a genome of 582,970 base pairs corresponding to about 480 proteins. No smaller organisms capable of freely reproducing themselves have been discovered. The organized complexity of these minimal species throws into relief the immensity of the task facing naturalistic explanations of how life originated.

Information and the genetic code

Cell metabolism and reproduction rely on cooperation between proteins on one hand and nucleic acids on the other. Proteins (also

---

2. S. Bardy, S. Ng and K. Jarrell, 'Prokaryotic Motility Structures', *Microbiology* 149 (2003), pp. 295–304.

3. J. I. Glass, M. Assad-Garcia, N. Alperovich, *et al.*, 'Essential Genes of a Minimal Bacterium', *Proceedings of the National Academy of Sciences* 103 (2006), pp. 425–430.

4. M. L. Thao, 'Cospeciation of Psyllids and Their Primary Prokaryotic Endosymbionts', *Applied and Environmental Microbiology* 66 (2000), pp. 2898–2905.

Nucleotide chemical structure

Phosphate (P)

Base
Adenine (A)

Sugar (S)

Schematic representations

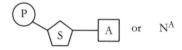

or N^A

Figure 1*: Chemical structure of a nucleotide with shorthand representations.*

enzymes) are large molecules which are made up of many amino acids, chosen from a basic set of twenty and linked together in linear fashion, in chains such as Gly–Phe–Ala–His–Met–Lys. They can be thought of as messages written in a twenty-letter alphabet. Proteins fold into specific three-dimensional shapes which are determined by the *order* in which the amino acids are linked. It is the exact three-dimensional shape which enables a protein to perform its specific task in the cell such as catalyzing a reaction or acting as a structural unit (Fig. 1).

DNA molecules are also long chains, made up from a set of four different nucleotides (N^A, N^G, N^C, N^T) which are linked together in a linear sequence [e.g. $-N^A-N^C-N^T-N^G-N^G-$]. In real life, two complementary DNA chains are held together by hydrogen bonds and they twist up into long regions of the familiar double-helix structure. The exact order of the nucleotides determines the information carried by a particular DNA strand. The DNA is therefore the information store, or memory bank, that instructs a cell how to build its own characteristic set of proteins. In all living cells, proteins and nucleic acids are related to each other via the genetic code. The order of amino acids in a given protein corresponds to the order of a set of nucleotides (i.e., a gene) located in the genetic DNA. In even the simplest cells the process of making proteins takes place in two stages. First, there is 'transcription', requiring an intricately adapted set of enzymes and RNAs to copy the information from the DNA.[5] In the second 'translation' step, this information is transported to a complex of RNA and proteins known as a ribosome, where a second set of enzymes recognizes the information and uses it to build a specific protein chain. Altogether over a hundred particular proteins are needed just for transcription and translation.[6]

When a cell divides, a copy of the genetic DNA containing all this information is passed on to the daughter cell, and so it is preserved with remarkable accuracy from generation to generation. Each species has its special DNA sequence, its genome, which contains most of the information needed to build itself. The cell biochemical machinery just has to read off the DNA sequence, decode it and then make the necessary proteins and structural units, so generating a new cell. The interdependence of DNA and proteins is very remarkable. The coded information in the genomic DNA sequence is useless without the protein-based translation machinery to transform it into cell components. But the instructions for production of this translation machinery are themselves coded on the genomic DNA.

The origin of such a system presents a paradox of the 'which came first: the chicken or the egg?' variety. The DNA information is needed to build the protein machinery but only the specific protein machinery can read the instructions! This set-up proclaims design about as loudly as any evidence could. The simplest conclusion, in harmony with Ockham's law of parsimony, must be that the two sets of bio-molecules were designed and assembled,

---

5. RNA is similar to DNA except that the sugar is ribose rather than deoxyribose and uracil replaces thymine as one of the heterocyclic bases.

6. For a detailed description of the gene expression process see for example: D. Voet and J. G. Voet, *Biochemistry* (New York: Wiley, ²1995), pp. 830–1065.

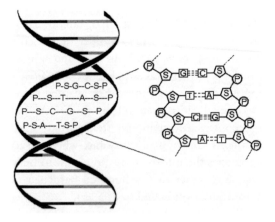

Figure 2: Sketch of DNA double helix structure.

ready for interaction with one another. Once the complexity of the mechanism by which the DNA domain communicates with the protein domain was appreciated, it became apparent that a gradualistic theory to account for the origin of such a coded system would be extremely problematic.

Could the first organism have formed by amino acids or nucleotides combining in random chemical fashion?

Before the first living organism came into existence, there would be no DNA with the right information to copy, and no enzyme-based cell translation machinery. Can mindless nature alone supply the vast amount of information needed to build an entity capable of reproduction? For the sake of argument let's suppose that a primordial soup existed on the earth containing amino acids and nucleotides.[7] These are then presumed to couple

7. The primordial (prebiotic) soup concept is beset with problems and is very implausible. For amino acids to form, the early atmosphere must have been without oxygen; but this seems improbable because oxygen is the most abundant element (47%) in the earth's crust and is over-whelmingly abundant in the hydrosphere. Soup components would

up to produce protein sequences and nucleic acid sequences respectively by purely random chemical transformations with no template copying. What is needed is just the right sequence of nucleotides in a DNA (or RNA) chain to start replication, and/ or just the right sequence of amino acids in an enzyme to catalyze replication.

For a set of just three amino acids coupling together at random there are six possible protein sequences. For four amino acids there are twenty-four different protein chains (Fig. 3). For five amino acids the number rises to 120 proteins. Random coupling would produce any and, given enough time, every one of these, but only one of the chains has the required biological activity.

For a protein to perform a useful function in a cell it must be able to fold into a particular three-dimensional shape. A minimum of around 100 amino acids is needed for functional shapes to result from folding. This poses a huge problem because the number of possible sequences rises exponentially as the length of the protein chain increases. Statistical calculations[8] have shown that the number of possible protein chains containing 100 amino acids, chosen from the set of twenty, is stupendously large, at about 10^{130}. It follows that the chance of one particular functional

---

chemically react with one another and be subject to serious degradative processes. Not a single nucleotide, let alone an RNA chain, has ever been made under plausibly prebiotic conditions. Geological evidence of a primordial soup is completely lacking in early Precambrian rocks, which are notably poor in organic and nitrogenous material. For a more detailed discussion, see C. B. Thaxton, W. L. Bradley and R. L. Olsen, *The Mystery of Life's Origin: Reassessing Current Theories* (New York: Philosophical Library, 1984), ch. 4, p. 42; R. Shapiro, *Origins: A Sceptic's Guide to the Creation of Life on Earth* (New York: Bantam, 1986).

8. M. Eigen, 'Self Organisation of Matter and the Evolution of Biological Macromolecules', *Die Naturwissenschaften* 58 (1971), p. 465; H. P. Yockey, 'A Calculation of the Probability of Spontaneous Biogenesis by Information Theory', *Journal of Theoretical Biology* 67 (1977), pp. 377–398; idem, 'Self-organization Origin of Life Scenarios and Information Theory', *Journal of Theoretical Biology* 91 (1981), pp. 13–31.

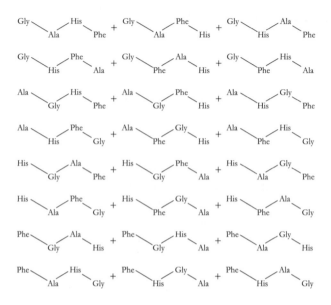

Figure 3: *The twenty-four protein chains formed by random chemical combinations of just four amino acids; Gly, Ala, His, Phe.[9]*

sequence forming by random combinations of amino acids is staggeringly and prohibitively small at 1 in 10^{130}.

In reality, amino acids have reactive side chains which will link, in a random chemical system, roughly 50 % of the time to yield non-proteinaceous chains. To allow for this, the probability must be multiplied by a factor of about 1 in 10^{30}. Purely chemical processes also produce equal quantities of the left-handed and right-handed forms of each amino acid (except glycine). However, functional proteins contain only the left-handed forms. The chance of one particular functional protein sequence forming

---

9. The last 12 appear to be the same as the first 12 but in fact, because the two ends of a protein are different, all 24 are separate and distinct molecules.

at random must be multiplied by a further factor of about 1 in 10^{30} to correct for the handedness factor. The total chance of a particular 100 amino acid sequence forming by random assembly becomes therefore: 1 in 10^{130} x 10^{30} x 10^{30}, i.e. 1 in 10^{190}.

The utter hopelessness of this minute chance is alleviated to some extent by the ability of enzymes to tolerate quite a lot of amino acid substitutions while still retaining their activity. Experimental determinations have been made, using several different strategies, of how the probability of random formation of a sequence is affected by amino acid substitutions that do not destroy enzyme functionality.[10] On allowing for this by one method, the probability of a functional enzyme of about 100 amino acids forming in a random process still turned out to be ultra-microscopically small at about 1 in 10^{63}. For a slightly longer 150 amino acid sequence, a different method of estimation gave a probability of about 1 in 10^{74}. In a prebiotic soup environment therefore, the total probability of a functional 100 unit protein forming would be 1 in 10^{63} x 10^{30} x 10^{30}, i.e. 1 in 10^{123}, and for a 150 amino acid protein this would be 1 in 10^{74} x 10^{45} x 10^{45}, i.e. 1 in 10^{164}. To form an idea of the impossibly small chance these numbers reveal, compare them with the chance of winning the national lottery jackpot, which is about 1 in 10^{9}, or the chance of finding one particular atom in the whole observable universe which would be 'only' 1 in 10^{80}!

The resources of material and time available in a prebiotic soup scenario would be utterly inadequate for the random assembly process to come up with a functional protein. The number of proteins, each of length 100 amino acids, that could pack into a 1-metre layer covering the whole surface of the earth would be

10. J. F. Reidhaar-Olson and R. T. Sauer, 'Functionally Acceptable Substitutions in Two α-helical Regions of δ Repressor', *Proteins: Structure, Function, and Genetics* 7 (1990), pp. 306–316; idem, 'Combinatorial Cassette Mutagenesis as a Probe of the Informational Content of Protein Sequences', *Science* 241 (1988), pp. 53–57; D. D. Axe, 'Estimating the Prevalence of Protein Sequences Adopting Functional Enzyme Folds', *Journal of Molecular Biology* 341 (2004), pp. 1295–1315.

about 10^{41} and the number that would be in a 1-millimolar soup in all the oceans would be about 10^{42}. These numbers are over eighty orders of magnitude smaller than would be required. The number of proteins that could pack into the entire volume of the observable universe would be 'only' about 10^{120}. It follows that the chance of a functional protein sequence forming spontaneously on the earth, even if random amino acid combinations had taken place at the fastest possible rate for a billion years is negligibly small.[11] In fact, it has been shown that if the entire resources of the universe had been devoted to making proteins at the fastest possible rate since the putative Big Bang the chance of formation of even one functional protein would still be negligible.[12] Gerald Schroeder compared a string of amino acids in a protein to a string of 488 letters in a sonnet. He made the same point this way:

> What's the likelihood of hammering away and getting 488 letters in the exact sequence as in 'Shall I compare thee to a summer's day'? You end up with 10^{690} trials . . . If you took the entire universe and converted it to computer chips . . . each one weighing a millionth of a gram and had each computer chip able to spin out 488 trials at, say, a million times a second . . . [producing] random letters, the number of trials you would get since the beginning of time would be 10^{90} . . . You will never get a sonnet by chance. The universe would have to be 10^{600} times larger.[13]

Nucleic acids are complementary to proteins and contain similar information, so the same conclusion is reached from a consideration of random combinations of nucleotides. The chance of a particular information-containing DNA (or RNA) sequence

---

11. The discovery of early pre-Cambrian fossil stromatolites in the Siyeh Formation, Glacier National Park, and in the Bulawayan Group, Zimbabwe, and of various biological marker molecules in the earliest crustal rocks, point to much less time available than this.

12. S. D. Meyer, *Signature in the Cell* (New York: HarperOne, 2009), ch. 10, p. 215.

13. G. Schroeder, quoted in A. Flew and R. A. Varghese, *There is a God* (New York: HarperOne, 2007), ch. 3, p. 77.

forming in a prebiotic soup is negligibly small. Furthermore, these odds refer to the chance formation of a single functioning protein or DNA strand. As indicated above, even the simplest reproducing organism would need a large number of such bio-molecules. It is virtually certain, therefore, that life did not originate by random chemical reactions in a prebiotic soup. Actually, this conclusion is not controversial. All reputable scientists who have studied the problem, whatever their ideology, concur with this view. It is a pity that popular texts on the origin of life make no mention of these odds.[14] Regrettably, popular books and media productions continue to confidently assert that 'life started by chance chemical processes in a prebiotic soup'.

Theories of self-assembly and self-organisation

Scientists have been aware of these fantastically low odds for decades but are still hopeful that a naturalistic way out of the impasse may be found. Wikipedia mentions over fifteen scenarios, some overlapping, that have been proposed to account for the origin of life, and this list is by no means exhaustive.[15] The existence of so many competing theories is itself evidence that they are all beset with serious problems and none of them is at all persuasive.

Early in the debate it was proposed that amino acids, or perhaps nucleotides, might have inherent physico-chemical properties that predisposed them to self-organize in biologically useful ways. Interest in this idea received great impetus when Dean Kenyon and Gary Steinman discovered significant chemical preferences in the association of one amino acid with others. In their book *Biochemical Predestination* they proposed that these differences in affinity led to preferential formation of some sequences over others and that this

---

14. Standard texts such as G. Zubay, *Origins of Life on the Earth and in the Cosmos* (San Diego: Academic Press, ²2000); D. W. Deamer and G. R. Fleischaker, *Origin of Life: The Central Concepts* (Boston: Jones & Bartlett, 1994), do not mention these odds and do not deal with the origin of information.
15. See http://en.wikipedia.org/wiki/Origin_of_life.

selectivity in turn might have led to the very sequences found in functioning proteins.[16]

The theory grew in popularity, but Kenyon himself began to doubt it and eventually repudiated it. The sequel to this mode of self-organization would be that the chemically predetermined amino acid sequences were somehow transferred into nucleotide sequences in DNA. However, experimental studies showed that the amino acid affinities discovered by Kenyon and Steinman did not correlate with actual sequence patterns found in known proteins.[17] Rather, the functional protein sequences had really been generated from information encoded in DNA and were not a consequence of any chemically directed assembly of amino acids. Information flowed from DNA to proteins and not the other way round.

There was still the possibility that self-organization and production of information could derive in some way from properties of the nucleotides. All four nucleotides contain the same sugar and phosphate units; they differ only in the nature of their heterocyclic bases. When they link up to form nucleic acids it is their sugar and phosphate units that bond together and each junction is the same type of phosphodiester bond. There is no contact between the heterocyclic bases of adjacent nucleotides. From a chemical standpoint it always seemed unlikely, therefore, that there could be any special affinities predisposing nucleotides to assemble in specific sequences. Nor has any such selectivity in nucleotide assembly ever been observed. Biochemist Bernd-Olaf Küppers concluded: 'The properties of nucleic acids indicate that all the combinatorially possible nucleotide patterns of a DNA are, from a chemical point of view, equivalent.'[18]

---

16. D. Kenyon and G. Steinman, *Biochemical Predestination* (New York: McGraw-Hill, 1969).

17. R. A. Kok, J. A. Taylor and W. L. Bradley, 'A Statistical Examination of Self-Ordering', *Origins of Life and Evolution of Biospheres* 18 (1988), pp. 135–142.

18. B.-O. Küppers, 'On the Prior Probability of the Existence of Life', in L. Krüger, G. Gigerenzer and M. S. Morgan (eds.), *The Probabalistic Revolution*, vol. 2 (Cambridge, MA: MIT Press, 1987), pp. 355–369.

Michael Polanyi was the first to clearly set out a further insight into the enigma of the information carried by DNA.[19] He drew attention to the difference between order and information. If letters in an alphabet were forced to always appear in certain sequences they could only transmit a limited set of meanings. He argued that DNA's capacity to convey information actually depends on the unconstrained ability of the nucleotides to couple in any arrangement, free from chemical or physical influences. If the bonding properties of the nucleotides favoured certain sequences, the capacity of DNA to convey information would be severely curtailed. He concluded: 'Whatever may be the origin of a DNA configuration, it can function as a code only if its order is not due to the forces of potential energy. It must be as physically indeterminate as the sequence of words is on a printed page.' Thus, nothing about the properties of either the amino acids or the nucleotides predisposes them to assemble in arrangements conducive to the start of self-replication. The idea that life is 'predestined' or 'inevitable' receives no support whatsoever from studies of protein or nucleic acid assembly. The biochemical predestination theory is now very generally discounted.

The RNA world[20]

By the mid-1980s it had been discovered that certain RNA molecules, called ribozymes, could behave like enzymes and catalyze some of the important cell reactions. Because of its great similarity to DNA, RNA could potentially store genomic information by means of its nucleotide sequences.[21] The idea took hold of a prebiotic world in which RNA, or possibly some simpler form called *pre*-RNA,[22]

19. M. Polanyi, 'Life's Irreducible Structure', *Science* 160 (1968), p. 1308.
20. See Meyer, *Signature*, ch. 14, p. 296 for a thorough discussion of the RNA world.
21. RNA is also composed of linear sequences of nucleotides.
22. Peptide nucleic acid (PNA), threose nucleic acid (TNA) and glycerol nucleic acid (GNA) have been considered as possible *pre*-RNAs.

could take on both roles, that of information storage as well as that of specific catalysis. The hope was that the chicken and egg enigma, associated with communication via the genetic code between the protein and DNA domains, would thereby be avoided. In the RNA-world hypothesis, a molecule of RNA capable of copying itself first arose by the chance combinations of ribose, phosphate and heterocyclic bases in some prebiotic soup. The complexity and functionality of the system gradually increased as a consequence of natural selection. In the next stage, the RNA molecules started to make proteins and eventually DNA emerged, acquired the genetic information, and took over the information storage role because of its greater stability. This scenario is currently well regarded in the scientific community and seen as the most promising way forward for origin-of-life research.

There are, however, many implausible assumptions and weaknesses in the theory that have prevented it from obtaining universal approval. There are no known chemical pathways for the abiogenic synthesis of the nucleotides needed for RNA assembly. The heterocyclic bases are unstable at the temperatures required by origin-of-life scenarios.[23] The formose reaction, which is supposed to have supplied the ribose sugar component of the nucleotides, does not produce sugars in the presence of the nucleotide bases or of amino acids.[24] Ribose is only one of many sugars formed in this reaction and ribose itself contains four reactive centres. Selection of the correct phosphate-sugar-base linkages, with the required stereochemistry, under prebiotic conditions would be a huge problem. Alternative strategies for RNA formation, which bypass the need for free sugars, have also been explored in the laboratory. In these experiments, the nucleotides were assembled by syn-

---

23. M. Levy and S. L. Miller, 'The Stability of the RNA bases', *Proceedings of the National Academy of Sciences* 95 (1998), pp. 7933–7938.

24. R. Larralde, M. P. Robertson and S. L. Miller, 'Rates of Decomposition of Ribose and Other Sugars: Implications for Chemical Evolution', *Proceedings of the National Academy of Sciences* 92 (1995), pp. 8158–8160; R. Shapiro, 'Prebiotic Ribose Synthesis: A Critical Analysis', *Origins of Life and Evolution of Biospheres* 16 (2006), pp. 283–284.

thetic sequences which started from glyceraldehyde-3-phosphate or equivalents. However, the problematic origin of glyceraldehyde and its 3-phosphate derivative under prebiotic conditions and the need for multiple purification steps makes this an implausible prebiotic route to RNA nucleotides.

RNA molecules are inherently less stable than DNA molecules and readily undergo hydrolysis. The fragility of large RNA molecules means that they easily unzip, and are prone to lose their coherence. Storing large amounts of information in RNA for significant amounts of time is not a practicable proposition.

The most formidable problem faced by the RNA-world hypothesis is that it relies on the chance assembly of particular operational RNA sequences already fit for task. It leaves unsolved the origin of this genetic information. The first self-replicating RNA molecules would have had to form by random undirected chemical combinations of nucleotides. The RNA world hypothesis simply assumes this happened but, as shown above, the odds against this are stupendous. The same problem is encountered at subsequent steps. RNA molecules are eventually envisaged as starting to make proteins. However, the hypothesis provides no explanation of where the information needed for the specific amino acid sequences required for functional proteins came from.

The RNA-world hypothesis has given rise to a great deal of interest amongst molecular biologists in making and studying RNA molecules. They seek to engineer ribozymes with better catalytic activity capable of carrying out more metabolic tasks. Some research has focused on modifying the sequences of naturally occurring RNA catalysts. In another approach, sets of RNA molecules (libraries) are screened for particular types of catalytic activity. The most active molecules are then isolated and variants are generated by mutating, or otherwise altering, some part of the sequence. The new crop of RNAs is then screened for activity and the most efficient molecules selected. The process is repeated until optimum catalytic activity is reached. It is quite evident that the latter method amounts to a process of 'directed evolution' with the selection being accomplished under the direction of the team of molecular biologists. Undoubtedly, results that are interesting and significant from a biochemical standpoint have been achieved using these methods. RNA molecules that can copy small sections of themselves have been engineered. RNA-polymerases that can extend existing sequences by up to twenty nucleotides have been produced,[25] as have short RNAs that can catalyze the formation of peptide bonds between amino acids.[26] These successes have been hailed in popular articles as evidence in support of the prebiotic RNA-world and as showing that artificial life forms will soon be generated in the test tube.[27]

Although ribozyme engineering has achieved some remarkable results, it is a fact that the great majority of metabolic tasks still require amino acid-based enzymes, and ribozymes capable of substituting for them have not been discovered. What is more, there are several obvious flaws in the claim that ribozyme engineering is a valid model for the prebiotic production of self-replicating organisms. In the first place, a crucial role in the development of the engineered RNAs was played by the intelligent molecular biologists who designed and carried through the experiments. Second, significant amounts of the information required for functioning RNAs was provided by intelligent selection of the primer RNA sequences and in the control of the experimental conditions. Third, the method, involving repeated phases of screening, selecting and variant production, actually models natural selection. Thus natural selection has been smug-

25. W. K. Johnston, P. J. Unrau, M. S. Lawrence, M. E. Glasner and D. P. Bartel, 'RNA-Catalyzed RNA Polymerization: Accurate and General RNA-Templated Primer Extension', *Science* 292 (2001), p. 1319.

26. H. S. Zaher and P. J. Unrau, 'Selection of an Improved RNA Polymerase Ribozyme with Superior Extension and Fidelity', *RNA* 13 (2007), pp. 1017–1026; F. Huang, Z. Yang and M. Yarus, 'RNA enzymes with two small-molecule substrates', *Chemistry & Biology* 5 (1998), pp. 669–678; P. J. Unrau and D. P. Bartel, 'RNA-Catalysed Nucleotide Synthesis', *Nature* 395 (1998), pp. 260–263; B. Zhang, and T. R. Cech, 'Peptide Bond Formation by In-vitro Selected Ribozymes', *Nature* 390 (1997), pp. 96–100.

27. J. W. Szostak, D. P. Bartel and P. L. Luisi, 'Synthesizing Life', *Nature* 409 (2001), pp. 387–390.

gled through the back door into experiments claimed to model prebiotic processes although, as pointed out above, natural selection cannot operate before the appearance of self-replicating organisms. The ribozyme engineering experiments do not really support a naturalistic origin of life. On the contrary, results from this field show that given a large measure of engineering input, originating from the intelligent minds of the molecular biologists, progress towards catalytically active sequences and replication can be made. As the input from human intelligence has grown, so the balance of the evidence has tipped in favour of the theory that reproduction and life originated from intelligent design.

Evolutionary algorithms

As the difficulties associated with chemistry-based prebiotic scenarios mounted, evolutionary biologists began to turn to computer programs designed to illustrate the emergence of functional organisms. The most widely known of these is Richard Dawkins' 'Weasel' program, described in his book *The Blind Watchmaker*.[28] Dawkins shows that it would be impossible to generate the 28-character phrase[29] 'methinks it is like a weasel', even in the lifetime of the universe, by a monkey typing at random a selection of letters from the alphabet. However, he wrote a computer program to carry out the actions of the hypothetical monkey but with a selection algorithm built into it. The programme begins by choosing a random sequence of twenty-eight letters. The algorithm duplicates this repeatedly, but with a certain chance of random error — 'mutation' — in the copying. The computer examines the mutant nonsense phrases, the 'progeny' of the original phrase, and chooses the one which, however slightly, most resembles the target phrase, 'methinks it is like a weasel'. The Weasel program is able

---

28. Richard Dawkins, *The Blind Watchmaker* (London: W. W. Norton & Co., 1986), ch. 3.

29. The spaces between words are included in the total character count.

to reach the target phrase in a matter of seconds. The program demonstrates that the preservation of small changes in an evolving string of characters (or genes) can produce meaningful combinations in a relatively short time as long as there is some mechanism to select cumulative changes, and as long as a target sequence is specified.

There are claims on the Web and elsewhere that the weasel program and later improved versions such as 'Ev'[30] model how biological information can be created from scratch. To achieve their rapid convergence, both the Weasel and Ev programs must be *supplied* with a meaningful target sequence before their selection algorithms can get to work. In the context of the origin of life therefore, the software *assumes* what it sets out to discover (i.e. the crucial nucleotide sequence(s)), so the whole process is an exercise in circular reasoning! These computer models are also open to the criticism that their selection algorithms do not really model any actual processes available in nature and in fact make use of additional supplied information. It is astonishing that evolutionary biologists still approvingly cite the Weasel and Ev software as evidence of how natural selection can produce new information.

A state-of-the-art software platform called 'Avida', written to study the evolution of digital organisms, and by analogy biological organisms, has attracted a lot of attention recently.[31] It has been claimed[32] that the Avida platform demonstrates that biological complexity can be generated by random mutations and natural selection amongst the digital organisms. Meyer has provided a detailed analysis of the Avida digital world which shows it lacks

30. T. D. Schneider, 'The Evolution of Biological Information', *Nucleic Acid Research* 28 (2000), pp. 2794–2799.
31. C. Adami and C. T. Brown, 'Evolutionary Learning in the 2D Artificial Life Systems Avida', in R. Brooks and P. Maes (eds.), *Proceedings of Artificial Life IV* (Cambridge, MA: MIT Press, 1994), pp. 377–381.
32. R. E. Lenski, C. Ofria, R. T. Pennock and C. Adami, 'The Evolutionary Origin of Complex Features', *Nature* 423 (2003), pp. 139–145.

realism as a simulation of biological evolution.[33] The logic functions selected in the program, in imitation of protein or nucleotide sequences in nature, contain too little information to realistically model the bio-polymers. The random search is thereby reduced to proportions that are manageable by the available resources. Then too, Avida comes already provided with a sizeable complement of pre-existing information. The digital organisms have been programmed with the capacity for self-replication. Avida presupposes these instructions and so does not explain how the information necessary to produce the first organism might have originated.

Intelligence and the origin of information

The ability of even the smallest cells to self-replicate depends on their inheriting DNA encoded with appropriate instructions, together with protein-based machinery capable of reading and actualizing them. In essence, there are four explanations 'in play' of how this extensive information first appeared (Fig. 4). Several scenarios rely either explicitly or implicitly on chance associations of biomonomers: a lucky throw of the dice, a fortunate coincidence. This explanation stretches credulity beyond reasonable limits because it is well established that neither nucleic acids nor proteins of sufficient length, complexity and specificity could have formed by chance combinations in either a prebiotc soup, or on the surface of clays, or at the margins of volcanoes, or on radioactive beaches, or close to deep sea vents or in any other proposed prebiotic scenario. The entire material and temporal resources of the universe are insufficient for the spontaneous formation of even one operational specified sequence.

Biologists always offer neo-Darwinian evolution as the sacrosanct explanation of increasing complexity and apparent design. Doubts about the ability of natural selection to accomplish the feats attributed to it have repeatedly been expressed by mathematicians,

---

33. Meyer, *Signature*, ch. 13, p. 271.

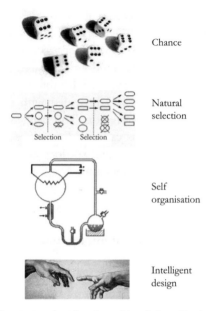

Chance

Natural
selection

Self
organisation

Intelligent
design

*Figure 4: Four proposed explanations of how information in DNA might
have originated.*

computer scientists, philosophers and other theoreticians.[34] Many
of these objections are explained in earlier chapters of this book.
Several influential scenarios seek to bring natural selection, in one
form or another, into play to explain the origin of life. However,
as shown above, natural selection cannot have preceded self-
replication, so appeals to it as the organizing and instructing force
in the prebiotic world must be dismissed as invalid.

Another explanation holds that self-organization is an emer-
gent property of complex molecules. In other words that uniform
'laws of self-organization' govern the appearance of non-periodic
sequences in DNA and proteins and that it is the business of
future molecular biology to discover them. That the known laws of

---

34. See, for example, W. A. Dembski (ed.), *Uncommon Dissent: Intellectuals
Who Find Darwinism Unconvincing* (Wilmington: ISI books, 2004); J. C.
Lennox, *God's Undertaker: Has Science Buried God?* (Oxford: Lion Books,
2007).

nature invariably describe regular, orderly events and phenomena is seriously at odds with this idea. The DNA nucleotide sequences do not show repeat units or any short- or long-term regularities. They are not ordered in the sense of atoms in a crystal, snowflakes, vortices in a fluid, or oscillating chemical processes.[35] The kind of specified complexity found in DNA is not the sort of property that can be described or predicted by a natural law. Furthermore, the freedom of nucleotides to be positioned in any order is an essential part of the ability of DNA to carry genetic information.

Instead of regularity, DNA nucleotide sequences bear a striking resemblance to letter sequences, words and sentences in written languages and to symbol sequences in computer programs. Letter groups of an extant language on a page convey meaning from one mind to another according to the rules of the language they are written in. Similarly, the characters programmed into a computer machine code instruct the computer to perform some function. Both these systems are analogous to DNA sequences that convey meaning, via the genetic code, to the cell protein-based nano-machinery. Messages communicated in written languages are produced by conscious intelligent agents. Instructions written in computer code also emanate from the minds of intelligent programmers. These analogies are very persuasive of the conclusion that the genomic information coded in nucleotide sequences also originated from an intelligent mind. Stephen Meyer puts it this way: 'Uniform and repeated experience affirms that intelligent agents . . . produce information rich systems.'[36]

We know that computers now exist in the world, although once they did not. To explain this fact we need more than just the design for a computer in a mind or on some virtual drawing board. The individual components must have been made and assembled with the right connectivity and then the system switched on, powered up or activated.

---

35. In the Belousov-Zhabotinsky reaction, for example, mixing a special set of chemicals sets up a system that self-organizes to perform a repeating cycle of reactions with associated colour changes.

36. Meyer, *Signature*, ch. 15, p. 329.

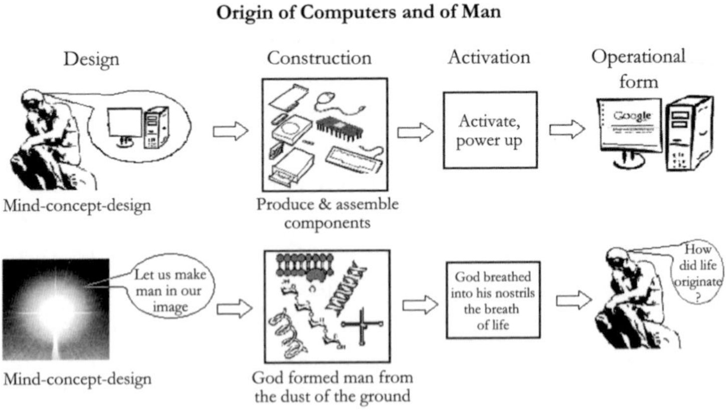

Origin of Computers and of Man

Figure 5: From mental concept to material reality: the origin of man parallels the origin of computers.

The same sequence of events explains how TVs, cars, and in fact any complex and specified structure or machine in the mechanical world, came into existence. The same sequence, from mental concept to operational biological form, is needed to explain the existence of complex and specified biological machines. The origin of life requires more than simply postulating that the genetic information for some simple self-replicating organism was conceived in a mind. Just like computers and cars, specified DNA sequences and their associated protein-based biological machinery, must have been made, assembled in the right configuration, and then activated (Fig. 5).

This scenario sounds strangely familiar, and with good reason because it has been around for a long time. Genesis 2:7 reads: 'The LORD God formed the man from the dust of the ground and breathed into his nostrils the breath of life, and the man became a living being.' The language is timeless and free of jargon. Of course, man was not the first living thing, but man is the only biological organism for which any detail was recorded. It is very significant that the creation sequence reported in Genesis: design – construction – activation, exactly parallels what we know is required to explain the origin of all other information driven machines. The trail of evidence from the discovery of cells and their complex internal structures, to decipherment of the non-periodic structures of proteins and DNA, to the realization that nucleotide sequences represent coded information, to the knowledge that intelligent minds are the only known sources of information, leads obstinately back to the traditional belief in creation first enunciated in Genesis.

CONCLUSION: SHOULD CHRISTIANS EMBRACE EVOLUTION?

Phil Hills and Norman Nevin

Having considered some of the key questions that arise from seeking to reconcile evolution with Christianity, we must face the question: Should Christians embrace evolution? Our answer is a resounding 'no' – absolutely not. Theistic evolutionists have failed to demonstrate a theology consistent with the supremacy of Scripture. They have reinterpreted Scripture in order to harmonize it with current understandings of the evolutionary paradigm. This approach has the potential of making our theology dependant on the changing perspective of scientific understanding as opposed to the unchanging character of the eternal word of God.

The uncertainty of science

In spite of the sound-bite science that suggests certainty, science is actually in a continuous process of inquiry as it explores the natural world. Many believe that science is an open environment with free exchange of ideas that will always follow the evidence wherever it leads. That may be the ideal, but that is not necessarily what happens in practice. Thomas Kuhn, the historian, in *The Structure of Scientific Revolutions*[1] argued that scientists work with a set of ideas to inform and develop their research until they reach a point where it is impossible to continue with that hypothesis. Until this position of impossibility arises, evidence challenging the prevailing hypothesis can be ignored, silenced, or indeed, modified.

The tipping point, when the prevailing scientific opinion is overturned, Kuhn described as a 'paradigm shift', from one way of knowing to another. This view was supported by Immanuel Kant, who argued that, 'Hypotheses always remain hypotheses, that is, suppositions to the complete certainty of which we can never attain.'[2] In *The Limits of Science*,[3] Peter Medawar considered that scientific truth is often thought the goal of the scientist's work, but there is no conclusive certainty beyond the reach of criticism. Those who question evolution are often treated as ignorant, idiotic or 'anti-science' because they have the audacity to challenge the accepted and prevailing consensus. However, history has recorded that consensus was often an obstacle rather than an aid to understanding.

The Nobel laureate, Julian Schwinger (regarded by some as one of the greatest physicists of the twentieth century), experienced the wrath of the scientific establishment and concluded, 'The pressure for conformity is enormous. I have experienced it in editors' rejection of submitted papers, based on venomous criticism of anonymous referees. The replacement of impartial reviewing by censorship will be the death of science.'[4] He was working in a field where the Massachusetts Institute of Technology had suppressed information, leading to the resignation of their chief science writer Eugene Mallove, who wrote about the issues in *Ten Years That Shook*

1. T. S. Kuhn, *The Structure of Scientific Revolutions* (Chicago: University Press of Chicago, ²1970 [1962]).

2. Sergio L. Fernandes, *Foundations of Objective Knowledge: The Relations of Popper's Theory of Knowledge to that of Kant* (Boston Studies in the Philosophy of Science, vol. 86; Boston: Springer, 1985), p. 72.

3. Peter Medawar, *The Limits of Science* (Oxford: Oxford University Press, 1984).

4. See http://en.wikipedia.org/wiki/Julian_Schwinger.

Physics.[5] Anyone interested in how the scientific establishment can treat those who challenge the prevailing consensus should do some research on Melvin Miles, Martin Fleischmann and Stanley Pons. One could illustrate again and again from this authoritarian attitude that the pressure to conform in science is indeed enormous. Brian Martin sums up the situation:

> Textbooks present science as a noble search for truth, in which progress depends on questioning established ideas. But for many scientists this is a myth. They know from bitter experience that disagreeing with the dominant view is dangerous – especially when that view is backed by powerful interest groups. Call it suppression of intellectual dissent. The usual pattern is that someone does research or speaks out in a way that threatens a powerful interest group. . . As a result representatives of that group attack the critic's ideas or the critic personally – by censoring writing, blocking publications, denying appointments or promotions, withdrawing research grants, taking legal actions, harassing, blacklisting, spreading rumours.[6]

This pressure to conform has long existed within various scientific disciplines but the recent efforts of Denis Alexander and Nick Spencer are seeking to persuade evangelicals that they must also conform. 'Rescuing Darwin'[7] has been the title they are working under to challenge Christians to embrace random mutation and natural selection as the driving force behind the development of life. However, new discoveries and developments in science are leading some prominent evolutionists and scientists to question the concept of Darwinism, particularly the sufficiency of natural selection to explain the evolution of form. Indeed, recently some evolutionists have discussed an Extended Evolutionary Synthesis

---

5. E. F. Mallove, 'Ten Years That Shook Physics', *Infinite Energy Magazine* 24 (1999); http://www.infinite-energy.com/iemagazine/issue24/tenyears.html.

6. B. Martin, 'Stamping Out Dissent', *Newsweek*, 26 April 1993, pp. 49–50; http://www.uow.edu.au/arts/sts/bmartin/pubs/93nw.html.

7. Nick Spencer and Denis Alexander, *Rescuing Darwin: God and Evolution in Britain Today* (London: Theos, 2009).

(EES). In July 2008, sixteen leading evolutionary scientists met at Altenberg, Austria, to consider novel approaches and concepts to evolution.[8] For some time there have been persistent rumours that the modern synthesis in evolutionary biology is incomplete. What will the final conclusion be? How long before science satisfies itself that it has answered crucial questions and has a robust and credible hypothesis that incorporates all the current data? Science is relatively clear about how little it understands and how much it still has to explore, but it would be extremely unwise to build one's theology around the shifting sands of a rapidly changing scientific field.

Theistic evolution's theology

The theology of theistic evolution necessarily denies any notion of a fall and curse that had a detrimental effect upon the natural world. It would be very difficult to do good forensic science if we acknowledge that the natural world was different prior to the fall and the curse. We would not simply be able to look at the world as it now is and to extrapolate from that how it used to be and to know what has happened in the intervening period. It is not sufficient for theistic evolutionists to make reference to Romans 8:20–21 – 'For the creation was subjected to frustration, not by its own choice, but by the will of one who subjected it, in hope that the creation itself will be liberated from its bondage to decay and brought into the glorious freedom of the children of God' – and then say theologians are not certain of what this means. A robust theology will wrestle with the text and seek to understand it. Rhetoric, on the other hand, seeks to remove the obstacle by a superficial statement that avoids the argument.

A theology that embraces evolution espouses the idea that God chose to use death, decay and the extinction of life forms as the best means of developing life. This presents a massive challenge to the nature of a good God who created a world that he was able

---

8. If you want to examine their pedigree and some of the positional papers, type 'Altenberg 16' into your internet search engine.

to describe as 'very good'. It makes death and decay good – but somewhere down the eons God then determined death to be our enemy. Embracing evolution demands that we decide when and why God changed his mind about the character of death. Until you have been given satisfactory answers to that question we urge you not to embrace evolution.

God obviously doesn't regard death as good nor one of the characteristics of the eternity he is preparing, for then there will be no more death, or sickness or suffering. However, it is also possible that some will enter that eternity without ever dying (1 Thess. 4:15, 17), not unlike Enoch (Heb. 11:5) and Elijah (2 Kgs 2:11). This means that death is not an essential preparation for eternal life. To add to the theological dilemmas of theistic evolution, apparently God has the capacity in a very short space of time to transform our lowly bodies and to take us into a perfect eternity prepared for us. This is a dilemma only in as much as he needed billions of years to create a world that was filled with disorder, death and disease, but needs only a moment to transform and translate us into a perfect new order.

Traditional Christian theology explains suffering, decay and death by reference to the fall, believing that the good creation of God was damaged and that death and decay entered as a consequence. God sent his Son to redeem us and to restore us to a place where everything in heaven and earth will be together, in harmony, and under the headship of Christ. It makes the sin of man responsible for the dysfunction in our world. A theology that denies a significant fall and denies that physical death is a result of mankind's sin makes God responsible for the suffering in our world. That is no little or light matter, and in the absence of a clear theology that explains this position and accords with Scripture it would be outrageous to embrace evolution. Darwin considered suffering in the world a strong argument against the existence of God. In his *Autobiography* he writes, 'this very old argument from the existence of suffering against the existence of an intelligent First Cause seems to me a strong one'.[9]

---

9. Charles Darwin, 'Autobiography' (1876), in Francis Darwin (ed.), *The Life and Letters of Charles Darwin*, vol. 1 (London: John Murray, 1888), pp. 307–313.

Interpreting the scientific data

The accusation levelled at Christians who do not embrace evolution is that we are opposed to science. That is not the case at all. The contributors to this book all have a high view of science and many have made it their life's work. Since the 1950s advances in biology, particularly in the field of genetics, have been astounding. However, it must not be supposed that the scientific data can only be interpreted in one way. Some of the chapters have sought to consider this and especially to consider much of the current data in the field of genetics.

One important area is that of chromosomal fusion. Humankind has 23 pairs of chromosomes whereas chimpanzees, bonobos and great apes have 24 pairs of chromosomes. Denis Alexander argues that 'the story of our 'missing pair' provides another great piece of historical sleuthing that reveals our shared ancestry with the apes'[10] and concludes that evidence makes it overwhelmingly likely that human chromosome 2 was derived from the fusion of two ancestral ape chromosomes (2p and 2q). Recent research[11] now makes it possible to directly compare the genomes of chimpanzee and humans. In addition to the difference in the number of chromosomes, there are numerous structural anomalies such as specific inversions (chromosomes 1 and 18) and numerous lineage-specific segmental duplications. The authors of this research conclude that genomic comparisons revealed numerous human-specific gains and losses of genes as well as changes in gene expression. In this book, Geoffrey Barnard, whilst accepting the probability of chromosomal fusion in human history, considers that evidence of common descent is unjustified. The fused chromosome is unique to the human and is not found in the great apes. Such a fusion must have taken place when the human population was extremely small and has been

10. Denis Alexander, *Creation or Evolution: Do We Have to Choose?* (Oxford: Monarch Books, 2008), p. 211.

11. H. Kehrer-Sawatzki and D. N. Cooper, 'Understanding the Recent Evolution of the Human Genome: Insights From Human-Chimpanzee Genome Comparisons', *Human Mutation* 28 (2007), pp. 99–130.

tolerated and inherited in subsequent generations. What is clear is that the numerous chromosomal variations between the human and chimpanzee suggest that these species do *not* have common ancestry.

Alexander writes, 'the record of our evolutionary past is indelibly inscribed within the DNA of every cell of our bodies. We are all walking genetic fossil museums.'[12] Around 97% of the human genome consists of DNA sequences that do not encode protein. They have been classified as 'junk' (non-protein coding) DNA. Scientists considered that non-protein coding DNA consisted of random sequences that had lost their coding ability, such as pseudogenes, long and short interspersed repeats and retroviral elements. Darwinists have long argued that the 'junk' DNA is evidence of fossil remains of the evolutionary history of the organism. Francis Collins writes that the 'junk' DNA has remained in the same location of the genomes, consistent with them having arrived in the genome from a common mammalian ancestor.[13] However, recent research has reversed previous scientific thought, confirming that the non-protein coding DNA, far from being genetic fossils, is dominated by sequences rich in functional information, such as coding for proteins, having major regulatory roles, controlling the transcription of genes and maintaining the structure of chromosomes.[14] The evidence of these findings has major implications for evolutionary theory. It is clear that the concept of 'junk' DNA has to be discarded.

It is necessary that those who are pressing Christians to embrace evolution are consistent with the scientific data. Natural selection is *not* considered by science to be a directed process in any way and certainly not directed by God. Such a view is not Darwinian. In his *Autobiography*, Darwin wrote, 'The old argument from design in nature, as given by Paley, which formerly seemed to me so

---

12. Alexander, *Creation or Evolution*, p. 200.

13. Francis S. Collins, *The Language of God* (New York: Free Press, 2006), p. 136.

14. The ENCODE Project Consortium, 'Identification and Analysis of Functional Elements in 1% of the Human Genome by the ENCODE Pilot Project', *Nature* 447 (2007), pp. 799–816.

conclusive, fails, now that the law of natural selection has been discovered. . . . There seems to be no more design in the variability of organic beings and in the action of natural selection, than in the course which the wind blows'.[15] If some theistic evolutionists wish to posit a different mechanism than natural selection (natural selection directed by God is not natural selection) for evolution, let them do so, but the appropriate way of doing that would be in the scientific arena and in peer-reviewed papers. Those like Alexander and Spencer, who are seeking to 'Rescue Darwin', must admit that Darwin adamantly opposed any idea of divine design in natural selection. Until this inconsistency is addressed we would want to persuade you not to embrace evolution.

Another anomaly that remains outstanding is the idea that evolution will not continue to progress beyond humanity. If random mutations and natural selection have the capacity to produce varying life forms, why would we assume that the process of evolution will not continue its onward march? The prevailing scientific opinion is not that evolution has stopped. This, of course, has significant implications for Christian theology, especially in light of the incarnation. However, if we are to do our theology based on scientific consensus then we need to engage this issue. Theistic evolution must challenge the prevailing scientific opinion and overcome it or else it must explain the implications for Christian theology of ongoing evolution. Until that is done satisfactorily you would be unwise to embrace evolution.

The heart of the matter

Alexander poses an important question, 'Where does new genetic information come from?',[16] and provides the standard Darwinian response that mutations 'cause changes in the sequence of amino acids in a protein' and combined with natural selection create new biological information. Is there any empirical evidence that

---

15. Darwin, *Life and Letters*.
16. Alexander, *Creation or Evolution*, p. 112.

mutations and natural selection have ever encoded a single gene with new information? We know that mutations are overwhelmingly neutral or deleterious. Such mutations have devastating consequences in human beings. They usually result in conditions incompatible with life or in serious physical and or mental impairment. It is clear that such mutations, rather than create new information, result in the disruption or destruction of information. J. C. Sanford, a plant geneticist, writes that he is not convinced that 'there is a single crystal-clear example of a known mutation which unambiguously created information'.[17]

The genome is not just a string of letters arranged in a code, spelling out a linear series of messages. Scientists now realize that the specified information stored in the DNA is orders of magnitude greater than was initially thought in the immediate wake of the genomic revolution.[18] The discoveries about the cells' informational system are phenomenal, with various levels of codes and storage. Stephen Meyer, Director of the Center of Science and Culture in Seattle, USA, in his book *Signature in the Cell* concludes that 'the linear and hierarchical arrangement of the genome is not what one would expect if the information in the DNA and the chromosomes had developed by undirected mutation and selection'.[19] The mathematician and evolutionist, Amir Aczel writes

> having surveyed the structure of DNA . . . having seen how DNA stores and manipulates tremendous amount of information . . . and uses this information to control life, we are left with one big question: what created DNA . . . was it perhaps the power, thinking and will of a supreme being that created this self-replicating basis of all life?[20]

---

17. J. C. Sanford, *Genetic Entropy and the Mystery of the Genome* (Dallas: Ivan Press, 2005), p. 17.

18. S. C. Meyer, *Signature in the Cell: DNA and the Evidence for Intelligent Design* (New York: HarperOne, 2009), p. 462.

19. Ibid., p. 469.

20. A. Aczel, *Probability 1: Why There Must be Intelligent Life in the Universe* (New York: Harvest, 1988), p. 88.

The strongest evidence for evolution that has been presented in 150 years is in the relative size of finches' beaks and the change in colour of some moths. This demonstrates variation, but it seems staggering that we would conclude from that the pathway of development of every living organism from an original life form. A 'just so' story cannot be treated as credible evidence. James Le Fanu, reviewing the scientific consequences of the Human Genome Project, argues that we stand on the brink of a tectonic shift in our understanding of ourselves that will witness the eclipse of Darwin's materialist evolutionary theory. The doctrine of Darwinism 'is not merely flawed or incomplete but its proposed mechanisms of natural selection as the "cause" of the diversity of living things is contradicted at every turn by the empirical evidence of science itself'.[21]

Why, with so little evidence to support biology's evolution-ary doctrine, would we completely revise orthodox theology to embrace such an unimpressive scientific position? Perhaps Steve Fuller, Professor of Sociology, hints at the answer to this question in Chapter 8. He argues that science is now treated as the defini-tive authority in much the same way that the Bible was treated in the past generation. He identifies the fact that the reliability of the Bible as the divine word has been questioned in many quarters, but points out the consequential, high cost of losing this unified sense of the truth. He contrasts the Protestant position on bibli-cal authority with the much more fluid interpretive method of Catholicism and asserts that Theistic Evolutionists are seeking to adopt this more fluid process but with science, not the Church, acting as the final authority. Fuller's perspective is particularly interesting because he is speaking as one who is firmly outside the camp of evangelical Christianity. This should raise alarm bells for any who are persuaded of the supremacy of Scripture. Steve Fuller has no commitment to the Bible motivated by personal faith. Yet as an academic with a particular interest in this subject he is fully persuaded that trying to harmonize Christianity with Darwinian

---

21. J. Le Fanu, *Why Us? How Science Rediscovered the Mystery of Ourselves* (London: Harper Press, 2009), p. 231.

evolution undermines the authority of the Bible. Unless you were willing to cede the authority of the Bible to the authority of science you would not revise orthodox theology to embrace biology's evolutionary doctrine.

No coherent, cohesive theology has yet been offered that would allow Christians to embrace evolution with integrity. Science has uncovered a great deal of empirical evidence that is challenging the Darwinian paradigm. Why then do so many want to embrace it? It appears that the only possible reason is the fear of appearing intellectually inferior to the academic consensus. There are many, including the contributors to this book, who with great intellectual acumen question the prevailing evolutionary paradigm, and there are others who are embarrassed to dissent from it. As Professor J. P. Moreland points out in *Kingdom Triangle*, 'Theistic Evolution is intellectual pacifism that lulls people to sleep while the barbarians are at the gates. In my experience theistic evolutionists are trying to create a safe truce with science so Christians can be left alone to practise their privatised religion while retaining the respect of the dominant intellectual culture.'[22]

Should Christians embrace evolution? Our answer is an unequivocal 'no'!

---

22. J. P. Moreland, *Kingdom Triangle: Recover the Christian Mind, Renovate the Soul, Restore the Spirit's Power* (Grand Rapids: Zondervan, 2007), p. 46.